Forced to Fail

Forced to Fail

The Paradox of School Desegregation

Stephen J. Caldas and
Carl L. Bankston III

PRAEGER

Westport, Connecticut
London

Library of Congress Cataloging-in-Publication Data

Caldas, Stephen J., 1957–
    Forced to fail : the paradox of school desegregation / Stephen J. Caldas and Carl
L. Bankston III.
        p.   cm.
    Includes bibliographical references and index.
    ISBN 0–275–98693–4 (alk. paper)
    1. Segregation in education—United States.   2. Educational equalization—United
States.   I. Bankston, Carl L. (Carl Leon), 1952–   II. Title.
    LC212.52.C35   2005
    379.2'63'0973—dc22   2005009817

British Library Cataloguing in Publication Data is available.

Library of Congress Catalog Card Number: 2005009817
ISBN: 0–275–98693–4

First published in 2005

Praeger Publishers, 88 Post Road West, Westport, CT 06881
An imprint of Greenwood Publishing Group, Inc.
www.praeger.com

Printed in the United States of America

The paper used in this book complies with the
Permanent Paper Standard issued by the National
Information Standards Organization (Z39.48–1984).

10 9 8 7 6 5 4 3 2 1

Contents

Acknowledgments

We would like to thank Col. John J. Caldas, Jr. (USMC, retired) and Christine Rossell of Boston University for carefully proofreading our work and offering suggestions to improve our book. We'd also like to thank our editor, Susan Slesinger, as well as Shelley Yeager, Seong Man Park, Kevin McGowan, Min Zhou, David Armor, David Prejean, David Thibodaux, Jim Flaitz, Clay Mc-Govern, Carol Broussard, Josh Benton, Roslin Growe, Gerald Carlson, and all the staff at Greenwood and Westchester Book Services for the various ways they helped to bring this project to completion. We would also like to acknowledge the logistical support provided by Sylvain Bernier, Richard Marceau, and the staff at the Centre de reserche et d'expertise eń evaluation (CREXE) of L'École nationale d'administration publique in Québec, Canada. Of course, we both owe a deep debt of gratitude to Suzanne Caron Caldas and Cynthia Bankston, who are not only wonderful wives and terrific mothers but also dedicated and caring public school teachers.

CHAPTER 1

School Desegregation:
A Policy in Crisis

THE RESEGREGATION OF AMERICAN SCHOOLS

At the end of the twentieth and beginning of the twenty-first century, public school systems throughout the United States were moving toward racial resegregation. After decades of efforts to place black and other minority students together with whites, students continued to attend schools populated by schoolmates similar to themselves in race and socioeconomic standing. This separation, moreover, was increasing steadily.[1]

The trend toward school racial resegregation has disturbing implications. Economic and social position in a modern society is largely a function of schooling. In fact, education has been identified as the key predictor of economic success.[2] If you want your child to succeed economically in the United States, you should ensure that he or she has the best education possible. However, your ability to do that depends on your own background. Researchers have found that the educational attainment of a child is closely connected to the occupational position of a parent. In other words, schooling is often the means by which economic position is passed from one generation to another. It is no coincidence that doctors are more likely to have parents who were doctors, but your local trash collector is much more likely to have parents who were high school dropouts. In perhaps the most influential educational study ever, *The Coleman Report*, published in 1966 and headed up by the renowned sociologist James Coleman, this reasoning was extended from individual families to schools. *The Coleman Report* maintained that quality of schooling is influenced not simply by an individual's own background, that is, his or her family and its resources, but by the backgrounds of schoolmates.[3] Not only is a doctor more likely to have parents who were doctors, but he or she is also more likely to have gone to a "good" high school and had classmates who also went on to prestigious, economically successful jobs.

Coleman argued that if a group of students from socially and economically disadvantaged backgrounds were isolated from the mainstream, as were most blacks during the Jim Crow period in the South, then this isolation could easily perpetuate the group's low educational levels and poor job prospects. The "disadvantages" of each member in this isolated group would be reinforced and perpetuated within their segregated schools as students "learned" from each other. Unfortunately, what the students would learn from each other would not equip them to rise above their group's already low social and economic status (also referred to as SES). Thus would be set in motion a cycle that would ensure a sort of permanent underclass or "caste." In their isolated condition, Coleman continued, the members of this caste would never receive the social and academic resources necessary to thrive in mainstream society. *The Coleman Report* would become one of the primary social science justifications for school desegregation. Although the logic and research underpinning *The Coleman Report* are valid and sound, this report would, with Coleman's own endorsement, be used to justify the ultimately damaging practices of busing, school district rezoning, and other desegregation practices discussed in this book. The common element unifying all these desegregation devices is decision making based solely on the race of individuals. Some of these desegregation strategies, particularly busing, would prove so destructive to schools and communities that Coleman himself would later publicly regret their use.

Contemporary academic researchers, commentators, and activists recognize that the racial resegregation of American schools has a number of sources. To some extent, they all acknowledge that the trend is a consequence of demographic change in the United States. In 1970, 15 percent[4] of American public school students were black. By 2000, this had increased to 17 percent. In 1972, the first year for which statistics are available for Hispanic students, Hispanics were 6 percent of all those enrolled in public schools. Twenty-eight years later, this proportion had tripled to 17 percent.[5] Moreover, the growth in the number and percentage of Hispanic students is projected to continue at a breakneck pace for at least another quarter-century. As the experts at the Harvard Civil Rights Project recognize,[6] one reason minority concentrations in schools are increasing is simply a question of mathematics: minorities constitute an increasing proportion of all students.

Segregation outside of schools is also widely recognized as a source of school resegregation. According to the influential book *American Apartheid* by Douglas Massey and Nancy Denton, residential segregation by race intensified in the late twentieth century.[7] In particular, minority members became more likely to be central city residents, whereas whites were increasingly suburbanites. In 1998, for example, a clear majority of African Americans (55%) lived in the central parts of cities, whereas only 22 percent of white non-Hispanic Americans lived in urban centers.[8] Black and Hispanic students, although minorities in the American population, made up over 60 percent of central city public school students in 2000.[9]

FAILURE OF WILL OR FAILURE OF COMMAND AND CONTROL?

Although the experts acknowledge the kinds of demographic changes discussed in the preceding section, the conventional wisdom among scholars and activists is that the primary source of school racial resegregation is a failure of political will or, perhaps, the success of political will of the wrong sort. For example, the articles in the influential 1996 book *Dismantling Desegregation*, edited by Gary Orfield and Susan Eaton, argue that although the U.S. Supreme Court initiated efforts toward racial desegregation with the *Brown* rulings, the court failed to clearly define in numbers and educational outcomes what truly desegregated schools should look like.

Thus, some have contended that the federal government, and particularly the courts, did not have a sufficiently clear image of schools to impose on American society, and this resulted in a conflict over strategies. They also contend that this lack of purpose and direction from federal authorities encouraged those who were seeking to subvert or avoid desegregation through white flight. It is true that by 1990, a relatively conservative Supreme Court began to deemphasize the more coercive aspects of school desegregation and to cede power to lower courts. This decentralization was especially notable in the court's affirmation of the concept of unitary status, allowing lower courts to decide if individual school boards had made good-faith efforts to comply with desegregation orders and, if such efforts had been made, to release school districts from judicial supervision.[10] This does not necessarily mean that courts were deliberately trying to subvert school desegregation.

Our studies have led us to believe, however, that much conventional wisdom about school desegregation is fundamentally wrong. The belief that government should be even more active in racially engineering school populations has fostered policies and programs that weaken American schools and communities. In fact, as we argue in this book, minorities, their schools, and their communities may have suffered the most. The problem, we contend, has not been insufficient centralized command and control over American schools. Rather, efforts at desegregation have ultimately been self-defeating precisely because they have sought to use public schools to redesign American society from above according to the blueprints of aloof social planners. And most Americans have been operating from a different set of blueprints than the social engineers.

In a command and control economy, the direction of the distribution of goods by a central authority leads to black market trading or to the flight of goods and people to freer markets. For similar reasons of self-interest, the command and control approach to school desegregation has produced evasive maneuvers by parents with a different vision for their children's education than the government would impose upon them. Moreover, we argue that America's children are much better off as a consequence of having concerned parents directing their education, rather than distant, disconnected bureaucrats with no particular interest in a specific child.

That court-ordered school racial desegregation runs truly counter to American values of individual choice was driven home to one of the authors at an educational research conference in Dallas in 2000. After his presentation on white flight from East Baton Rouge parish schools as a result of a particularly ruinous court order, a Chinese researcher who had emigrated from Communist China only a few years earlier approached him. She marveled that even in Communist China individuals had more choice about where they could attend school than in the supposedly free United States. Since she did not want to put her child in the low-performing Dallas school that a court order would mandate, she had moved outside the city limits.

Parents trying to avoid court-mandated desegregation orders they believe run counter to their children's educational interests have exercised one of four options. This concerned Chinese parent had employed the most popular maneuver of parents subverting desegregation orders for the good of their children: flight from controlled to noncontrolled school districts or avoidance of controlled districts altogether. She moved to a more affluent suburban school district. The other three options available to parents are choosing segregated tracking within so-called desegregated schools (for example, putting your child in the "gifted program"), abandoning the public schools altogether for nongovernment-controlled private schools, and increasingly, opting out of formal schooling altogether (homeschooling).

REDISTRIBUTING CHILDREN'S "SOCIAL CAPITAL"

Attempts to create a more egalitarian society through central planning are essentially redistributive. That is, the government takes from the group that "has more" and gives it to the group that "has less." The American federal income tax is but one example of generally accepted governmental redistribution in a modern society. The government collects proportionately more money from wealthier citizens to help fund the myriad social programs typical of highly developed countries. Many of these social programs, like public assistance, are targeted to helping less-advantaged citizens.

Governments, however, do not simply redistribute their citizens' incomes. They may also attempt to redistribute other, less tangible kinds of capital possessed by individuals and groups of individuals. Part of the logic underlying school desegregation is the redistribution of students' "social" capital, which, the planners believed, would lead to more "academic" capital. Following the line of sound reasoning in *The Coleman Report*, students benefit from attending schools with relatively privileged schoolmates. If there are few of these privileged schoolmates in one school, but more of these privileged schoolmates in another, then redistribution involves moving the students themselves around. Predominately black schools were seen, accurately, as having concentrations of "disadvantaged students" with less social and academic capital. Middle-class white schools were viewed, again accurately, as institutions with students from more-advantaged backgrounds possessing more social capital, and as a consequence, more academic capital as well. In other words, socially advantaged white students were better students earning better grades.

But what is this "social capital" that a classroom full of middle-class students possesses so much of, and how does simply being exposed to their collective social capital cause improved school performance? As we explain in more detail in Chapter 4, social capital can be viewed as a product of our social relations with others.[11] A mother cradling her young child in her arms and reading him a book that emphasizes hard work, honesty, and doing well in school is creating social capital. Groups of children playing together in a schoolyard are sharing and reinforcing the collective social capital that they have received in their homes. They do so in the things they tell each other, the attitudes they display toward learning and teachers, and the hobbies and interests they share with each other. The parents of these same children, in their interactions with each other on the golf course, at church, or at their children's high school football games are strengthening their collective social capital and generating yet more social capital. This occurs through their exchange of information about how school systems should be operated, enthusiasm about the latest books they have read, or swapping of stories about their experiences helping their seventeen-year-olds apply to universities.

Although you cannot see them, these networks of interactions between parents, children, and members of a community are a resource that is an investment much like a financial investment. The more you talk with your children, share the experience of a visit to the zoo with them, and place them in peer groups of children with like-minded parents, the greater the investment in the fund of social capital available to your children. Moreover, this investment can be turned into a profit. The social capital predominant in middle-class families and communities has been linked to doing well in school.[12] Given the work of Coleman and other social scientists, government has come to understand this concept and has been trying to redistribute the "resource" of middle-class social capital to high-poverty minority groups through school desegregation. The hope has been that minority children, too, will benefit from these investments in social capital.

Unfortunately, one of the difficulties with the redistribution of capital, whether it is economic or social, is that it implicitly benefits the have-nots at the expense of the haves. Think of the income tax example. Whereas we all benefit from federal government investments of taxpayer dollars in roads and the military, there are some very large programs, like Medicaid, Headstart, and Aid to Families with Dependent Children (now replaced by Temporary Assistance to Needy Families) that benefit essentially only those in poverty. Moreover, many of the poor recipients of these programs pay no taxes at all. Of course, it can be argued, and it is to some extent true, that we all benefit from services provided to the poor. That is why most of us dutifully, if perhaps grudgingly at times, pay our taxes. However, when government efforts at redistribution are perceived as particularly egregious or unjust, there is little motivation for the haves to participate in this sharing, and they rarely do so voluntarily.

This means, again, that redistributive programs perceived as detrimental to the interests of the haves require coercion and continual vigilance against those who seek to escape complying with "the plan." It means, further, that governmental agents who seek to redistribute resources commit themselves to the exclusive interests of the have-nots and cannot pretend to be broadly representative.

THE FALLACY OF "DIVERSITY"

Coercive desegregation proponents have sometimes sought to mask the redistributive character of their program by claiming that students from all backgrounds benefit from diversity. They contend that all students benefit by attending school with people who are different from them. The diversity advocates argue that both advantaged and disadvantaged students benefit by learning about cultural variations that broaden their understandings of the world.[13] Although there are undoubtedly things that all of us can learn from each other, it is difficult to see why school desegregation would take any effort at all, much less invasive court actions, if everyone derived clear benefits from it. If diversity per se were really a desirable characteristic for schools, then one would have to conclude that students from safe, secure neighborhoods learn more when they go to school with students from neighborhoods with daily shootings or that middle-class young people learn valuable lessons from being in classes with peers from families and communities ravaged by drugs and violence.

In truth, as we will demonstrate in this book, since the 1970s arguments for the racial redistribution of students have not been based on the benefits of diversity but on creating greater equality of opportunity for historically deprived groups (recall *The Coleman Report*). Members of disadvantaged minorities in the United States come from families with relatively low incomes and limited experience with educational systems and from neighborhoods suffering from a multitude of social problems. Redistributing students has been a way of attempting to break down isolation in these families and in these communities. But a realistic view must acknowledge that when advantages are redistributed, disadvantages are also necessarily redistributed. This very important social fact—that learning is a two-way street—has been almost completely ignored by courts, social scientists, and educational planners. This truth has not, however, been ignored by parents—the ultimate judges in the equation.

Many of the disadvantages of some minority students, in addition, actually seem to have increased over time, making predominantly minority schools ever more unattractive to the white or black middle class. Crime, sometimes of the most brutal sort, has become increasingly serious in minority neighborhoods during precisely the period of judicially enforced desegregation in the United States. On any given day, obituary sections of newspapers in major metropolitan areas around the country report the deaths from gunshot wounds of young black men. The perception is backed up by statistics. The U.S. Justice Department reports that blacks were six times more likely to be murdered than whites and seven times more likely to murder than whites in the year 2000.[14] The case of Milwaukee is typical of what is happing in many American cities. Whereas the homicide rate for white youth aged 15–25 has decreased 24 percent in this large midwestern city over the past twenty years, the comparable rate for blacks has increased a whopping 69 percent.[15]

Why do we see this increasing index of social disintegration in black communities? It is almost certainly in part related to the collapse of the black family. In 1965, the late Senator Daniel Pat Moynihan referred to the "tangle of pathologies" associated with the disintegrating black family, at a time when 70 percent of black families were still headed by two parents.[16] Though the politically liberal Moynihan received much flack for his candor, in retrospect he may deserve credit as one of the more fair-minded and prophetic of modern social critics. During the decades of desegregation, the single-parent family, a structure strongly associated with poor academic achievement and behavioral problems among children, became the predominant family form among African Americans. In some academic circles it has become unpopular to insinuate that differences exist in the quality of family structures. Modern thinking is increasingly tending toward a relative view of families, that one structure is as good for children as another. Many research studies do not support this viewpoint, however. Moreover, the great sociologist James Coleman recognized the link between the single-parent family and significantly diminished social capital. According to Coleman, "The physical absence of adults may be described as a structural deficiency in family social capital. The most prominent element of structural deficiency in modern families is the single-parent family."[17]

We are not suggesting that people who live in crime-ridden neighborhoods or who grow up in communities in which two-parent families are rare should be blamed for their circumstances. Group characteristics are consequences of historical and social structural influences over which individuals often have little control. But we will point out that trends such as these give middle-class families a legitimate interest in seeking to avoid having their own children share in this aspect of "diversity" that less-privileged children may bring to schools.

UNINTENDED CONSEQUENCES

Even when it is not utterly inconsistent with the interests of many of the people in a locality, centralization of control can still create problems. The active involvement of individuals in a community or an organization depends on their sense that the community or organization not only is their own but also is under their direction. The more a court or distant federal bureau dictates what happens in a locality, the less people have a sense of ownership. This is an especially dangerous situation for schools, since both commonsense and scholarship suggest that active parental involvement is one of the most essential foundations of a successful school.[18] In the following pages, we will show how and why the federal takeover of K–12 education has alienated families from their local schools, undermining that quintessential foundation of a healthy, vibrant, and free society.

The alienation produced by the efforts of our central government to equalize the distribution of student advantages has also had serious economic consequences, in our view. As citizens with the financial means to contribute to schools begin to feel that the local schools do not belong to them, the willingness to make sacrifices for funding declines. Tax measures become more difficult to pass. The movement of middle-class students to private schools or suburban districts that are relatively free from judicial oversight means that the middle-class stakeholders in school systems decline in numbers as well as in involvement. Typifying this middle-class logic was a very candid letter to the editor in a Louisiana district undergoing the pains of a coercive desegregation court order:

> I whole-heartedly disagree with forcing my son and other children to be bused to predominately black or white schools. . . . I moved in [this particular school's district] and not [into a high poverty school's district] to send my son there because of their wonderful test scores . . . but if the powers that be continue to alienate our children, we will continue to send our children to private schools. This means even less money to rebuild your public schools and less money for teacher pay raises . . . everyone has a choice to live in any school district of their choosing . . . I mean, what is next, Judge [anonymous], are you going to say that it's unconstitutional to live in a predominately white or black neighborhood?[19]

Predictably, the desegregating school district in which the cited parent lives had driven thousands of white students from its public schools and went from having a large surplus of funds prior to forced busing, to a huge deficit.[20] Along with a decline in economic support for school systems, a weakening of local civic cultures may also result from federal attempts at social equalization through schools. In the United States, public schools are more than places where children learn lessons. Schools are social centers of communities. They are places where adults make contact with each other through Parent-Teacher Organizations (PTOs), where clubs and youth groups meet in the evenings, and where community meetings are held. Schools occupy special places in the webs of voluntary associations that enable Americans to cultivate practices of public participation. When neighborhood schools are combined to erase differences between neighborhoods, when students are moved from one school to another each year, or when students are bused to schools far from their homes, government disrupts the participatory ties within a local community.

Concerned parents in one tight-knit, rural Louisiana town trying to keep their above-average-achieving community school from being shut down and their children bused to a below-average-achieving school in another distant community tried to intervene in the desegregation case on their own behalf. The U.S. Justice Department responded to the parents' efforts at civic involvement by telling them, "There is no 'right' on the part of parents to maintain neighborhood schools." One of the parents answered, "The government will not dictate where my children should go to school based on the color of their skin . . . we're looking for home schooling or a private school."[21] Given his figurative slap in the face from the federal government for performing his civic duty, does this sound like an individual who will continue his support for public education? Moreover, as we will explain in more detail in Chapter 2, the Justice Department's stance in this particular case is completely contrary to the Supreme Court's decision in *Brown*, where the high court actually rewarded Linda Brown's parents for their efforts to send her to a neighborhood school and then proclaimed their support for the right of all parents to send their children to neighborhood schools "irrespective of race or color."[22]

Desegregation, as it has been practiced since the 1970s, can have consequences other than white flight and middle-class black flight. It can weaken the habit of voluntary association that the insightful Frenchman Alexis de Tocqueville described almost 175 years ago as a foundation of American society.[23] Disrupting communities can diminish the supply of that intangible good, social capital.[24] By taking neighborhood-based schools away from the people who surround them, government removes a critical means of forming effective ties among a community's residents.

For this reason, efforts at the redistribution of social resources may not only undermine more affluent communities; these efforts may also hurt the low-income minority communities these policies are ostensibly designed to help. In fact, the consequences may be even more severe for those with the fewest financial resources. A local school may be the only basis for social organization in a poor neighborhood. If, as we will argue, one of the greatest disadvantages of the poorest in contemporary American society is a lack of effective social ties within families and communities, then in the long run policymakers do minority neighborhoods a grave disservice when imposed policies take away local schools in the name of equalization.

So, although coercive desegregation can create an inconvenience to the better off in society by driving them out of desegregating schools and systems, the negative consequences of this destructive form of governmental redistribution may fall heaviest on the poorest citizens who have many fewer options than the one dictated by the government. Coercive desegregation not only drives away the local source of taxes the middle classes can provide a school system, giving them a sense of ownership, but also can destroy neighborhood minority schools and the community cohesion such institutions provide. And, as we intend to make clear in these pages, it is not a good idea to totally entrust the safekeeping and education of your child to any government. The research suggests that the best educational directors a child can have is his or her concerned parents.

A NOBLE, MISGUIDED VISION

Our study of the topic has led us to believe that school desegregation did not begin to falter because of a failure by the federal judiciary or the Attorney General's Office to enforce a vision of a new racially just world. We recognize that courts did become more willing to release school districts from desegregation orders toward the turn of the century. The 2002 end of court-ordered desegregation in Charlotte-Mecklenburg, North Carolina, where judicially mandated redistributive desegregation began in the early 1970s, was a symbolic event. But the courts did not begin this shift away from sledgehammer desegregation activism because judges lost their appetite for social justice. The change was a response to public demand for some way to end an undemocratic, socially destructive, and ultimately self-defeating intervention in the lives of cities and towns across America.

If federally enforced school desegregation has indeed been such an utter failure, though, why is it still the conventional wisdom of so many intelligent, well-intentioned advocates and academics? We think that the answer to this question is that school desegregation is more than a plan of action that people judge on the basis of success or failure, costs and benefits. It has grown out of efforts to resolve deep contradictions between American political values, on the one hand, and social realities, on the other.

Let's face it: Publicly criticizing the desegregation of schools is not easy. The word "desegregation" implies to many Americans something more than a policy. It carries the weight of a moral imperative. Not long ago one of the authors had a conversation with a newspaper reporter writing a story on desegregation litigation in her Midwest metropolitan area. The reporter remarked that many of the region's staunch academic advocates of continued court action that she had interviewed admitted putting their children in private schools or mostly white suburban schools. She thought it curious that people would be so dedicated to an ideal that they did not support with their own actions. One ardent education reformer in Louisiana who actually acted on her ideals felt she had to set a public example by sending her two sons to majority black schools in Baton Rouge. Her sons eventually found themselves in remedial college classes and never obtained college diplomas. She later lamented her decision. She confessed publicly, "I probably sacrificed Chip and Drew [her sons] for my principles."[25]

As we will discuss in more detail, we think that the actions of most parents, regardless of ideology or color, are based on the immediate interests of their own children. But if their ideals and their actions are contradictory, and if they are unwilling to change their actions, why don't they change their ideals? Why are even opponents of coercive desegregation so often morally defensive? Why do policies apparently at odds with public behavior and community cohesion seem to occupy the ethical high ground? Can there be any doubt that the inner cities of the major urban centers in this country are worse off than they were before forced desegregation?

To understand the moral and political power of contemporary school policies, it is important to look at those policies within the context of historically evolved values regarding human rights, opportunities, and racial inequality. Efforts to use schools to create racial equality are part of the broader idea of civil rights developed over the course of centuries. A close examination of the concept of civil rights and of how school policy has emerged from this concept can clarify the goals and dilemmas of racial policy in education.

THE GENESIS OF CIVIL RIGHTS

Strictly speaking, the term "civil rights" refers to the legal rights of citizens. Over the course of history, though, the meaning of the term has gradually evolved to mean the individual rights of *categories* of people that require government protection. The concepts of individual rights and of the rights of categories of people can be traced to the same origin: the emergence of the modern market society.

The seventeenth-century philosopher John Locke argued that all human beings are born with rights by the sheer fact of human nature. This thinking became an ideological foundation for the extension of European civilization in the New World. Those who founded the United States were greatly influenced by the philosophy of universal natural law and natural rights. The American Declaration of Independence, the chief author of which was

Thomas Jefferson, justified the American revolt against the English crown using arguments derived from the philosophical tradition of Locke. The Declaration stated that all men "are endowed by their Creator with certain inalienable rights."

The Virginia Declaration of Rights, also largely Jefferson's work, in 1776 sought to guarantee basic democratic rights to citizens of the state. This document became the model for the first ten amendments to the Constitution of the United States, known as the Bill of Rights. These rights, possessed by all American citizens as reflections of their essential equality as human beings, were expressions of what is often called negative freedom. In the philosophical tradition of Locke, European and American liberals in the late eighteenth and early nineteenth centuries tended to see freedom primarily as freedom from government interference in the lives of individuals. This is a powerful idea in the history of Western civilization, one that still animates much public debate more than two centuries later. To put in perspective how far the Western ideal of freedom from government has evolved over the last 1,300 years, contrast Jefferson's thinking with the following description of government "typical of the Oriental methods of Baghdad," a Muslim caliphate in the eighth century:[26]

> The police formed an important part of the intelligence service, and their duties included interference in the minutest details of daily life, while in every city a swarm of local officers, judges, tax-gatherers, and stewards of the Crown lands reduced still further the liberty of the subject.[27]

Is it any surprise that the Chinese immigrant mentioned earlier, having emigrated from a country with a long history of suppression of individual rights, would find judicially ordered school desegregation in the United States—a country born of Enlightenment thinking—so anti-Western?

This emphasis on negative freedom derived from ideas first associated with the modern market economy. The market economy encouraged ideas of negative freedom, that is, freedom from political interference. In a market economy, social relations depend on people buying and selling their time, labor, and goods. So, a market economy tends to emphasize the rights of people to be free from compulsion in buying and selling time, labor, and goods. This historical economic basis of the ideology of liberty has led some critics of the market system to characterize that ideology as a mask for exploitation.[28] However, a reasonable response to those critics would be that market societies have generally been successful in meeting human needs.[29]

Beyond the material success of the market, though, the ideas of abstract individual rights created by capitalism have been and continue to be essential for the security and autonomy of modern citizens.

Still, even though the negative freedom of the citizen is both economically and politically necessary, the ideology of individual liberty remains incomplete. People do act as individuals, but they always act as individuals within groups. Families, friendship circles, clubs, companies, religious institutions, and the like, always shape what actions are possible for individuals. This will become an important point in this book as we discuss how the group settings of individuals can exist in a state of tension, or even conflict, with ideas of individual opportunities. In American history, though, the direction of individual life-chances by social setting has been a part of an even more profound contradiction. The ideology of individualism has developed alongside a system of human bondage.

The same market society that produced concepts of abstract human rights also refashioned the age-old institution of slavery to create new categories of people. The seeking of profit, which was the driving force of the economy that began to develop in Europe at the opening of the modern period, produced a society in continual expansion. During the same decade that Columbus reached the shores of the New World seeking competitive trade routes to Asia, the Portuguese began purchasing slaves from kingdoms along the West African coast.

Columbus did not succeed in finding his trade route, in part because he had underestimated the size of the globe, but chiefly because there was a large landmass obstructing the westward journey from Europe to Asia. Still, European expansion managed to make use of the obstructive continent as an outlet for surplus population and as a place for producing consumer goods for the European market. Sugar and tobacco, two of the most successful export products, were plantation crops. They required heavy investments of labor on extensive tracts of land. The growth of plantation economies in North and South America encouraged the importation of slave labor to meet the demand for large numbers of workers. This importation of people from the coast of Africa created a niche for a caste of workers, identifiable by appearance and ancestral place of origin, within a market economy.[30]

Caste may be perfectly acceptable in many societies. In the society that developed in North America, though, it contradicted the fundamental ideology of negative freedom. This contradiction was exemplified in the life of Thomas Jefferson, advocate of individual liberty and holder of more than 200 slaves. Jefferson agonized over the issue of slavery, but he nonetheless retained his own slaves.[31]

The contradiction between beliefs about liberty and the enslavement of one-fifth of early America's population shaped beliefs about race over the course of the nation's history.[32] One way of resolving this contradiction was to define those humans who were denied basic rights as belonging to a special category. In order to justify the bondage, slaveholders argued that their slaves were childlike and needed the protection of their masters. Thus, the influential apologist for slavery Henry Hughes argued in his *Treatise on Sociology* (1854) that the simple slaves as well as the masters benefited from the arrangement. In another version of this solution, it was argued that liberty for slaves would be dangerous to others, as well as to the slaves themselves, since blacks were inherently savage.[33]

Americans whose ancestry could be traced to Africa, then, were denied individual rights on the basis of group membership. With the end of slavery, the question of the status of blacks in American society took on a new urgency. One solution, the most consistent with American political values, was to dissolve the group exclusion of blacks and admit them as individual citizens without distinction from other citizens. Another solution, widely favored among even antislavery whites in the nineteenth century, was to remove former slaves from U.S. soil and resettle them elsewhere. This proved to be unrealistic, in part because members of the formerly enslaved group continued to be a valuable labor force. The third solution, the least consistent with national political values, was to maintain the black population as technically not enslaved, but subordinate to whites.

RECONSTRUCTION AND THE ORIGINS OF "AFFIRMATIVE" PROTECTION OF GROUP RIGHTS

During the early years of Reconstruction, Radical Republicans in the U.S. Congress attempted to implement the first solution to the question of black status. They managed to pass the Civil Rights Act of 1866 over the veto of President Andrew Johnson. Consistent with the ideology of individual rights, the bill declared black Americans to be citizens and to have equal rights with all other citizens. However, while this action was based on Jeffersonian ideas of personal liberty, it was also different from those ideas in at least two important respects. In the earlier American expression of Locke's ideas about the autonomy of the individual, freedom was a consequence of governmental inaction. People were free to the extent that the government did not interfere with them. Inaction was not an option for the federal government under the Radical Republicans, though. Congress had to actively protect the rights of the newly enfranchised blacks, otherwise whites and local governmental and nongovernmental organizations would quickly take those rights away. Thus, this key piece of legislation not only guaranteed equal protection of the law in contracts, lawsuits, trials, property transactions, and purchases; it also prescribed penalties for interfering with this equal protection.

The second way in which the Civil Rights Act of 1866 revised older ideas of individual rights was that the act was, paradoxically but understandably, not aimed at individuals. It sought to protect the individual liberties of a people based on group membership. This can be identified as the source of the "group rights" often criticized in recent times.[34] But to see clearly the origins of governmental protective action aimed at groups, one needs to understand that black Americans were collectively threatened after the Civil War by local whites who would try to resolve the question of black status by putting all blacks into quasi-slavery.

The term "civil rights," then, began to shift from simply meaning the rights of citizens, to having the connotation of minority group rights ensured through the active intervention of the federal government in state and local affairs. Of course, this new approach to civil rights was a variation on one of the central themes of American political life from the nation's beginning, namely, the question of how much power should belong to the national administration and how much should belong to state and local authorities. Ideologies of state and local control had long been tied to the political and social systems of the slave states. These ideologies were cited as justification for the secession of the Southern states, and Confederate apologists still maintain that the Civil War was not a war over slavery but a struggle between decentralized and centralized visions of the American polity.[35] With Reconstruction, though, the contradictions of American civil society took on the form of two competing sets of rights. From the states' rights perspective, political authority should be as close as possible to local communities. From what was becoming the civil rights perspective, the power of authorities below the federal level had to be severely restricted because local communities in the occupied South were undemocratic in structure and would, without outside interference, quickly take away the liberties of a huge section of the citizenry.

RETREAT FROM RECONSTRUCTION AND THE PROTECTION OF GROUP RIGHTS

The United States did become more unified and centrally controlled as a result of the Civil War, and this was never reversed. But part of the compromise to obtain the cooperation of the former Confederate states in the transformed nation was the end of federal intervention on behalf of the black population in those states. The U.S. Congress passed two more pieces of civil rights legislation in the 1870s: the Civil Rights Act of 1871 (the Enforcement Act), which was intended to overturn laws preventing black Americans from voting, and the Civil Rights Act of 1875, which sought to guarantee freedom of access to public places and to give federal courts jurisdiction over cases of violation of this freedom. In the following years, though, the civil rights perspective went into a long period of neglect. Reconstruction ended in 1877, the troops who could protect black citizens were withdrawn, and Congress and the judiciary began to acquiesce to Southern imposition of the third solution to the question of black status. Blacks were largely consigned to a state of serfdom. To make matters worse for blacks, in 1883 the Supreme Court declared the Civil Rights Act of 1875 unconstitutional.

From the end of Reconstruction until after World War II, the idea that the federal government should become involved in local affairs to protect oppressed minority group members stayed at the margins of American public life. As the country left the Civil War behind and entered a period of rapid industrial expansion, the situation of minorities attracted less political attention. Other groups, in addition to black Americans, were excluded from full participation in American life at this time. In the southwestern part of the country, which the United States had taken from Mexico following the Mexican-American War of 1846–1848, the immigration of white Anglos made Hispanics a minority who were subordinated to the new majority. The far west, especially California, had become home to large numbers of Chinese: over 225,000 Chinese arrived in the United States between 1850 and 1882. The Chinese could not become U.S. citizens, and American political parties exploited anti-Chinese feelings. In 1867, anti-Chinese California Democrats won widespread victories in state elections. By 1882, discrimination against Chinese had become a part of U.S. federal law: the U.S. Congress passed the Chinese Exclusion Act in that year, barring the immigration of Chinese laborers.

The retreat from civil rights continued through the first half of the twentieth century. The Supreme Court upheld the "separate but equal" principle in the *Plessy v. Ferguson* decision of 1896, which declared that it was legal to segregate blacks from whites, as long as "equal" facilities were offered to both. Laws enforcing segregation, known as Jim Crow laws, followed this decision in most southern states. By 1950, the following states had state laws requiring racial segregation: Alabama, Arkansas, Delaware, Florida, Georgia, Kentucky, Louisiana, Maryland, Mississippi, Missouri, North Carolina, Oklahoma, South Carolina, Tennessee, Texas, Virginia, and West Virginia. The four states of Arizona, Kansas, New Mexico, and Wyoming did not require segregation, but they did allow local governments to pass ordinances for segregation.

DEVELOPMENT OF BLACK SOCIAL CAPITAL AND THE
STRUGGLE FROM BELOW

In the absence of governmental assistance, black Americans, the nation's largest and most oppressed minority group, began to develop institutions of their own to pursue their collective interests. Black church congregations emerged in the United States during the years immediately following slavery and served as centers of black community life "second only to the family."[36] These congregations were important centers of social and political mobilization, as well as the sharing of information. One of the most comprehensive studies of the black church in America in recent years introduced the subject by remarking, "Not only did it [the black church] give birth to new institutions such as schools, banks, insurance companies, and low income housing, it also provided an academy and an arena for political activities, and it nurtured young talent for musical, dramatic, and artistic development."[37] The black church, in short, became an essential source of black social capital.

Perhaps the most important explicitly political organization of black Americans has been the National Association for the Advancement of Colored People (NAACP). The NAACP was founded in 1910 as a response to lynching. Although a number of whites were prominent in the NAACP, the brilliant black scholar and activist W.E.B. DuBois became its leader. At the same time that the NAACP came into existence, the white philanthropist Mrs. Ruth Standish Baldwin and the black social worker and scholar Dr. George Edmund Haynes founded the Committee on Urban Conditions in New York to work to lessen the discrimination and other problems faced by blacks moving to the northern city. Merging with several other organizations over the following decade, the organization became known in 1920 as the National Urban League.

Black Americans mobilized in labor associations, as well as in religious and political groups. In the railroad industry, black workers confronted discrimination by creating their own unions, struggling against exclusive white affiliations, and relentlessly pursuing redress in the courts.[38] One of the most active and effective of the black labor organizations was the Brotherhood of Sleeping Car Porters, organized and led by A. Philip Randolph.

The modern concept of civil rights, as it emerged in the years following the Civil War, was largely a top-down model of relationships between government and citizens. Ironically, though, the mid- to late-twentieth-century Civil Rights Movement was, at least during its most effective years, primarily a bottom-up form of social action. The institutions that black Americans created through the years of oppression and social exclusion served, ironically, as means of working for equality and inclusion. In September 1940, after the military draft had been established, Walter White of the NAACP and T. Arnold Hill of the National Urban League (NUL) met President Franklin D. Roosevelt to discuss racial discrimination in the armed forces and in defense industries. When Roosevelt took no action, Randolph of the Brotherhood of Sleeping Car Porters began to organize a black protest march on Washington, D.C. Under this pressure, President Roosevelt issued Executive Order 8802, creating the wartime Fair Employment Practices Committee.

Until the middle of the 1960s, governmental action to intervene on behalf of black Americans was reactive in character. It was a result of pressure created by the mobilization of black institutions. The threatened march on Washington, D.C., on the eve of World War II was an early stage of this mobilization, which manifested itself in a number of other strategies for obtaining civic equality for African American citizens. In addition to putting moral pressure on national political leaders, the NAACP, through its Legal Defense and Educational Fund, pursued equality through the courts. It may be revealing that the name of the fund is usually shortened to "Legal Defense Fund."[39] Recognizing that local governments were generally dedicated to maintaining a racial caste system, the lawyers of the NAACP pinned their hopes on bringing cases before the federal courts.

In the late 1940s, under the leadership of Legal Defense Fund director Thurgood Marshall, the NAACP began a struggle to end the segregation of American educational institutions. At first, legal efforts concentrated on graduate and professional schools on the grounds that exclusion from these whites-only institutions usually left aspiring black students without any options at all and therefore such exclusion could not claim the justification of "separate but equal." By 1950, though, the NAACP turned its attention to public schools and began a series of lawsuits that argued that segregated schooling had led to gross inequalities between the schools attended by white children and those attended by black children. These suits culminated in the famous *Brown v. Board of Education of Topeka* decisions, in which the Supreme Court declared that racial discrimination in education was unconstitutional and called for admission to public schools on a racially nondiscriminatory basis.[40]

The legal struggles of the NAACP illustrate a complicated paradox in the history of civil rights in the United States. The concept of civil rights, as it had developed during Reconstruction, implied the protection of a category of people by the central, national government against local oppression. This protection was brief, and the oppressed people turned to developing their own formal social institutions and social capital. But those institutions were

largely excluded from the social and political settings immediately surrounding them. For most of the twentieth century, black institutions could
not serve as a means of getting representatives onto city councils or school
boards. Mobilization was therefore aimed at pressuring federal powers to re-
sume the abandoned interventions of Reconstruction. Bottom-up organization had created social capital, but this capital could only be invested in
top-down efforts at reform.

As judicial efforts to bring about the desegregation of American schools
from above proceeded slowly and painfully, new grassroots struggles to
achieve racial equality came to life in the Civil Rights Movement. A defining
moment in the bottom-up push for equality of rights can be dated to 1955, a
year after the Supreme Court declared school segregation unconstitutional.
A seamstress, Ms. Rosa Parks touched off the protests when she refused to
give up her seat on a bus in a section reserved for whites and was arrested.
The young Rev. Martin Luther King, Jr., with a base in a black religious institution, achieved prominence by organizing a successful boycott of the bus
system.

Even the grassroots efforts of the Civil Rights Movement necessarily appealed to central government intervention to overcome local discrimination.
Four months after Rosa Parks's brave stand, lawyers for the NAACP argued
the case against discrimination on public buses in the Federal District Court,
which ruled against segregated seating. The U.S. Supreme Court upheld the
ruling in *Gayle v. Browder* (1956). In other situations, as well, action from
below provoked responses from the center. In 1960, protestors, primarily students, participated in widespread sit-in demonstrations against segregated
lunch counters and other segregated public facilities. In a series of cases, beginning with *Garner v. Louisiana* (1961), the Supreme Court upheld the right
of protestors to use restaurants and other public facilities.

A RETURN TO RECONSTRUCTION

While black demands for equal citizenship met with resistance from local
governments, particularly in the South, they also pushed the federal government into returning to a legislative agenda that it had abandoned with the
end of Reconstruction. The Civil Rights Act of 1957 created the Civil Rights
Division of the Department of Justice, and it gave the U.S. attorney general
the power to sue on behalf of black citizens who had suffered discrimination
in federal elections. This power to sue was expanded as the Civil Rights Division was charged with enforcing provisions of the Civil Rights Acts of 1960,
1964, and 1968 and the Voting Rights Act of 1965.[41] By the end of the 1960s,

private organizations such as the NAACP were no longer alone in bringing suits to desegregate schools or to pursue other civil rights activities. The Civil Rights Division had become a powerful advocate with enormous financial resources. The development of this division of the Attorney General's Office meant that the federal government came to play a dual role in desegregation lawsuits. It provided both the judiciary and attorneys for parties who charged that a given school system was illegally segregated, by an expanding definition of segregation also created by the federal government. Now, the machinery of all three branches of the federal government was committed to desegregating schools. During the first Reconstruction, the federal government was split in its commitment to civil rights for blacks, with the legislative branch (the Radical Republicans) taking the lead and the executive branch (especially under the first President Johnson) resisting federal interventionism.

We are not suggesting that it was in any sense a mistake for civil rights activists to work through Washington, D.C., to combat discrimination throughout the nation. They had few other choices. Moreover, civil rights legislation has been beneficial to the United States in securing the right to vote for disenfranchised American citizens, in limiting discrimination in housing and in the use of public facilities, and in myriad other ways. Still, even the most beneficial programs may have unfortunate and unforeseen consequences. The late-twentieth-century return to Reconstruction, though understandable when seen in the context of our nation's long history of racial discrimination, was committed to a self-defeating perspective on school policy.

BLINDERS OF MORAL COMMITMENT

The moral drama of the Civil Rights Movement made it difficult for anyone to question actions undertaken in the name of civil rights. Memories of schoolchildren facing screaming bigots, of Freedom Riders being beaten by angry mobs, and of peaceful demonstrators falling before snarling police dogs are still with us. Black and white Americans reacting with revulsion to the centuries of injustice culminating in these memories have tended to accept as just and reasonable any efforts intended to create a more racially egalitarian society. Those who raise doubts about whether the efforts work or are worth the costs paid run the risk of being identified with the side of the screaming bigots and the angry mobs—a strong disincentive indeed.

As we have argued, the development of the concept of civil rights over nearly a century and a half of American history has meant that efforts at making a more racially egalitarian society have come to mean federal intervention, especially by judicial means, in local affairs. Since schools became a focal point for overcoming racial injustice by the middle of the twentieth century, a commitment to racial justice often came to mean the attempt to redesign American society by means of judicial control of schools.

In Chapter 2, as we look at the political and legal history of school deseg-regation, we will argue that the moral momentum of civil rights led to pro-gressively greater and more intrusive federal interventions in American schools over the 1960s and 1970s. The view that a better society could and should be achieved by central planning to redistribute students became deeply entrenched in many sectors of government and academia. It became, in our view, the dominant worldview, a "guiding light." Even after school de-segregation provoked a quiet white desertion of many school districts and losses of social capital in schools and communities, the machinery of school desegregation continued to grind on in many localities. Indeed, some deseg-regation cases grind on blindly today, even if few of the parties directly in-volved seem to understand the larger logic behind what are often self-defeating educational plans and policies.

A poignant example of how officials caught up in efforts to desegregate schools have lost sight of the big picture is illustrated by the following ex-change that took place recently in a federal district courtroom. In response to parental concerns that a court order that involved closing black schools and busing black students could hurt education, one government official stated that the issue was, not to improve education, but to further desegregate the schools.[42] Wearing the blinders of political and moral commitment, the ad-vocates of desegregation policies failed (and still fail) to see the destructive effects of those policies for American schools and communities.

CHAPTER 2

How Did We Get Here?

THE LONG LEGAL ROAD

Now examine how the federal government's approach of using schools to "redesign" American society evolved in a long series of court decisions. We turn to a consideration of how the broader society influenced these judicial decisions and how the federal government modified its policies in response to changing times. The historic *Brown* decision of 1954 was not made in a vacuum. To truly understand *Brown*, one must go back in history and review the unpleasant Jim Crow period of "separate but equal." Brown was a direct response to what was occurring in the United States during this period of "American apartheid."

The America of the early twenty-first century is in some respects not at all comparable to the America of 1954. The desegregation remedies crafted by the federal courts and handed down over the last half-century may have made sense in the context of their times, but now some seem archaic and anachronistic in the light of present social, political, demographic, and educational realities. Even so, the *Brown* decision remains as refreshing and relevant as it was fifty years ago. Unfortunately, the courts have strayed from its central rationale.

Once we understand how *Brown* came about, we can move forward with greater insight into making sense of the fifty years of desegregation litigation and policies that follow *Brown*. This tumultuous half-century of school desegregation can be divided into six distinct periods. The first is the period from *Brown I* (and subsequently *Brown II*) to the Civil Rights Act, when many school systems vigorously resisted desegregating. This timeframe included Eisenhower's mobilizing the National Guard to escort black children to Little Rock High. It also included Prince Edward County, Virginia, closing its schools for five years rather than desegregate. The second period includes the few years of "freedom of choice" immediately following the Civil Rights Act of 1964. School systems, faced with the dilemma of either desegregating or losing federal funding, opted for the money. For a brief few years, blacks were not barred from attending white schools, but neither were they coerced to attend.

The third period, which dates to the epochal 1968 Supreme Court *Green* decision, is the period of the most coercive and destructive federal court orders. This period is typified by massive busing and rezoning based solely on race. It is also the period of huge waves of whites fleeing desegregating school districts, never to return. Seeing the damage being done by their unpopular sledgehammer tactics, the fourth period of desegregation is characterized as a time of legal restraint. Here, we see courts defining the limits of legal action in desegregation cases. For example, the courts draw the line on cross-district busing, a tactic that if implemented could have quite possibly doomed public education in the United States. The fifth period is marked by the judiciary's willingness to release "compliant" school districts from the scrutiny of federal oversight. We finally see significant numbers of districts being granted "unitary status" and control of school districts returned to popularly elected school boards.

We are now at the beginning of the sixth period of desegregation since the *Brown* decision. This period is typified by a rethinking of how government should deal with race in the schools, in part as a consequence of rapidly changing demographics, and in part as a consequence of two high-profile cases. Courts, policymakers, and scholars now have a half-century of accumulated experience with school desegregation from which to derive useful lessons. The United States could be on the cusp of completely abandoning the race-based assignment of students. Yet, if two recent court cases and the comment of a Supreme Court Justice offer any clues, we may be entering a whole era of obsession with race in the public schools, or what could become a proxy for race—student socioeconomic status.

Before considering *Brown* and the seminal court cases that followed, we must first review one of the most unpleasant periods in American racial history. This era began more than a century ago with one of the most ignominious Supreme Court decisions ever handed down.

AMERICAN APARTHEID

Following the removal of Yankee troops from Southern soil in 1876, which had been stationed in the former Confederacy to enforce post–Civil War Reconstruction, the South quickly put the black man "in his place." And his place was not among whites. Southern state legislatures, which had been racially integrated for the first time in history, were once again "whites-only" institutions as blacks were disenfranchised and whites voted their own back in office. Within twenty years of Reconstruction's end, blacks were *de facto* completely segregated from whites in most areas of Southern society. One of those areas was in transportation. In 1890 Louisiana passed a statute relegating blacks to their own separate train cars. In a planned challenge to Louisiana's law, a New Orleans Creole named Homer Plessy, who was one-eighth black, boarded a "whites-only" car. He was summarily ejected. Plessy sued based on racial discrimination, arguing that his Fourteenth Amendment "equal protection" rights had been denied him. The case eventually wound its way to the docket of the U.S. Supreme Court. In *Plessy v. Ferguson*,[1] the high court ruled in favor of the states' right to make distinctions based on race and to provide "separate" accommodations for blacks—provided they were "equal." In his powerful and reasoned dissenting opinion, Justice Harlan argued that the Constitution was "color blind." His concerns went unheeded. Armed with the law of the land, the rest of the South raced to pass laws mandating *de jure* racial separation between whites and blacks in virtually every area of Southern society. This included restaurants, theaters, schools, churches, and even cemeteries. These accommodations were certainly separate but rarely, if ever, equal.

The South entered into a period of legal apartheid much as did South Africa at the same time. In fact, Mahatma Gandhi, a British-trained lawyer, was thrown from a "whites-only" train car in South Africa for his "brown-skin" only one year after *Plessy*. Like Plessy, Gandhi used his experience to challenge South Africa's race laws—with only slightly better results. Like a spreading cancer, Jim Crow legislation passed in states and localities across the South not only disenfranchised blacks politically but also kept them at arm's length. The white power establishments relegated the grandchildren and great grandchildren of slaves to their own impoverished—and legally powerless—spheres of little influence at the margins of white Southern society. With the law on their side, white power elites ensured that blacks were politically barred from challenging their new condition, which was in many ways little better than that of their enslaved ancestors. As noted in the last chapter, blacks did, however, maintain their own healthy social and political institutions, most notably the church. Black communities, though separate, remained strong. The NAACP, founded in 1910 to defend and extend black rights, began its long and methodical struggle to overturn the *Plessy* "separate but equal" doctrine.

The *Plessy* ruling was quickly applied to schools. In 1899 the Supreme Court upheld a Georgia school board's action to close a black high school but continue taxing the whole district to support its white high schools. The displaced black high school students were "encouraged" to continue their educations in parochial schools.[2] The black plaintiffs sued, arguing as in *Plessy*, and as in most cases that would follow, that the law was not being applied equally and thus violated the Fourteenth Amendment "equal protection" clause. Blacks were paying taxes to support white high schools, but they had no high school of their own. They asked to be allowed to attend the existing all-white district high schools. The state of Georgia upheld the school board's actions. On appeal, the U.S. Supreme Court did not interfere in the board's refusal to keep black students from attending the white high school. In logic reminiscent of the antebellum period, the high court ruled that the entire issue was a state matter, not a federal one. It had washed its hands of the issue.

Then, in the 1908 case of *Berea College v. Commonwealth of Kentucky*,[3] the high court upheld a Kentucky law that mandated that no educational institution could provide instruction for blacks and whites unless classrooms for each respective race were at least twenty-five miles apart. Berea College was a private institution created in 1855 for the express purpose of educating blacks and whites together. At one point, fully 50 percent of the student body was black. However, in upholding Kentucky's Jim Crow legislation, the high court significantly extended the "separate but equal" doctrine to include not only private institutions, but higher educational institutions as well. The "separate but equal" doctrine was now all but enshrined in stone in many American communities and American schools.

BLACK GRASSROOTS RESISTANCE TO "SEPARATE BUT EQUAL"

The 1930s saw the beginning of the most serious challenges to the legally segregated South. The NAACP sued the University of Missouri to allow blacks into its law school. Blacks had no other means to obtain law degrees in the state. The case reached the Supreme Court, and the high bench ruled against the state. The Supreme Court argued that blacks had to be admitted to the all-white law school, since no "separate" facilities were available for blacks.[4]

As discussed in Chapter 1, World War II marked an increasing awareness of enforced inequality among African Americans. As American blacks fought to free other oppressed peoples around the globe, the war fueled their own struggle for racial equality and full inclusion in American society at home. In the military, blacks demanded and were ultimately granted legal rights equal to those of their white comrades-in-arms. In 1948 Truman signed Executive Order 9981 that mandated the racial integration of America's armed forces. The Korean War of 1950 to 1953 saw the first racially integrated combat units since the Civil War, and these served as a model for how blacks and whites could successfully integrate in other social spheres.

A Supreme Court decision in 1950 would be the biggest setback to that date for the "separate but equal" doctrine. Because there was no Texas law school for blacks, a black man named Herman Marion Sweatt sued for admission to the University of Texas law school. The state of Texas responded by hastily slapping together a woefully inadequate black law school in the basement of a building. The NAACP and its lead attorney, the future chief justice Thurgood Marshall, brought Sweatt's case before the U.S. Supreme Court and argued for his admission to the white University of Texas law school. The high court agreed with the persuasive arguments of the skillful Thurgood Marshall and ruled that the new black law school was hardly "equal" to the white law school.[5] Sweatt won the case, setting a high court precedent acknowledging that "separate" educational facilities for blacks were not necessarily equal. The reality was that they were almost never equal and, indeed, were usually grossly inadequate.[6] The successful rationale used in the *Sweatt* case would become important legal fodder in Marshall's assault on the Topeka Board of Education just four years later.

Political pressure and consensus continued building throughout the early 1950s to re-enfranchise blacks and grant this group expanded civil rights, even if few at first envisioned the broad scope of the movement that was about to be unleashed. Some institutions, even in the Deep South, could see the handwriting on the wall and began desegregating before the momentous *Brown* decision. For example, the first black admitted to the then Southwestern Louisiana Institute, now the University of Louisiana, was admitted only two months after the *Brown* decree, without fanfare or white community resistance.[7] However, it still took a lawsuit to get her in.[8]

THE EARTHQUAKE OF *BROWN I*

It is the *Brown v. Board of Education of Topeka* decision of 1954 that marks the modern period of school desegregation and, indeed, the entire Civil Rights

Movement. The high court decision said in effect that virtually every public school system in the South was in violation of the law, since black children were refused the right to attend all-white schools. The Supreme Court, in ruling in favor of ten-year-old Linda Brown seeking admittance to an all-white school in her Topeka, Kansas, neighborhood, concluded tersely: "In the field of public education the doctrine of 'separate but equal' has no place. Separate educational facilities are inherently unequal." As momentous as *Brown* was, the specifics of the court decision were not as draconian as many court orders that would be handed down after 1968. For example, nowhere in *Brown* do we see a hint of the busing, rezoning, and clustering of schools that would typify the aggressive desegregation remedies to come twenty years later, in the 1970s. The *Brown* decision was beautiful in its clear simplicity: "School children irrespective of race or color shall be required to attend the school in the district in which they reside and that color or race is no element of exceptional circumstances warranting a deviation of this basic principal."[9] With these words, the court seemed to endorse the concept of the neighborhood school as well as Justice Harlan's earlier colorblind attitude toward race. If blacks lived in the same geographical locality as whites, they could not legally be prohibited from attending the local school with whites because they had the same status as students—not "black" students or "white" students—just students. Though the court's dictum may seem mild by comparison with the more race conscious "affirmative" judicial actions of twenty years later, its ruling was still revolutionary for its time. Indeed, it was so revolutionary that it triggered defiance and protest throughout the South that would continue for more than a decade. Several southern governors swore that schools would not desegregate under their administrations.

When it became clear that simply ordering schools to abide by the high court's ruling was not enough to change decades of apartheidlike educational practices, the high court issued a second decree in 1955, sometimes referred to as *Brown II*.[10] This second ruling ordered districts to desegregate with "all deliberate speed." *Brown II* also charged federal district courts with overseeing implementation of the high court's ruling, as well as crafting "remedies" for individual school districts under their jurisdictions. As we will soon see, this empowerment of federal district courts to devise their own desegregation plans would prove to be a mixed blessing.

Southern intransigence continued. In 1957 President Eisenhower was forced to take the unprecedented action of ordering National Guard troops to escort seven black children into a formerly all-white high school in Little Rock, Arkansas. This audacious federal intervention, the first of its kind since northern soldiers occupied the South during Reconstruction, seemed to simply embolden southern segregationist leaders, who campaigned on platforms of school racial segregation. Singing governor Jimmy Davis of Louisiana (of the "You Are My Sunshine" fame) threatened to shut down the entire New Orleans public school system rather than allow school racial desegregation to proceed. The Virginia Assembly actually did pass legislation authorizing the closing of any school that allowed blacks and whites to attend together. Then, in 1959, the Prince Edward County school board in Virginia did just that: it shut down the entire school system for five years rather than allow black children to sit next to white children in the same classroom.

Some limited school desegregation in the South did begin taking place in the early 1960s. For example, New Orleans drew national attention when it finally allowed blacks to attend formerly all-white schools in 1961 (in spite of Governor Davis's segregationist bluster and white parents who called themselves "the cheerleaders" harassing black children enrolling for the first time in all-white schools). Still, progress was plodding, and there was much resistance and foot-dragging until the passage of the Civil Rights Act of 1964. Then, everything began changing.

A SEA CHANGE OF CIVIL RIGHTS

The Civil Rights Act of 1964 did more than guarantee unprecedented rights for groups of individuals. It also allowed the federal government to withhold federal funding from those school systems that discriminated based on the categories of *race*, religion, or national origins (emphasis added). With the passage of the Elementary and Secondary Education Act (ESEA) of 1965, which included billions of dollars for new federal programs such as Headstart, the Free and Reduced Price Lunch Program, and Title I compensatory educational funds, the federal government now had a very big carrot . . . and an equally big stick.

The job of breaking down white southern resistance to school desegregation was made even easier by the changing tides of societal and political attitudes toward civil rights for blacks. Martin Luther King, Jr.'s "I Have a Dream" speech at the Lincoln Memorial in 1963 drew a quarter million whites and blacks pressing for full inclusion of African Americans in mainstream American society. Scenes of peaceful civil rights protesters contrasted sharply with images of southern white police officers brutally enforcing segregationist policies against nonviolent white and black resistance. By the early and mid-1960s it was clear to most Americans which group had the morally superior position. Memories of burly cops bludgeoning helpless black protesters for merely sitting at the "wrong" restaurant counter were seared deeply into the American collective consciousness. The way was being prepared for a torrent of federal legislation and high court edicts that would have an uncommon moral underpinning that few would dare challenge.

In 1964, the U.S. Supreme Court ruled against the Prince Edward County school board, ordering the district to reopen schools.[11] The high court decision outlawed state action authorizing the closing of schools to avoid desegregation. The ruling also forbid states from funding private, "segregationist academies," as private schools for whites only would come to be called.

FREEDOM OF CHOICE

Within several years after passage of the Civil Rights Act, most *de jure* school segregation came to an end, as southern school systems lifted their legal bans on blacks and whites attending school together. This brief period of educational history is referred to as the "freedom of choice" era, since students ostensibly had the choice about whether or not to attend a school with children from another race. There is evidence to suggest that during the "freedom of choice" period, most southern school systems effectively complied with the 1954 *Brown* decision, dismantling their "dual *de jure* segregated systems" based on race.[12]

In reality, however, there was intense social pressure among whites, and to some extent even among blacks, to attend schools populated by students from their own race. Moreover, some districts found creative ways to stymie meaningful desegregation. Finally, blacks and whites simply tended to live in different areas. Attending a school in one's neighborhood district usually meant attending a one-race school. For all these reasons, including a strong desire to create truly racially balanced schools, the high court handed down a decision that would have consequences for schools and communities almost as profound as *Brown*. This decision would ultimately be the death knell not only of school choice but also of viable and vibrant public education in many areas of the United States.

"AFFIRMATIVE" ACTION

The tumultuous year of 1968 marked perhaps the closest that American society came to disintegrating since the Civil War of a century earlier. Indeed, it was a year marked by uncommon violence on several fronts. The United States was embroiled in another divisive war, which was to become exponentially more divisive with the explosive Tet Offensive in early February. The communists in South Vietnam launched attacks on 150 villages and cities that shook American confidence in its government to the very core. The Johnson administration had been misleading American citizens about United States success in Southeast Asia, and Tet fueled a growing antiwar movement in the United States that would eventually change American foreign policy and bring an end to the first war America ever lost.

But Tet was only the beginning of violence in 1968. The year continued with the assassination of Dr. Martin Luther King, Jr. in April that cast a long shadow over the whole nonviolent Civil Rights Movement he had lead. Disillusionment swept the black community, and angrier black voices began to attract more attention and respect. The country was still racially on edge when Robert Kennedy, another icon of the Civil Rights Movement who was on his way to becoming the Democratic nominee for president, was cut down by a crazed assassin's bullets in early June. Then, all hell broke loose during the sizzling summer of 1968. Increasingly violent black protests lead to the burning of numerous inner cities, including Detroit, Buffalo, Newark, and the nation's capital city, Washington. The black radical movement, symbolized by the founding of the Black Panther Party for Self-Defense in 1966 (later shortened to just Black Panther Party) would reach a pinnacle of sorts in 1968 following the murders of Dr. King and Robert Kennedy. Finally, to cap off the most violent summer on American soil since 1864, erupted the chaos and bedlam in August that was the Democratic National Convention in Chicago. Not since the presidential election of 1860 had the American political process been marked by such confusion, division, and acrimony.

It was in this explosive social atmosphere of 1968 that the high court handed down its equally seismic *Green* decision. The liberal leaning court ruled that the New Kent County, Virginia, school board's "freedom of choice" desegregation plan was neither working nor constitutional.[13] That it was not working was beyond question. As the court noted, In three years of operation not a single white child has chosen to attend Watkins school . . . and 85 percent of the Negro children in the school system still attend the all-Negro Watkins school. In other words, the school system remains a dual system.

Neither was the New Kent County school system unique. In systems across the South where "freedom of choice" was the policy, very few blacks attended white schools and almost no whites attended black schools. In *Green* the high court ruled that such school boards were "clearly charged with the affirmative duty to take whatever steps might be necessary to convert to a unitary system in which racial discrimination would be *eliminated root and branch* [emphasis added]." Moreover, the court added that any desegregation plans had to promise *"immediate* [emphasis added] progress toward disestablishing state-imposed segregation" toward the end that systems did not have "a 'white' school or a 'black' school, but just schools." So, the court, in effect, moved from the pre-*Brown* period of "state-imposed segregation" to the opposite extreme of state-imposed desegregation. *Green* marks the beginning of racial social engineering in America's public schools.

Since most southern systems indeed had either "white schools or black schools," enforcing the Supreme Court's order to undo so systemic and ingrained a social reality would be the educational equivalent of the unsettling social revolution then sweeping the country. The *Green* decision went on to delineate six specific areas where school systems needed to desegregate in order to become "unitary" (i.e., get the courts out of running your school system), and these have since become known as the Green Factors. These areas were (1) student assignment, (2) teacher assignment, (3) facilities, (4) transportation, (5) extracurricular activities, and (6) staff (administration). The court decision specifically mentioned rezoning as a legitimate desegregation tool, moving away from the *Brown I* decision supporting the concept of neighborhood district schools.

Thus, we see a sea-change in judicial thinking on school desegregation, as school districts were now mandated to immediately seek to racially mix student populations. Rather than moving toward Justice Harlan's ideal of a "color blind" Constitution or Dr. King's vision of children who were unaware of the shading of each others' skin, the country embarked on a course of hypersensitivity to student race. Teachers were now ordered to count the number of white and black children in their classes on a daily basis. *Green* marks the opening salvo in the affirmative action era of school desegregation, the period of most active and in many instances intrusive judicial meddling in the operation of local school districts. The consequences for many white and black students, as well as their schools and communities, would be disastrous.

MAXIMUM FEDERAL INVOLVEMENT

The social tumults of the 1960s continued into the next decade, with 1970 marking the year of the largest antiwar protests ever witnessed on American soil. It also marked the year of the largest rock concert in history in Woodstock, New York, which epitomized an era of high hopes and inspired Charles Reich's melodramatic prose in his bestselling book *The Greening of America*, where he envisioned a hippie utopia coming to pass in America.[14] The idealism on display in both of these largely youth-directed activities would eventually contribute to ending America's longest war. This idealism and activism was also evident in two early 1970s desegregation cases that would further extend judicial reach into local school district decision making.

The first major desegregation case decided by the Supreme Court in the 1970s was *Swann v. Charlotte-Mecklenburg Board of Education* (1971).[15] Though some elements of the *Swann* ruling were remarkably balanced, insightful, and even visionary, other elements would later be used to justify some spectacular failures in the racial engineering of school populations. *Swann* was the high court's first explicit endorsement of busing as a legal remedy to end racial desegregation in formerly *de jure* segregated school districts. Additionally, the justices in the *Swann* ruling upheld the constitutionality of "pairing" and "grouping" of noncontiguous school zones (gerrymandering), endorsed majority to minority transfers with mandatory transportation, and allowed the use of racial target ratios as desegregation tools. In *Swann* the "moral momentum" of the Civil Rights Movement reached a pinnacle with regards to the court's greatest manipulation of schools as instruments to redesign not just attendance zones, but society itself. By 1971, the sheer speed and weight of the movement had swept up individuals and groups and carried them along for a ride that was not always easy to steer or resist. To quote Reich, "The transformation that is coming invites us to reexamine our own lives."[16] Indeed!

A second early 1970s high court desegregation ruling that significantly extended judicial involvement and oversight in local school district affairs was the case of *Keyes v. School District No. 1, Denver*.[17] Prior to *Keyes*, only school districts that had a history of previous statutory *de jure* dual school systems, such as those found in the former Confederacy and border states, were ordered by courts to desegregate. In other words, before 1973, *Brown I* had only been applied to school systems that had by official legal action established two separate (dual) systems of schools, one for blacks and one for whites. In *Keyes*, however, the court ruled that the Denver, Colorado, school board "by use of various techniques such as the manipulation of student attendance zones, school site selection and a neighborhood school policy, created or maintained racially or ethnically (or both racially and ethnically) segregated schools."

The *Keyes* case thus opened up school systems across the entire United States to legal desegregation action, provided it could be proven that "school authorities have carried out a systematic program of segregation affecting a substantial portion of the students, schools, teachers, and facilities within the school system."[18] On the one hand, the courts were finally acknowledging the reality that it was not only southern school districts that had unconstitutionally segregated schools and students based on race, however subtle the discrimination. On the other hand, the vast judicial efforts to redesign school districts that had concentrated on the South would now be extended to nonsouthern school districts and communities throughout the United States. Moreover, it was very difficult for school districts charged with racially discriminatory actions to defend themselves, and they were almost always found guilty, whether or not there had actually been discriminatory intent.[19] The existence of racially identifiable schools was in itself sufficient evidence of a discriminatory and culpable system. Northern and western school systems ordered to desegregate were, like their southern counterparts, mandated to achieve certain prescribed racially balanced ratios. As in the South, this would prove an almost impossibly elusive feat, with predictably destructive consequences for schools, communities, and entire school districts.

BOSTON BURNS

One of the most celebrated of northern desegregation cases that underscored the cataclysmic damage that an all-powerful judicial decree could wreak occurred shortly after the *Keyes* case, in Boston. In 1974 the Boston school district was found guilty of *de jure* segregation and was ordered to implement one of the most ambitious mandatory student reassignment plans ever devised by a court. The plan ordered thousands of blacks from the northern part of the city bused to the southern part, and white students from South Boston ("Southies," of whom many were Irish-Americans) bused northward. Students being bused from their neighborhood schools could literally wave to other students being bused in from far away to take their places. Following rioting and bus burnings by incensed white parents, whites began fleeing the system by the thousands, never to return. The percentage of white students in the average minority child's classroom in Boston decreased every single year from the beginning of forced busing in 1974 to the turn of the twenty-first century, during which time the system went from 57 percent to 15 percent white.[20]

Somewhat ironically, the Boston school system was declared unitary in 1989, after it had lost most of its white students. However, race-based school assignments continued until 2000—as did white flight—until the practice was supposedly abandoned as a policy following a parent-initiated lawsuit. Apparently, however, some policies just die hard, and the practice continued. So, the Boston school system was sued yet again in 2002 for considering the race of students in school admissions. Only this time, the school board was accused of discrimination against white, and not black, students.[21]

The command and control approach to school desegregation of the type imposed upon the citizens of Boston was supposed to usher in a new social order of racial peace, harmony, and equality in this former abolitionist stronghold. Unfortunately, the social planners overlooked the fact that schools are not just expressions of political goals; they are social environments embedded in American communities. Policies cannot succeed if they are inconsistent with the interests of individuals, social groups, and communities. Obviously, parents in Boston did not see hour-and-a-half bus rides to distant schools in faraway communities as in the best interest of their children.

A MIGHTY SOCIAL FORCE

As social movement theory would predict, some of the moral underpinnings of the civil rights era became institutionalized in governmental policies like affirmative action and judicial rulings like *Green, Swann,* and *Keyes.* In the face of a dramatic struggle to right the wrongs of the past, it became increasingly difficult to voice opposition to even unproductive policies without seeming racist, narrow-minded, or just plain cold-hearted.

Nowhere was the pressure to conform to enforced utopian morality more intense than on America's college and university campuses, fresh from their moral victory in helping to end what was widely considered an immoral war in Vietnam. The somewhat bizarre case of Professor David Armor provides a glimpse into the political and social atmosphere prevalent in academia at the time. Prior to the Boston busing debacle of 1974, Armor, who was an associate professor in social relations at Harvard University, had discovered in a voluntary pilot study that busing black Boston students to white suburban schools generated few academic or social benefits for the bused students and in fact may have hurt them. He submitted his research for publication to the *Harvard Education Review* but was told by the editor that his findings were too controversial (and not that they were inaccurate). The editor told Armor that the journal was still feeling the heat from the Arthur Jenson research it had recently published, which claimed the black-white IQ gap was hereditary.

However, as chance would have it, Armor bumped into the future senator Daniel Patrick Moynihan on an airliner. At the time, Moynihan was a professor of government at Harvard and an independent social thinker in his own right. Sitting together on the flight, Moynihan listened sympathetically to Armor's story and then encouraged him to submit his article to the more widely circulated *Public Interest,* with which the professor of government was affiliated as a member of its publication committee.[22] Armor's evidence that busing was not working was published in *Public Interest,* picked up by the popular press, and widely disseminated in leading newspapers around the country. His findings created a bit of a firestorm and prompted an academic adversary at Harvard to go as far as stealing his data.[23] Even though Armor's scientifically rigorous study was published, widely read, and available to the courts, its central findings were entirely ignored when the judiciary and policymakers crafted Boston's desegregation order a few years later. The policymakers listened only to the proponents of busing, believing that these were voices of social justice.

SETTING LIMITS

While the decade of the 1970s was the period of greatest extension in judicial power over local school districts ordered to desegregate, there were also several seminal cases that defined the limits of court action. The previously mentioned *Swann* case of 1971, while authorizing several affirmative desegregation remedies, including busing, also stated that school districts could not be held responsible for racial imbalances caused by demographic factors beyond a school board's control, and that

> neither school authorities nor district courts are constitutionally required to make year-by-year adjustments of the racial composition of school bodies once the affirmative duty to desegregate has been accomplished and racial discrimination through official action is eliminated from the system.[24]

In other words, once a system was declared unitary, it did not need to constantly readjust the racial balance of schools according to previously set court ratios.

Among the most pivotal decisions of the 1970s to set judicial restraints was *Milliken I*,[25] which banned cross-district desegregation remedies. The significance of the 1974 *Milliken* high court decision cannot be overstated. The Court of Appeals had ruled with the plaintiffs that in order to meaningfully desegregate the majority black Detroit City School district, cross-district busing with the fifty-one majority white suburban districts would be necessary. Had such an action been ruled constitutional—and enforced—it is conceivable that the Detroit metropolitan area would look quite different today. With forty years of experience and hindsight to inform us, it is highly likely that as lower-socioeconomic students filled Detroit's suburban schools, many affluent blacks and whites would have either put their children in nonpublic schools or fled the Detroit metropolitan area altogether.

More significantly, however, had *Milliken I* been decided in favor of the plaintiffs, a precedent would have been established allowing cross-district busing in every metropolitan area whose core city was found to operate a *de jure* segregated school system. Thus, not only would the schools and communities of Detroit's metro area have been transformed but it is possible that the schools and communities surrounding Denver, Boston, New Orleans, Baton Rouge, Dallas, Houston, Los Angles, and many other metropolitan areas would also have been radically changed. The Supreme Court's overriding principle established in *Milliken I* was that "the scope of the [desegregation] remedy is determined by the nature and extent of the constitutional violation." In other words, the punishment has to fit the crime.

In general, the ban on cross-district busing held in the years following *Milliken I*. One exception was in Louisville, Kentucky. There, the Supreme Court allowed the merging of predominantly black Louisville schools with surrounding public schools in 1975 on the grounds that both city and suburbs had together maintained segregated schools and that both would therefore have to bear the "burden" of the remedy (see Chapter 5). The resulting Louisville riots, in which angry whites protested, made national news but failed to sway the course of legal history.

An important principle originally set forth in the *Swann* case, which stated that there were limits to judicial reach in dismantling dual school systems, was applied and elaborated upon in a famous case involving the Pasadena City Board of Education.[26] The Pasadena, California, school board, which had been found to have unconstitutionally segregated schools, submitted a plan in 1970 that racially balanced all schools in the district. The court accepted the plan. Four years later, however, the original plaintiffs in the case brought suit against the board because the minority population in several schools once again exceeded 50 percent. In reviewing the court of appeals decision, the Supreme Court ruled in favor of the board, which it decreed had no control over the subsequent resegregation of Pasadena's schools. It elaborated on the earlier *Swann* principle, stating that "neither school authorities nor district courts are constitutionally required to make year-by-year adjustments of the racial composition of student bodies once the affirmative duty to desegregate has been accomplished."[27]

Importantly, the court recognized that once a system had in good will imposed a desegregation plan that was approved by all parties in a case, the district could not be held accountable for subsequently shifting racial compositions of schools resulting from changing residential demographics. Had the court ruled differently, the desegregation histories of many districts could have evolved in radically different ways.

UNITARY STATUS AND THE END OF OVERSIGHT

From very early in the desegregation drama, some school districts' deseg-regation plans were deemed adequate to undo "previous vestiges of *de jure* segregation," and these systems were released from federal judicial oversight in short order. The high court itself recognized the importance of local con-trol over schools, and in several important rulings it defined strict limits to judicial interference in local educational affairs. The process by which a for-merly "dual system" school district could be declared "unitary" had to be worked out in the courts case by case. The parameters set forth in the 1968 *Green* decision were among the first specific guidelines for determining whether or not a system could be declared unitary. Other guidelines followed.

An issue that arose fairly early on was the length of time the federal dis-trict courts could exercise oversight after a school system was in compliance with the court-ordered plan. Oklahoma City, which was ordered to desegre-gate in 1961, was still found to have vestiges of its dual system in place eleven years later in 1972. The court ordered the board to adopt a more stringent de-segregation remedy, which the board faithfully implemented to the satisfac-tion of the court. Five years later, in 1977, the district court released the Oklahoma City school system from court oversight, ruling, "substantial com-pliance with the constitutional requirements has been achieved." Five years later, however, another suit was filed against the board to reopen the case be-cause of the board's new student assignment policy. The case eventually wound its way to the Supreme Court, which ruled that since Oklahoma City had been decreed unitary, the case could not be reopened unless the school system was found in violation of the Fourteenth Amendment "equal protec-tion" clause. The court declared that "from the very first, federal supervision of local school systems was intended as a temporary measure to remedy past discrimination . . . decrees are not intended to operate in perpetuity."[28]

Another important principle laid down by the Supreme Court in the *Oklahoma City* case was that districts only had to eliminate vestiges of past *de jure* discrimination "to the extent practicable."[29] As we have seen from the de-structive consequences of the chaotic Boston and Baton Rouge cases (and the even more bizarre Kansas City, Missouri, case that we discuss later), there has apparently been a lot of wiggle room in the interpretation of what is "prac-tical." The fact is, what was deemed a practical remedy for a desegregating school system was often more a function of who was the federal district court judge adjudicating the case than of the actual specifics of the case.

Another major issue to be resolved was whether or not a system could be released piecemeal from court supervision. In other words, could a system be freed from court oversight on one or more Green Factors at a time, while the courts continued supervision on those factors not yet adequately addressed? In *Freeman v. Pitts,* which involved the suburban Atlanta county of DeKalb, the high court pronounced that this was indeed a constitutionally and pragmatically sound approach to returning control to local boards. DeKalb County had achieved its racial balancing goal in the first year of implementation, but subsequent demographic shifts in the county meant it could not meet its stated objective in each the following sixteen years. Still, the district court declared that the DeKalb County system was unitary in student assignment, since the system had undone the previous *de jure* injury. The lower court also declared the system unitary on every other Green Factor except teacher and administrator assignment. The case was appealed and eventually landed on the high court's docket, which ruled that systems could be released piecemeal from judicial oversight. The Supreme Court went on to affirm that systems could not be held accountable for shifts in residential housing patterns beyond their control and that "racial balance is not to be achieved for its own sake"—a wise pronouncement, but one that was not always heeded by lower courts.

In 1999, a federal district court judge ruled that Charlotte-Mecklenburg was at last unitary on student assignment and could no longer use race-based student assignment to schools or school programs. Ironically, the system was declared unitary after the parents of a white child filed a lawsuit claiming that the district was violating the Fourteenth Amendment "equal protection" clause and discriminating against their child based on race. In other words, the district was practicing "reverse discrimination." The six-year-old was refused admittance to a gifted program because "all the slots available to non-blacks had been filled." Though appealed, the full Fourth District Circuit Court of Appeals eventually upheld the lower court ruling. The court of appeals ruling was itself appealed to the U.S. Supreme Court, which refused to hear the case. Thus came to an end one of the most celebrated desegregation cases in history.

THE FUTURE OF DESEGREGATION LITIGATION

The Connecticut Conundrum

What does the future of desegregation litigation hold? The Connecticut case of *Sheff v. O'Neill,* and its tentative settlement in 2003 may provide a glimpse into the new age of desegregation litigation.[30] In this landmark case the Connecticut Supreme Court potentially opened up an entirely new strategy for plaintiffs in school desegregation cases. The state court ruled that the Hartford public school system violated students' rights by not providing an equal educational opportunity to its largely poor black and Hispanic students, as prescribed in the state's constitution. Moreover, in *Sheff* the court ruled that the *de facto* racial, ethnic, and economic segregation of Hartford's schools was unconstitutional. This is a radical departure from having to remedy *de jure* segregation, which was the standard applied in previous federal court cases, as well as economic segregation, which had never been targeted by a federal desegregation case. In addition, Hartford was ordered to institute cross-district desegregation remedies to rectify the racial and ethnic segregation of the capital city's schools, a practice largely abandoned elsewhere after the 1974 *Milliken* decision.

Sheff removed desegregation from the federal courts and made it a state issue. The state of Connecticut constitution requires that an "equal educational opportunity" be provided to all Connecticut students. The U.S. Constitution has no such clause and does not even contain the words "school" and "education." If dealt with as a state and not a federal issue, previous federal court rulings based on the Fourteenth Amendment do not necessarily apply. In other words, where a district like Boston had been found guilty of *de jure* segregation, the remedy ordered by the court was meant to undo the damages caused by *de jure* segregation. But the Hartford case was based, not on a previous *de jure* segregation injury, but on an entirely different legal rationale: the equal educational opportunity clause of the Connecticut state constitution. Thus, the remedy to rectify the transgression of an "unequal" educational opportunity could be much more radical indeed.

The plaintiffs brought the case against the Hartford school district in 1989. In 2003 the plaintiffs in the case won a partial victory, with the Connecticut Supreme Court awarding a tentative settlement of $45 million to the impoverished Hartford district over a four-year period to decrease *de facto* racial and economic segregation. However, the state of Connecticut's Office of Fiscal Analysis estimates that the cost of the desegregation remedies, which included building two new magnet schools per year for four years, is likely to soar to $89 million.[31] The whole plan, involving several suburban districts that surround Hartford, is estimated to cost a much steeper $245 million.[32]

Since the case focused on *de facto* racial *and* socioeconomic segregation, *Sheff* could inspire similar lawsuits against other states in which districts are segregated into rich and poor but have been exempt from desegregation litigation because they have no history of *de jure* school segregation. According to the desegregation expert Richard Kahlenberg,[33] this could potentially re-open the legality of cross-district busing, something ruled unconstitutional for *de jure* racial desegregation purposes in the 1974 *Milliken* case. More recently, Kahlenberg has argued that metropolitan socioeconomic desegregation reme-dies could be entirely defensible and could free plaintiffs from previous fed-eral court rulings severely limiting desegregation strategies based on race.[34]

We agree with Kahlenberg that the *Sheff* case may indeed have tremendous implications for reinstituting cross-district busing and other "affirmative" strategies for the purpose of "socioeconomic" integration. However, in states where poverty and race are closely correlated, as they are in most states, there is little material difference between socioeconomic and racial segregation.[35] As such, we predict that similar undesirable consequences would follow from the affirmative desegregation remedies suggested by Kahlenberg.

The *Sheff* case already has some disturbing elements. One similarity is the open-ended nature of the settlement. The plaintiffs in the case have the op-tion of asking for additional funding in 2007 if the racial, ethnic, and eco-nomic isolation of Hartford's students have not been significantly reduced. Given the track record of previous inner-city desegregation efforts, the plain-tiffs may well be approaching the supreme court of Connecticut with hat-in-hand in the coming years. Also, the Hartford district is counting on the surrounding suburban districts to supply middle-class students for the eight new magnet schools ordered built to comply with the settlement, while lim-iting the number of Hartford minority students who can attend these schools to 30 percent per school. In the event that the students in the surrounding suburban districts do not participate in the "build it and they will come" plan to the extent envisioned, the Hartford district could be left with half-empty schools—but the whole bill to run them. Transportation costs, too, are con-servatively projected to run into the millions of dollars. The Hartford expe-rience, if it develops along this less optimistic but more logical progression, could foreshadow what is in store for other districts in the future.

Given that whites, blacks, and Latinos tend to live in different neighbor-hoods in most parts of the United States, *de facto* segregation is a fixture of American communities. This is true because neighborhoods tend to be seg-regated by class, and the middle class is disproportionately white, whereas the underclass in the United States is disproportionately black and Latino. Should state courts begin to desegregate schools according to socioeconomic status, which would undoubtedly involve busing and rezoning, the conse-quences are likely to be just as disruptive and destructive as efforts to racially desegregate schools have been.

Supreme Court Schizophrenia

The year 2003 saw another landmark case that could potentially impact the future of school desegregation in the United States. In the University of Michigan cases *Grutter v. Bollinger*[36] (law school admissions) and *Gratz v. Bollinger*[37] (undergraduate admissions) the U.S. Supreme Court handed down its most significant affirmative action decision since the *Bakke* case of 1978. The Supreme Court ruled that the University of Michigan's undergraduate admission policy of awarding points solely based on an applicant's race was unconstitutional. However, the high court upheld the university's interest in fostering "diversity." The court also upheld the university's law school policy of giving preferences to racial minorities in its admissions procedures, significantly moving beyond the racial restrictions of the *Bakke* decision a quarter-century earlier.

The high court's schizophrenic rulings in the *Grutter* and *Gratz* cases do not directly involve K–12 schools. Still, they do have potential implications for elementary and secondary education that have already prompted action. For example, in light of the high court's ruling, Little Rock, Arkansas, officials were considering eliminating using race as the sole criteria for admittance to some magnet schools.[38] On the other hand, though, the 2003 ruling reiterates the high court's position that the state has an interest in diversifying the racial composition of state institutions and in accomplishing this goal can consider the race of individuals in governmental selection processes. This part of the ruling has Texas, which had eliminated the use of race in admissions to state public universities in 1996, scampering to figure out how to reintroduce race as a criteria for admission to its University of Texas medical school.[39]

Justice Ruth Bader Ginsburg, in her dissension from the court's majority ruling in the undergraduate case, stated, "The stain of generations of racial oppression is still visible in our society, and the determination to hasten its removal remains vital." Ginsburg thus reveals that there is thinking on the Supreme Court that undoing the vestiges of racial oppression, which school desegregation has been attempting to accomplish, has yet to be achieved. Moreover, her statement implies that governmental action to undo these vestiges is still necessary and, indeed, "vital." Thus, we still see a judicial orientation at the highest levels of American government that is favorable for upholding the use of race as a factor in school admissions.

Justice Sandra Day O'Connor, speaking for a majority of the court, did indicate that she thought the end of racial preferences in university admissions was in sight—but such preferences were still necessary for the time being.

She wrote, "We expect that in 25 years from now, the use of racial preferences will no longer be necessary to further the interest approved today." It would be interesting to know upon what logic O'Connor based this prediction. Does she envision the elimination of the minority-white achievement gap within a quarter-century, so that minorities will be able to compete on the level playing field of university academic admissions requirements? If so, her position implies that she foresees a significant improvement in minority K–12 education. Given the trend toward the continued resegregation of American public schooling and the association of segregated minority schooling with vastly inferior academic outcomes—especially for African American and Hispanic students—O'Connor's vision seems overly optimistic. One outcome of the *Grutter* decision seems more certain: In the words of another legal scholar, it will likely "lead to confusion, to controversy, and to litigation."[40]

Will plaintiffs pursue the socioeconomic desegregation of schools through state courts as a means of attempting more racial desegregation? According to Dr. Charles V. Willie, professor of education (emeritus) at Harvard University, the answer is yes. Willie points out that "states are the ultimate authority in education . . . and plaintiffs know that states have deep pockets."[41] If Willie's prediction proves true, this could entail a new round of extensive judicial intervention in American schools aimed at redistribution on socioeconomic rather than racial grounds. If, as we argue in this book, racial redistribution has not worked, there is no reason to believe that the socioeconomic version would, even if race and socioeconomic status were not so intertwined in American society.

In the next chapter, we explore demographic changes in the United States and the increasingly complex racial and ethnic makeup of American society in general and American schools in particular. Demographic changes, particularly the growth of single-parent families, have frustrated efforts to redesign American society through the judicially directed engineering of the schools. At the same time, the nation's growing racial and ethnic complexity puts the largely black-white nature of most desegregation litigation out of step with the increasingly multiracial, multiethnic makeup of America. We show how the growing diversity of our nation makes it ever more difficult to put into practice designs for achieving social justice through race-based policies.

CHAPTER 3

The Demographic Transformation of America

A CHANGING SOCIETY

This chapter examines some of the demographic changes that have affected the United States in general, and in schools in particular, since the 1954 *Brown* decision. We look at the changes in family structure, particularly among black families, over the last half-century in the United States. We also consider the effects of immigration on American society in general and on American schools in particular. Then, we discuss the continuing strong connection between race and poverty. We consider how these demographic characteristics have affected racial desegregation goals and policies.

Family structure in the United States has changed dramatically since the 1950s. Other family types—most notably the family headed by the single-parent mother—have increasingly supplanted traditional two-parent families, in which the vast majority of whites and most black children were raised through the 1960s. Whereas most white children are still reared in two-parent families, the majority of black children are now reared by single mothers. This demographic trend has had disproportionately adverse consequences for the black community and schools with large numbers of African American children. One of the most notable negative consequences for schools having large numbers of students reared in single-mother families, and coming from communities dominated by other children reared in mother-only families, has been an increase in disruptive behavior. The other major problem associated with mother-only families is lowered academic achievement.

Where children from these often-disadvantaged circumstances are concentrated in schools, teachers report that learning environments are significantly degraded for all children, including those from two-parent families.[1] An important implication of this growing problem for school desegregation has been that middle-class white and black parents are likely to seek other educational options for their children rather than enroll them in schools with large numbers of low-SES black children. This phenomenon, known as white flight—and now middle-class black flight—has sabotaged efforts across the United States to racially balance schools and in many cases has left school systems worse off than before desegregation policies were implemented. Though the motivations of white parents removing their children from minority schools have been questioned, we suggest that most of these parents are simply acting out of rational self-interest for the well-being of their children.

Another major demographic trend of the last two to three decades has been the phenomenal growth of the Hispanic population in the country, largely as a result of immigration. In 2002 Hispanics surpassed African Americans to become the largest minority group in the United States, constituting approximately 13 percent of the total U.S. population.[2] This new demographic reality raises concerns about linguistic as well as racial segregation.[3] We consider the implications of this new and perhaps even more intransigent segregation of Hispanics, who attend schools as segregated as African Americans. Hispanics typically have below-average standardized test scores, high poverty rates, and very high dropout rates—higher than African Americans. Hispanics are also even more likely to attend schools dominated by other poor children than are African Americans. Many Hispanic children come to school with either limited-English or no English skills and thus have the additional handicap of deficient language skills compounding their poverty and isolation. In addition, for purposes of many affirmative action programs, Hispanics are treated as a historically underrepresented, disadvantaged minority—just as blacks are.[4] Nine years before the *Brown* ruling, Gonzalo Mendez sued the Westminster school district in Orange County, California, leading the courts to order the district to stop segregating Mexican American children.[5] At the time, though, Hispanic students were a much smaller group and integration meant dropping legal barriers to attendance, not coming up with designs for attendance. Efforts to re-engineer American society through the schools by moving around categories of the underprivileged would become ever more complicated as the categories themselves continually changed.

Still another important demographic trend over the past few decades has been the unprecedented Asian immigration to the United States, which has filled schools with often large numbers of poor Asian students who, like Hispanic children, often have little or no English-language skills. However, unlike poor blacks and Hispanics, Asian immigrants are much more likely to thrive socially and academically, even in segregated learning environments. Asian students are, however, more likely than other minority groups to attend schools with greater percentages of middle-class whites. The fact that a category of poor, limited-English proficient students tend to do well academically, even in segregated schools, has undermined some of the early, key intellectual assumptions of desegregation—that attendance in a multicultural school environment was in and of itself a positive influence on academic achievement.[6] Whereas some researchers contend that even whites do better academically in schools with some black students,[7] much research has found the opposite to be the case.[8] In 2000, the average Asian student attended a school that was on average 19 percent Asian, compared to the average black or Hispanic student who attended schools that were on average 57 percent black and Hispanic, respectively.[9] However, this was largely because Asian Americans constituted a much smaller group as a proportion of the American population. Still, while Asians were relatively concentrated, they had much greater exposure to white students than did either blacks or Hispanics. In the 1999–2000 school year, 46 percent of the average Asian student's schoolmates were white, compared to 28 percent of the average black student's schoolmates and only 25 percent of the average Hispanic student's schoolmates.[10] As we will discuss, despite the fact that Asians were generally first- or second-generation arrivals in the United States, their levels of school performance were similar to those of whites, rather than to those of the other two groups. This may suggest that it is not diversity per se that is so important, but the kind of student diversity that matters. In schools with large numbers of Asian and white students, the average student performs better academically. However, students in schools with large percentages of black and Hispanic students, who have traditionally not done as well academically, also do less well academically—regardless of their race. It is the academic preparedness of the majority of a school's students, not a school's multicultural flavor, that sets the academic press of a school's learning environment.

Finally, we consider an unfortunate socioeconomic fact of American life. Minority students, particularly black and Hispanic students, have historically suffered from much higher poverty rates than students from the majority white population. Over the course of the late twentieth century, new kinds of poverty became much more common, especially among minority groups. We do not suggest that minority young people or their families are somehow to blame because many of them are poor. However, we will suggest that the association between race and poverty in the United States means that redistributing students by race is essentially redistributing a type of poverty in schools that lowers the academic achievement levels of all students.

FAMILY STRUCTURE

As policymakers attempted to remake American society through the schools, American society remade itself. One of the most notable trends in family life in the United States was the increasing prevalence of single-parent families. Divorces became more common through the 1960s and 1970s, increasing from 2.2 divorces for every 1,000 people in the population in 1960, to 3.5 for every 1,000 people in 1970, and 4.8 in 1975. The divorce rate peaked in 1980, with 5.2 divorces for every 1,000 individuals. Throughout the 1980s and into the 1990s, the divorce rate remained constant at about 4.7 to 4.8 divorces for every 1,000 people. In terms of probability of divorce for married couples, about one-half of couples aged 25–34 who married in 1980 were expected to divorce at some point during the course of their marriage. By 1989, two researchers predicted that two-thirds of all first marriages would end in divorce.[11]

Divorce, then, was one factor contributing to the increase in one-parent families. After 1980, though, the divorce rate began to level off. Most of the increase in single-parent families since then came from childbearing by mothers who had never been married. In the United States, in 1960 only about 5 percent of all births were children born to unmarried mothers. By 1980, slightly under 20 percent of children were born to unmarried mothers. Ten years later, this increased to about 30 percent of all births in the United States.

As Figure 3.1 shows, black and white differences in unmarried births have been a part of the American landscape for a long time. Older studies of this phenomenon frequently maintained that the prevalence of unmarried black parents was a consequence of the cultural heritage of slavery.[12] Historian Herbert W. Gutman challenged this assumption in his influential study of black family life under slavery, in which he maintained that slaves had struggled to keep families intact.[13] Other historians also argued that monogamous, nuclear families were the norm for slaves, although slave families may have been more democratic and egalitarian than white families of the same historical period.[14] If so, why nearly one-third of black births were already occurring outside of marriage by the Depression era would be difficult to explain.

We have already discussed the development of ideas about school desegregation during the critical years of the 1960s. During these years, also, unmarried birth rates began to increase dramatically among both blacks and whites. Part of the reason for this trend is that the connection between unmarried pregnancy and unmarried birth grew closer as fewer pregnancies

Figure 3.1
Unmarried Births among Whites and Blacks, 1930–1934 to 1990–1994

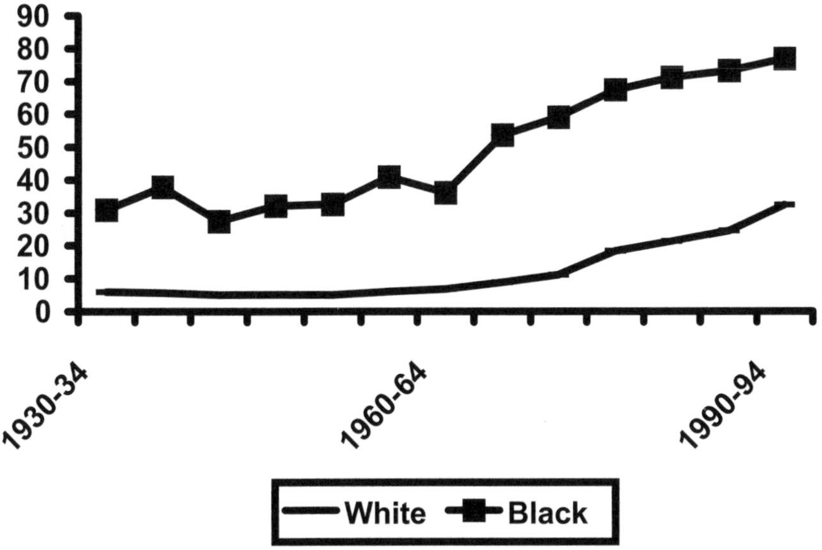

Amara Bachu. *Trends in Premarital Childbearing, 1930–1994* U.S. Census Bureau, Current Population Reports. U.S. Government Printing Office, 1999, 2.

were followed by marriage than in earlier years.[15] The near universality of the decline in post-pregnancy marriages and in the growth of unmarried births strongly suggests that developments in late modern society are conducive to single parenthood. Some of these developments may include the large-scale entry of women into the labor force,[16] the growth of government as a potential source of economic support,[17] and the weakening of normative bonds within families and communities.[18]

Although unmarried pregnancies have increased among all groups, the years since the 1960s have seen the sharpest rise among black women. White births outside of wedlock have reached approximately the level of black births outside of marriage during the 1930s and 1940s. For black Americans, unwed parenthood has actually become the norm, with well over 70 percent of births in this group occurring to single women in the mid-1990s. Some of these unmarried mothers do marry and form two-parent families. For the most part, though, black children live not just in mother-only families, but in mother-only families in which the father has never been a continual presence.

Some of the problems that attend this rising form of family structure are economic.[19] Single-parent families, especially those headed by single women, have a much greater probability of living in poverty than do two-parent families. Even were the only difficulty economic, this would greatly complicate efforts at school desegregation. Families that have the means to avoid putting their children in low-income environments, whether these environments are in neighborhoods or in schools, tend to do so. However, the problems associated with family structure are not solely economic. Researchers have generally found that children from single-parent families are more likely than other children to engage in substance abuse, to display aggressive or violent behavior, and to suffer from a variety of psychological problems. Students from one-parent families also show a greater tendency to display behaviors and attitudes toward school that result in poor school performance.[20] Writing in the July/August 1996 issue of *Society*, David Popenoe summarized research findings: "Based on the findings of longitudinal studies that follow children over time, children growing up in single-parent families, compared to children growing up in intact families, are two to three times more likely to have emotional and behavioral problems when they become teenagers. These findings largely hold true even when families from the two groupings at equivalent income levels are compared, suggesting that structural and experiential and not just economic factors are at fault."[21]

The increase in single-parent families has had particular significance for questions of race and school desegregation. Nearly four decades ago, Daniel Patrick Moynihan touched off a storm of controversy when he argued that the high proportion of single female-headed families among black Americans threatened black children with a "tangle of pathologies." Some of his critics denounced his views as racist; others claimed that his concerns embodied patriarchal and antifeminist assumptions about the superiority of male-headed households. In the ensuing years, the conventional wisdom purveyed by sociology textbooks has consistently held up *The Moynihan Report* as an example of the "culture of poverty theory," which is identified as a reactionary line of thought that "blames the victim" of social injustice by claiming that socially disadvantaged statuses are products of inferior cultures.

In retrospect, Moynihan deserves credit as one of the most fair-minded and prophetic of modern social critics. As William Julius Wilson has acknowledged in the insightful volume *When Work Disappears* (1996), Moynihan did recognize that the unstable black family was the consequence of the American socioeconomic structure. Moynihan simply maintained that having been produced by an unequal and discriminatory economy, one-parent families yielded unfortunate results of their own.

Since the publication of *The Moynihan Report*, the remarkable rise of one-parent families in American society in general has been particularly marked among African Americans. Figure 3.2 shows the proportions of two-parent,

Figure 3.2
Distribution of Family Structures among White and Black Families Containing Minor Children

White Families

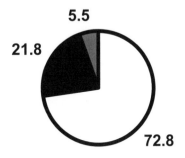

5.5

21.8

72.8

☐ Married couple   ■ Single female   ▨ Single male

Black Families

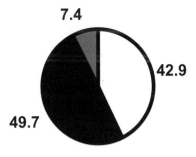

7.4

42.9

49.7

☐ Married couple   ■ Single female   ▨ Single male

U.S. Census of Population and Housing, Census 2000.

single-male, and single-female households among white and black families containing children under eighteen years of age, as reported in the 2000 U.S. Census. Over 70 percent of white family households with children were headed by two parents in that year, but a clear majority of black family households contained only one parent. Moreover, since these two pie charts show only the distribution of family households, they actually present underestimations of white-black differences in family structure because black two-parent households tended to contain fewer children than black single-parent households, whereas the reverse was the situation for whites. Thus, data from the 1996 Current Population Survey of the U.S. Census Bureau showed that only 36 percent of black children were living in two-parent families, compared to 79 percent of white children.[22]

Our research suggests that those concerned about the growth of the single-parent family have missed some of the most serious difficulties created by change in family structure. Families do not influence only their own children, and children are not socialized only by their own families. Children bring influences from their families to their peer groups and, in peer groups, share the influences of their backgrounds with one another. Children, then, are not simply affected by the composition of their own families; they are also influenced by the family compositions of all those around them. The undesirable consequences of one-parent families, then, are not additive, but exponential when those from this type of home are concentrated in a social environment.

What contemporary institution brings young people together, producing social environments from peer groups? The answer to this question is obvious. It is the same institution chiefly responsible for preparing young people to take positions in our socioeconomic structure—the school. Considering the school as a social environment leads us to the following line of reasoning: (1) Black American children are much more likely than white American children to live in single-parent families. (2) Children from single-parent families show much higher rates of behavioral and attitudinal problems than do other children. (3) Schools with large concentrations of children from single-parent families will therefore tend to be plagued by behavioral and attitudinal problems. (4) Schools with large concentrations of black children will tend to be disproportionately plagued by behavioral and attitudinal problems because these will be precisely the schools with large concentrations of children from single-parent families. (5) Children in schools with large concentrations of black children will therefore be faced with disadvantageous school learning environments. These disruptive learning environments will in general lead to lower levels of school achievement for all students in those schools, regardless of the students' own race or family background.

This series of syllogisms indicates that prevailing family structure may be a major barrier to achievement and upward mobility for children in majority black schools. It also suggests that white efforts to avoid black school districts may often be motivated by the desire to avoid school environments dominated by children from one-parent families, and not simply motivated by irrational prejudice. An article published in 1998 found that the negative association between percentages of black students in schools and levels of school achievement could be statistically attributed to the prevalence of single-mother-headed families in those schools.[23] The problem of minority schools, in other words, did not appear to be race per se. Instead, the problem seemed to be the concentration of single-parent families in those schools. As the percentage of black children in single-parent families has grown to a majority, racial redistribution has, essentially, become the same as the redistribution of the family structures that dominate schools. This can either enhance or hurt the academics of schoolchildren. In Louisiana, where a large proportion of the public school population lives in single-parent families, teachers report that negative student behavior is the primary reason they leave the profession.[24]

DEMOGRAPHIC CHANGE: NEW STUDENT POPULATIONS

The population of the United States has been changing throughout the period of judicial efforts to redistribute student social capital through desegregation. The greatest part of this change has been dramatic increases in the Hispanic and Asian populations of the United States as a consequence of immigration during the years following 1965.

Many of the same social currents that led the United States to struggle for a more racially and ethnically egalitarian society also encouraged a growing complexity in the nation's ethnic makeup. Roughly a century ago, the United States saw one of its largest waves of immigration between 1880 and the late 1920s, when 27,788,140 immigrants reached the United States. This wave began to slacken after 1924, when the U.S. Congress passed highly restrictive immigration legislation. Likewise, the Depression and World War II contributed to low immigration.

The Immigration Act that the United States passed in 1924 limited immigration by establishing quotas of migrants that the United States would accept from other nations. These quotas were heavily biased in favor of northern and western Europe. By the middle of the 1960s, issues of civil rights and discrimination had become central topics in American political life. In this climate, the quota system was seen as discriminatory and prejudiced against non-European peoples.

In 1965, therefore, the U.S. Congress revised the nation's immigration law, replacing quotas from individual countries with a worldwide ceiling of immigrants. Some migrants, such as refugees or immediate family of U.S. citizens, were not counted in this ceiling. The number of immigrants who could be accepted from each country was equal. The act also set up preferences, or priorities, for potential immigrants. The highest priority was family reunification, which meant that family members of both citizens and noncitizens living in the United States were given preference over all others wishing to immigrate.

The Immigration Act of 1965 had two consequences. First, overall immigration increased sharply in the late 1960s and then continued to rise steadily in the decades that followed. Second, people began to arrive from parts of the world, especially Asia and Latin America, which had sent few migrants to America earlier in the twentieth century. During the late twentieth and early twenty-first centuries, about half of all legal immigrants to the United States in each year were arriving from Latin America and about one-fourth were arriving from Asia.

In addition to legal immigrants came substantial numbers of illegal immigrants. Precisely how many immigrants were entering the country without the required documents is difficult to know, but most estimates suggest around 300,000 per year. Many of these were temporary labor migrants, but by the end of the twentieth century this number probably included at least 4 million people without U.S. citizenship or immigration documentation. The majority of these people were either Mexicans or Central Americans who had crossed the border into the United States.

During the single decade from 1990 to 2000, Hispanics increased from 21.9 million (8.8% of the U.S. population) to 35.3 million (12.5% of the U.S. population). Asians at that same time grew from 7.3 million (2.9% of the population) to 12.3 million (4.4% of the population).[25] The dramatic impact of population change was intensified by geographic concentration. In 2000, a little over 43 percent of all Hispanics were in the West, mainly in California, and another 33 percent were in the South, primarily in Texas and Florida, although there were also fairly sizable populations in Georgia and North Carolina.[26] Nearly half of all Asians were in the West, again in California, and another fifth were in the Northeast. Despite their relatively small numbers, Asians were so concentrated that eleven American cities were 20 percent to 49 percent Asian and twenty-nine cities were 10 percent to 19 percent Asian.[27]

The new population groups intensified the minority domination of many locations in the United States. According to a U.S. Census Bureau brief issued in August 2001, "the Black population is still highly concentrated—64 percent of all counties (3,141 counties) in the United States had fewer than 6 percent Black, but in 96 counties, Blacks comprised 50 percent or more of the total population."[28] About three-fifths of the total black population of the United States lived in only ten states. Although New York and Chicago had the largest black populations in 2000, Detroit, Philadelphia, and Houston all had black populations between half a million and a million.[29] While this concentration of the black population was not new, the growth of Hispanics meant that in many, especially urban, parts of the United States, populations would be largely either black or Hispanic or both black and Hispanic. In 2000, 77 percent of all Hispanics in the United States lived in the seven states with Hispanic populations numbering at least a million. Half of all Hispanics lived in California and Texas. Nearly one-third of all Hispanics in the United States lived in New York, Los Angeles, Chicago, Houston, Philadelphia, Phoenix, San Diego, Dallas, San Antonio, El Paso, and San Jose.[30] New York and Chicago, in addition to being centers for the Hispanic population, had the largest black populations in the country.[31] The rapidly increasing Asian population was also highly concentrated in many of the same locations as Hispanics and in some of the same locations as blacks. Over half of Asians in the United States in 2000 lived in California, New York, and Hawaii. The largest concentrations of Asians were in New York and Los Angeles.[32]

The growth of the new minorities was even more marked in U.S. public schools than in the population at large. In 1972, nearly eight out of every ten public school students in the United States were white. By 2000, this had gone down to just over 60 percent. Black students consistently made up about 15 to 17 percent of the public school population. Most of the proportional growth was among Hispanics, who were only 6 percent of public school students in 1972, but 17 percent in 2000, exactly equal to blacks. The "other" category, made up primarily of Asians, increased from 1.5 percent in 1972 to over 5 percent in 2000. Thus, in the early 1970s minority students made up 22 percent of pupils and were mostly black, but in 2000 nearly 40 percent of pupils and were equally divided between blacks and Hispanics. Readers should also note that the proportion of minorities in the public school population was consistently larger than the proportion of minorities in the population at large. By the middle of the twenty-first century, then, when U.S. Census projections indicate that whites will be a bare majority in the United States and one of every four Americans will be Hispanic, most public school students will not be white Anglos, and Hispanic pupils will greatly outnumber blacks.

Nationwide proportions are, of course, a bit misleading. Racial and ethnic categories of students are not evenly distributed among regions or among neighborhoods. Regionally, the West, particularly California, is notable for its concentration of Hispanics and Asians as a result of the post-1965 wave of immigration just discussed. In the West, public school students went from being close to three-quarters white Anglo to being almost evenly divided between white Anglos and so-called minorities. Blacks were only about 6 percent of public school students in the region during the entire period, but Hispanics went from 15 percent in 1972 to over 30 percent in 2000, and the "other" category (again, nearly synonymous with Asian/Pacific Islander) grew from under 6 percent to about 12 percent at the end of the twentieth century.

In the West, then, minority public school students were generally not black at the opening of the new century, but Hispanic or Asian. By contrast, whites still made up close to three-quarters of public school students in the Midwest in 2000. In the South, whites were a scant majority (55.1%) by the end of this period; but there, minority students were still predominantly black (45% of all students). Even in the South, though, Hispanics had increased from 5 percent of all students in 1972 to 16 percent in 2000.[33]

HISPANIC EXPLOSION

The post-1965 growth of the Hispanic population has had major consequences for efforts at school desegregation in a number of locations. Los Angeles, America's greatest contemporary immigrant center, entered the desegregation arena at the beginning of August 1963, when the parents of Mary Ellen Crawford and several other schoolchildren filed suit in Los Angeles Superior Court on behalf of "all Negro and Mexican-American pupils" in the L.A. school district.[34] Clearly, school desegregation outside the South was already more than a strictly black-white issue even at this early date.

The L.A. school desegregation struggle drew national attention in 1979 when, motivated by events in Los Angeles, the California public passed Proposition 1, which prohibited any more busing to achieve school desegregation than required by the federal government. However, the population of Los Angeles was already changing in ways that would make any real desegregation impossible. When the Crawford case began, the L.A. school district was more than 55 percent white Anglo, and blacks were the largest non-white group. When the Crawford case finally ended, in March 1989, immigration to Los Angeles and white flight from desegregating schools had combined to transform the L.A. school district into one that was 59 percent Hispanic, 17 percent black, 16 percent white Anglo, and 6 percent Asian/Pacific Islander.[35] By the end, the placing of students in L.A. schools no longer meant distributing mostly black and some Hispanic students among white schools that were unfairly barring minorities. It meant deciding where comparatively small proportions of black students and even smaller proportions of white Anglo students would attend school in a predominantly Hispanic system.

The expansion of the Hispanic population as a complication in school desegregation also affected locations outside of California. Texas, with its long border with Mexico, was another center of America's growing Hispanic population. In Dallas, relatively far from this border, during the short period from the 1996–1997 school year to the 2002–2003 school year, whites decreased from 11 percent of all students in the school district to only 7 percent. In the same brief period, Hispanic students went from 49 percent to 59 percent of students, whereas black students decreased somewhat from 42 percent to 33 percent (see Chapter 5). Most of the white students were concentrated in just a few schools, but even if they were widely distributed there would not have been enough whites to desegregate any institution. Diversity in this situation meant schools in which blacks and Hispanics came into contact with each other, not schools in which minority students would attend schools with whites.

The rapid growth and geographic concentration of the Hispanic population that greatly complicated efforts at juggling categories of students in California and Texas also occurred in other parts of the United States throughout the last quarter of the twentieth century. A 1987 report issued by researchers at the University of Chicago headed by desegregation activist Gary Orfield concluded, "More Latino children are attending segregated schools than before, while the segregation of black students is virtually unchanged from the early 1970s."[36] Across the United States, the percentage of Latino students attending schools labeled as intensely segregated (90% minority or more) grew from 23.1 percent in 1968 to 28.8 percent in 1980 and 31 percent in 1984. Hispanic students in New York and Illinois were particularly segregated, with over 59 percent of Hispanics in New York State and over 41 percent in Illinois attending schools that had more than 90 percent minority enrollment.[37]

The dramatic growth in Latino segregation during the 1970s is particularly noteworthy because this was the decade of the most fervidly interventionist policies in the pursuit of racially and ethnically balanced schools. Although some experts have insisted that segregated schools should be blamed on insufficient judicial and legislative zeal in enforcing desegregation policies,[38] their own data have indicated that the concentration of Latino students was proceeding rapidly at just the time when the policy zeal was greatest. Attempting to direct the flow of the arriving wave of Latino students was as effective as King Canute's efforts at commanding the tides.

By the end of the twentieth century, not only were schools in the United States still identifiable by race, but Hispanic students had become even more separate from whites than black students were. Figure 3.3 uses data from the National Center for Education Statistics to show that in 1999 about 45 percent of white pupils in the United States attended schools that were over 90 percent white, and nearly three-quarters of whites attended schools that had less than one-fourth minority enrollment. In contrast, 37 percent of Latinos and 36.7 percent of blacks were attending those "intensely segregated" schools that were at least 90 percent minority. Most Latinos (56%) were in schools that were three-quarters minority or more, whereas almost half of blacks were in schools that were three-quarters minority or more.

The growth of the Hispanic student population, then, both intensified *de facto* school segregation and complicated it. Although Hispanic students were separated from whites by policy in earlier years, Hispanics grew more segre-

Figure 3.3
Percentage Distribution of White, Black, Hispanic and Asian Students in U.S. Public Schools, by Racial Composition of Schools, 1999

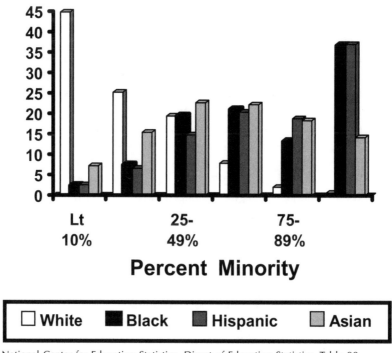

National Center for Education Statistics, Digest of Education Statistics, Table 98.

gated during the era of official policies aimed, not at separating them, but at diversifying student populations. Part of the reason for this growing separation was simply the expansion of the minority population in general and the expansion of the Hispanic population in particular. It is much more likely that schools will be composed primarily of minority group members when they make up nearly 40 percent of the population than when they make up only 20 percent. Regional and urban concentrations contribute to this group size effect. Hispanics make up most of the public school students in Los Angeles because they are most of the young people in Los Angeles, just as most New Orleans public school students are black because it is a majority black city.

Another important part of the reason that Hispanic students tend to be even more separate from whites than blacks are, though, is that whites avoid schools with large Hispanic enrollments. This is not simply a matter of ethnic or linguistic prejudice. One of the common indicators of a "good high school," for example, is the rate of school completion. Schools with high dropout rates can legitimately be seen as problem institutions, both by administrators and by parents.

As Figure 3.4 shows, Hispanic students have had extraordinarily high dropout rates since American schools began keeping records on them. In the early 1970s over one-third of people in this group aged 16–24 were "status dropouts"; that is, they were not in school and they had not completed high school. Although this fluctuated some over the last three decades of the twentieth century, the rates did not go down as they did for black and white Americans. Although the source of these rates may be open to debate, the consequences are clear: non-Hispanics may avoid schools with large Hispanic concentrations precisely because of the high dropout rates.

The influx of Spanish-speaking students also brought special demands to schools. Among young people in this age group who spoke Spanish at home, 36 percent spoke English with difficulty, compared to 24 percent of young people from Asian-language homes, 28 percent of young people from other European-language homes, and 29 percent from homes at which miscellaneous other languages were spoken. English abilities were particularly limited in the Spanish-speaking five- to nine-year-old group, in which 43 percent spoke English with difficulty.

We do not believe that English is in any way inherently preferable to Spanish, nor do we suggest that speakers of one language are necessarily better students or classmates than students of another. Indeed, one of the authors of this book reared his children in French and intentionally avoided speaking English in his home.[39] Still, it should be clear that schools with large numbers of Hispanic students need to devote time and resources to classes

Figure 3.4
White, Black, and Hispanic Status Dropout Rates (among Ages 16–24), 1972–2001

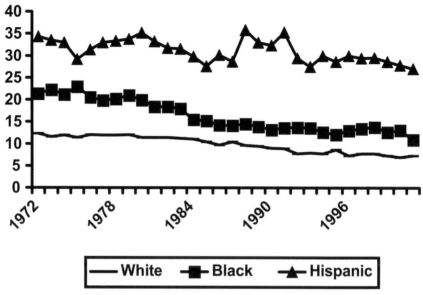

U.S. Department of Commerce, Bureau of the Census, Current Population Survey (CPS), October 1972–2001.

specializing in language minority students. Given the finite nature of all resources, this means these classes often come at the expense of other academic possibilities. Theoretically, Spanish-speaking students could enrich academic programs by teaching their own valuable linguistic skill to students from monolingual English families. This is the theory behind two-way bilingual programs.[40] Still, it requires a good deal of wishful thinking to conclude that immersion in a school populated by minority-language students will contribute to the overall educational advancement of students in a society's majority language. The academic edge would almost necessarily go to students surrounded by speakers of the majority language. When we combine the difficulties posed by the growth of a language minority population with the extraordinarily high dropout rates and problematic social environments associated with a disproportionate number of Hispanic students, it should be easy to see that the increasing diversification of the American student population poses daunting challenges for those who would mandate ethnic and racial redistribution.

THE ASIAN ADVANTAGE

The growth of the Asian school population posed a different kind of problem. Whereas black and Hispanic students were, by statistical averages, underachievers on most measures, Asians were overachievers. Whereas Hispanics had extraordinarily high dropout rates, Asians had the lowest dropout rate of any group. In 2000, only 3.5 percent of Asians aged 16–24 were not in school and had not finished school. During the period October 1999 to October 2000, proportionately fewer Asians dropped out of the tenth and eleventh grades than whites, blacks, or Hispanics.[41]

Figure 3.5 shows verbal and mathematics SAT scores for white, Asian, Hispanic, and black students from 1986–1987 to 2000–2001. Consistently, whites and Asians were the high scorers, whereas blacks and Hispanics were the low scorers. Asians scored somewhat lower than whites did on the verbal test, a fact that is not surprising considering that many Asian students were first or second generation Americans living in homes that spoke languages other than English. Despite this, Asians still did better than the other minority group members. In mathematics, Asians outdid all the others. We discuss race and test scores in much more detail in Chapter 7.

A California education demographer who studied preparedness for the University of California (UC) system found that 54.4 percent of the state's Asian high school graduates had completed the coursework required for entry into the UC system in 1986–1987, compared to 31.7 percent of white Anglo graduates, 23 percent of black graduates, and only 16 percent of Latino graduates. Asians had by far the highest rates of course completion in advanced mathematics, physics, and chemistry.[42] As a result of their high levels of achievement and preparedness, by 2002 Asians made up a quarter of all the students admitted to the UC system not counting Filipinos (listed separately in UC enrollment figures[43]) and 30.3 percent of students with Filipinos included in the Asian category. At the two top campuses of the UC system, Berkeley and UCLA, Asians constituted 32.8 percent and 35.0 percent, respectively, of newly admitted students without Filipinos, and 36.5 percent and 38.3 percent, respectively, with Filipinos included in the Asian category. Even without Filipinos, Asians were the largest ethnic category of new admissions at UCLA and were almost equal to whites as the two largest ethnic categories at Berkeley.[44]

Outside of California, also, Asians made up many of the nation's highest achievers. For example, Boston's elite Boston Latin School was, at the end of the 1990s, 24 percent Asian, although Asians made up only 9 percent of stu-

Figure 3.5
Verbal and Math SAT Scores, 1986–1987 to 2000–2001, by Race and Ethnicity

Verbal Scores

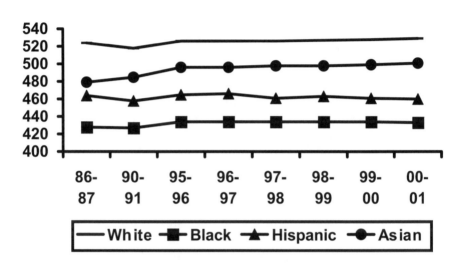

Math Scores

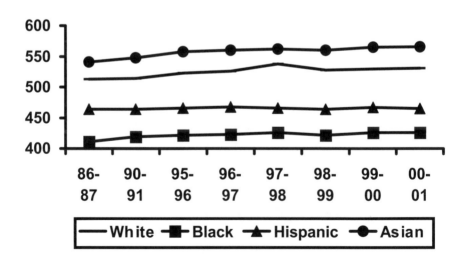

dents in the city's public schools.[45] The school district was 48 percent black, 28 percent Hispanic, and 15 percent white. Reports of a 1998 suit against Boston by a white student who was denied entry in order to maintain racial diversity indicate that if admission to Boston Latin had been solely on the basis of grade point averages and test scores, enrollment in the entering ninth grade class would have been 56 percent white, 23 percent Asian, 9 percent black, and 7 percent Hispanic. However, Boston Latin maintained a policy of allowing only the top half of the newly admitted on the basis of rankings alone. For the second, lower half, students were admitted on the basis of percentages in the school's qualified applicant pool, combined with rankings.[46] This resulted in an entering class that was 44 percent white, 24 percent Asian, 21 percent black, and 10 percent Hispanic. Clearly, both Asians and whites had the desire and ability to enter the pool of qualified applicants to the school at rates that were vastly disproportionate to their representations in the district. These figures also raise the distinct possibility that all the whites and nearly all the Asians who made it into the school were admitted as part of the top half. Regardless of the strained efforts to achieve diversity, Boston Latin was a school that was over two-thirds white and Asian in a school district that was more than three-quarters black and Hispanic. It is unlikely that anyone would have foreseen this at the beginning of busing in Boston in the early 1970s, when whites were a majority of public school students, Asians were only 3 percent, and Hispanics were only 8 percent.[47]

We do not necessarily suggest that Asians should be seen as a "model minority" to be emulated by other groups. The Asian category is made up of a variety of national backgrounds, and, although relatively high achievement seems to characterize most Asian subgroups, there is variation. More important, it is not entirely clear just what it is about Asians that could be emulated, since the reasons for their apparent academic success are debated.[48] In addition, Asian youth are often affected by a variety of family problems[49] and by delinquency.[50] (In the next chapter we offer some insights into why Asian students do so well in school.) Still, their generally high level of accomplishment does pose problems for the redistribution of minority students. If desegregation is to be seen as a matter of mixing the disadvantaged with the advantaged, in which slot should Asians fit? Judged by school achievement, we could treat Asians and whites the same, as members of the "academically privileged," and treat both blacks and Hispanics as the "academically underprivileged." If so, then we would need to limit the access of Asians to preparatory schools such as Boston Latin and to elite public universities such as Berkeley and UCLA. In fact, we would need to limit Asian access much more dramatically than white access, since Asians are much more overrepresented in many of the highly desirable schools. The "from each according to ability, to each according to need" logic of redistributive desegregation, if carried out consistently, would penalize Asians for their achievement.

Because of their high level of achievement, Asians were gravitating toward top schools in cities with large minority populations for the same reasons that whites were. Their parents wanted them to go to the best schools possible and, unfortunately, this meant going to schools with the smallest numbers of blacks and Hispanics. In Boston, for example, school results closely matched their racial compositions. For example, in the majority white and Asian Boston Latin, 96 percent of students scored in the highest performance category of "advanced" or the next highest category of "proficient" in English language arts in 2002. In mathematics, 97 percent of students scored in these categories. In science and technology, 61 percent scored at these levels. By contrast, at the majority black and Hispanic Brighton High, percentages of students classified as "needs improvement" or "failing" were 77 percent in English and language arts, 91 percent in mathematics, and 99 percent in science and technology. Most students at Brighton were classified as "failing" in both mathematics and science and technology (56% and 86%, respectively).[51]

Although Boston's top schools, with their overrepresentation of whites and their even greater overrepresentation of Asians were some of the best in the nation, the Massachusetts Department of Education rated schools overall in Boston "low" in English language arts and "very low" in math in 2002. In 2002, the state gave performance level ratings of "failing" in English language arts to over one-third of Boston's tenth graders (36%), and ratings of "failing" in both mathematics and science and technology to a majority of the district's tenth graders (52% and 65%, respectively).[52]

In July 1999, faced with lawsuits claiming that race-based assignments to schools discriminated against whites seeking entry into the system's elite schools, the school committee of Boston decided to end racial assignments of students to schools. The decision met with criticism from some quarters. Harvard's Charles V. Willie, one of those responsible for designing Boston's controlled choice system proclaimed that "to choose a student assignment plan that is based largely on neighborhood is to re-segregate the city." Willie's protestations seem bizarre when we consider that no school could possibly be meaningfully desegregated in a district that, in 1999, was only 16 percent white, a percentage that would continue to drop into the new century.

Many of Boston's schools contained almost no white students. Charles H. Taylor Elementary School, for example, was 92 percent black in 2000–2001. Agassiz Elementary School was 75 percent Hispanic and 21 percent black. Blackstone Elementary was 71 percent Hispanic and 26 percent black.

Brighton High was 53 percent black and 34 percent Hispanic. In Boston, "desegregated schools" at the opening of the twenty-first century meant schools where whites would go to school with Asians and blacks would go to schools with Hispanics.

THE PROBLEM OF POVERTY

Over the course of the era of judicially mandated desegregation, as we have demonstrated, the minority population of the United States grew much larger and more diverse, creating new problems for those who would redistribute students. During that same period, the single-parent family became the norm for black families. Both of these demographic trends, we will argue throughout this book, tended to mean that redistributing minority students has generally meant redistributing disadvantages. At the same time, a new manifestation of economic disadvantage plagued many minority students and the schools that they attended.

Figure 3.6 shows percentages of children living below the poverty level in the United States from 1974 to 2002. Throughout this quarter of a century, the white poverty rate has generally hovered at about one out of every ten white children. The Asian poverty rate (available only since the late 1980s) declined dramatically, from one-fourth of the Asian children in 1987 to just fewer than 12 percent in 2002. This may have been partly a consequence of the economic adaptation of the Southeast Asian refugee groups, which were still fairly new to the United States at the end of the 1980s.

The greatest and most persistent economic disadvantage appeared among the populations of Hispanic and black children. Situations for both of these groups improved during the decade of the 1990s, but both continued to show extremely high poverty rates. Even with the gains of the last decade of the twentieth century, about one-third of black children (32.3%) and over one-fourth of Hispanic children (28.6%) were living below the poverty level. Minority poverty was still a prominent part of the American landscape at the half-century anniversary of the *Brown* decision.

Not only were black and Hispanic children more likely than others to live in poverty, they were more likely to live in extreme poverty. Over 15 percent of black children and over 11 percent of Hispanic children were in families living at below half the poverty threshold. Although these children were statistical minorities in the American child population, black and Hispanic children together comprised more than 63 percent of all children at this level of extreme poverty.

Although poverty is defined as a lack of income, it is more than that, and

Figure 3.6
Percent of Children Below Poverty Level, 1974–2002, by Race and Ethnicity

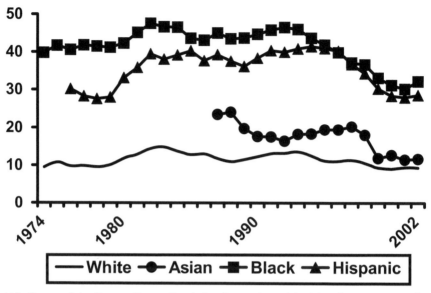

U.S. Bureau of the Census, Current Population Survey, Annual Social and Economic Supplements. Poverty and Health Statistics Branch/HHES Division.

there are different types of poverty. During the 1970s and 1980s, a new kind of poverty became evident.[53] Journalists in the latter decade helped to popularize the term "the underclass."[54] This concept has been criticized for expressing the supposed "culture of poverty" theory that attributes economic disadvantage to the behavioral shortcomings of the poor.[55] However, one does not need to accept behavioral or cultural explanations to recognize that a new kind of poverty had become much more common.

The old poverty was that of the working poor in rural areas or in the factory neighborhoods of cities. The new poverty has been characterized by unemployment (especially male unemployment), by concentration in inner-city areas, and by single-parent family structure. We have already devoted substantial attention to family structure by itself, since this is a race-related phenomenon that cuts across class lines. However, we should also emphasize, at this point, that changing family structure is also one of the strands in a demographic knot of socioeconomic problems.

At the beginning of the twenty-first century, a majority of black Americans (53.1% in 2000) and nearly half of Hispanic Americans lived in central city areas, compared to about one-fifth of white Americans. One of the clear difficulties for assigning students to schools by race is that this urban concentration of minorities means that students of different groups live in different places. On the eve of the 1974 *Milliken I* decision that banned cross-district busing, desegregation planners across the country were looking for ways to merge minority urban school districts with heavily white suburban districts. Watching the Detroit case anxiously, the Board of Education of New York City declared in February 1974 that "state and national officials and lawmakers cannot ignore the fact that the correction of the growing isolation of our poor minority groups in urban schools is each year becoming less and less a condition with which large city boards of education can deal alone."[56]

In Chapter 6, we will argue that if the Supreme Court had permitted cross-district busing, the result would not have been integration, but new evasive strategies as the middle classes would seek to avoid having inner-city, underclass poverty imposed on their own children's schools. For now, we simply want our readers to recognize that the urban isolation of minority groups that was becoming increasingly evident as judicially mandated desegregation reached a peak was a part of the rise of a new kind of poverty.

The sociologist William Julius Wilson has argued that the root of this new kind of poverty has been joblessness, specifically male joblessness. According to Wilson, the postindustrial disappearance of urban jobs left members of minority groups concentrated in neighborhoods where work had largely disappeared. This tended to undermine marriage and it led to a wide range of "ghetto related behaviors." Without working and without employed role models, minority young people were growing up deprived of opportunities, experiences, and expectations that might lead to upward mobility.[57]

One may question Wilson's model of causation. In a previous book, we have pointed out that it is difficult to ascribe the decline in marriage among black Americans to inner-city joblessness, since the decline has occurred in the black middle class as well as in the putative underclass. If single-parenthood is a problem apart from mere poverty, as we have argued earlier in this chapter, then problems of minority family structure should not be considered as only part of the new poverty in American society. Still, the new poverty does exist, and we believe that Wilson has accurately described its nature, even if he may be a little off regarding some of its causal relations.

A majority of blacks and a heavy preponderance of Hispanics not only live in inner-city areas but also make up most of the residents in the low-income sections of these areas. Figure 3.7 shows the composition of the inner-city poor population who were living in families with children below age 18 in 2002. Hispanics are proportionately less likely to live in inner-city areas than

Figure 3.7
Composition of the Population of Inner-City Poor Families with Children, March 2002

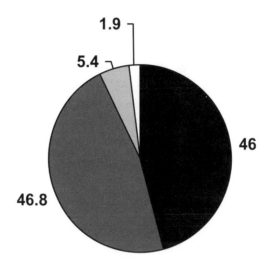

blacks are. However, Hispanic families make up the single largest percentage of poor inner-city families with children. This is because Hispanics are the largest minority group overall, and Hispanics, like blacks, have high rates of poverty, in general, and of children living in poverty, in particular.

In this figure, we can see that thinking about the inner-city poor as a racial and ethnic minority population is not a matter of stereotyping or misleading generalizations. The vast majority of poor families in central city areas in the United States are indeed either black or Hispanic. If concentrated poverty is a problem then, it is a problem that is strongly associated with minority status.

The second characteristic of the new poor identified by Wilson, male joblessness, holds up fairly well for blacks but shows mixed results for Hispanics. Official male unemployment rates in 2001 were 11.9 percent for blacks, 6.5 percent for Hispanics, and 4.1 percent for non-Hispanic whites. These percentages are misleading, though, because the most discouraged or alienated individuals drop out of the labor force altogether and are not looking for work. Ironically, the chronically unemployed do not appear in the official unemployment statistics at all.

In Figure 3.8 we use U.S. Census data to calculate percentages of men aged over 16 and under 65 who were neither employed nor pursuing educations from 1970 to 2000. At the top, we present results for whites, blacks, and Hispanics throughout the nation. Hispanics were not included in the data in 1970. Below that, we present results on men living in central city areas from 1980, when data on these areas became available, to 2000.

Using this broader but more accurate definition of unemployment, we can see that joblessness rose over the course of the late twentieth century, but that it rose particularly sharply among blacks and Hispanics during the 1990s. In the minority-dominated central cities, rates of male joblessness were slightly higher than in the United States in general. By 2000, 36 percent of black men and 29 percent of Hispanic men at traditional working ages who were living in urban centers had no jobs. We should note that these figures applied throughout the city centers, not to the dramatically poor areas, where it may well be the case that most adults have no jobs.[58]

If we look only at men below the poverty level, we can see that the nonworking poor increased as a percentage of all the poor in these ethnic groups and that the increase was especially marked among black men. From 1970 to 2000, the percentage of low-income black men who were not working rose from 38 percent to 63 percent. In inner-city areas, nonworkers among inner city black men increased from 50 percent in 1980 to 65 percent in 2000. Among low-income Hispanic men, inner-city unemployment was not as high as it was among blacks, but it did rise from 36 percent to 48 percent.

Both blacks and Hispanics, then, show high levels of concentration in inner-city poverty. In addition, they both show high levels of male joblessness, either through officially recognized unemployment or through nonparticipation in the labor market. This can result in serious problems for children in minority-dominated poor urban areas. Poverty not only is common, it has more and more become the poverty of a surplus population, of men who have no work to give their lives direction.

New Orleans psychologist Beverly Howze noted the impact on children of male joblessness in the new poverty. While working with low-income, school-aged boys, she asked them, "What do men do?" The answers of these boys, none of whom were living in families with fathers, ranged from " '[T]hey sleep, beat their wife, drink' to '[T]hey kill'."[59] These children certainly do not represent all minority students, but the new poverty in American society has ensured that there are enough minority children with backgrounds similar to those of these boys to make redistribution of pupils by race an extremely questionable and problematic effort.

Figure 3.8
Male Unemployment and Labor Force Non-Participation, by Race, 1970–2000

Throughout U.S.

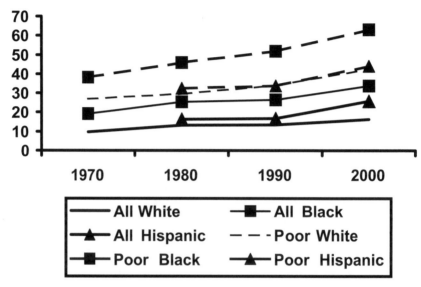

In Central City

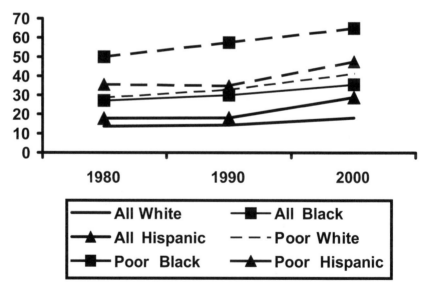

U.S. Bureau of the Census, 1 Percent Public Use Microdata Samples (PUMS), 1970–2000.

DEMOGRAPHICS AND SCHOOL DESEGREGATION

The demographic changes we have been discussing created a new social environment to which families would respond. The explosion of single-parent families among black Americans created problematic situations in minority-dominated schools. We are not arguing that African Americans or any other group of people are somehow to blame for changes in American family structure. Individuals make decisions that may have desirable or undesirable consequences, but statistical tendencies among categories of people are products of larger social forces. The forces that have led to a rise in single-parenthood among Americans in general and to particularly high rates of single-parenthood among black Americans continue to be matters of debate among social scientists.

Our intention is not to judge, but to point out that societies, as complex and continually changing sets of human relations and beliefs, do not lend themselves readily to central planning and design. The dream of the planners has been to erase the discrimination and inequality of the past by deciding on desirable racial mixes in schools and assigning students to create those mixes. But schools are reflections of the communities from which they draw their students, and communities are themselves the products of families—two points we address in some detail in the next chapter. While the planners were making blueprints for schools, minority families were changing in ways that would make their model educational institutions unrealizable. Redistributing students on the basis of race did not just mean putting white children into schools with black children; it meant trying to impose the problems of communities suffering from family breakdown and poverty on young people from other communities.

The rapidly changing ethnic composition of the United States, similarly, should remind us that those who seek to remake a society work in a material that slips through their fingers as they try to mold it. If desegregation means putting minority students in schools with substantial numbers of white students, this will be more difficult to accomplish when the minorities begin to make up close to half of a population than when they make up only a fifth. As supposed minorities become ever more varied in background and needs, the proper distribution of categories becomes more difficult to determine, much less to achieve.

If schools with concentrations of black students tend to suffer the consequences of family breakdown, schools with concentrations of Hispanic students are plagued by high dropout rates and low achievement. At the same time, schools serving Hispanic pupils need to devote resources to the needs of many students who are not proficient in English. As a result, schools with large black and Hispanic populations became places that those with the means and desire to acquire good educations might reasonably seek to avoid. This is especially true if parents are seeking school environments with the highest levels of academic press and achievement. Because of the growth in the Hispanic population since 1965, these two populations now make up one-third of all students and the overwhelming majority of students in many urban areas. In most locations, school desegregation is no longer a matter of scattering a few historically disadvantaged minority group members among the relatively advantaged members of the mainstream; it means dispersing the latter among schools plagued by social problems.

Asians, who made up one out of every twenty students nationally and about one out of every eight students in the West, posed a special difficulty for strategies to redistribute students by racial and ethnic categories. Despite being relative newcomers to the United States, many Asians managed to achieve entry into elite educational institutions. As we have seen in the case of Boston, this very fact tended to segregate Asians from blacks and Hispanics. A purely egalitarian approach to the provision of educational opportunities would deny high-achieving Asians their places in top schools such as Boston Latin and move them, instead, to some of the nation's worst institutions. A recent Chinese American parent strike in San Francisco highlights the problem of denying Asians entrance into high-performing schools based solely on their race. Chinese American families were "fighting assignments to low-performing schools in heavily Latino and African American sections of town."[60] This incident followed the end of race-based busing in San Francisco, but it highlighted the school district's continuing efforts to juggle school racial concentrations.

Changing family structure and a growing, more diverse minority population were accompanied by the development of a new form of poverty. Although proportionately somewhat fewer minority children were living in poverty at the beginning of the twenty-first century than earlier, their impoverishment had become more concentrated, and joblessness had become a way of life for many of the men around them. To be sure, it was precisely this isolation that desegregation activists have wanted to break down. But, as we will argue in the next chapter, schools are the products of families and communities. To the extent that schools draw their students from desperate, disorganized, and violent neighborhoods, the schools themselves will be desperate, disorganized, and violent places.

CHAPTER 4

It Takes a "Certain Kind of" Village to Raise a Child

In Chapter 3, we looked at some of the ways in which a rapidly changing society can confound the aims of top-down government social engineers. A society consists of relationships among people. The racial and ethnic mix of communities, the social expectations we have of each other, and the social hierarchies in which our relationships are situated are continually changing on their own. These changes are outside the control of the social planners. People respond to the dynamic world around them according to their own goals and interests, not according to blueprints for behavior set down by governing authorities. Think for a moment: Did you choose your friends, your spouse, your job, or your neighborhood based on a government directive?

Societies, in other words, are not responsive to organization from the top down because they organize themselves from the bottom up through the decisions and interactions of human beings. This is especially true of a well-educated citizenry with the resources to construct their lives and the lives of their families according to their own dreams and plans. Indeed, such is almost a birthright of Americans, articulated in one of our most sacred founding documents, which declares that one of our rights is "the pursuit of happiness."

Of course, societies can organize themselves in various ways, some arguably preferable to others. Some human communities may be more or less violent than others. Some may be relatively cooperative, whereas others are characterized by individual rivalries or distrust among groups. Some may achieve political, educational, or academic goals efficiently, whereas others seem to flounder in inefficiency. This question of how societies organize themselves, and the questions of how schools are involved in this self-organization, brings us to the concept of social capital.

WHAT IS SOCIAL CAPITAL?

The term "social capital" has become popular among social scientists in recent years. The concept incorporates the idea that the way we behave is not simply a consequence of our own individual actions, but the product of patterns of social relations with others.[1] Social capital develops from our involvement in interlocking social relations or "interpersonal attachments."[2] It is the beneficial product of these personal interactions that, though invisible, can be used in advantageous ways—like doing well in school. Few emotionally and mentally stable persons are islands unto themselves. Indeed, we thrive on social interaction.

We can think about our patterns of social relations—parents with children, coworkers on the job, or neighbors at a community barbeque—as a form of "capital." These human interactions are like resources invested in future outcomes, much as the possession of financial resources or educational resources may be seen as investments. However, just as one can make a bad financial investment, one can make a bad social capital investment as well. Hanging with "bad company" is not a wise investment in social capital and may give a poor return. The hermit is simply an individual who makes no social capital investment at all—and gets no return on his investment.

Among the best-known theorists of social capital are the sociologist James S. Coleman and the Harvard political scientist Robert D. Putnam. Coleman was concerned with how family and community relationships can produce good students. He argued that "close, emotionally intense, bounded networks among parents and other adults surrounding children" enable groups of parents "to establish norms and reinforce each other's sanctioning of the children."[3] We have all heard of (and if we are lucky, actually live in) tight-knit communities where a neighbor at the end of the block feels free to correct another parent's child who is misbehaving—and not only does the child obey, but the parent is happy her child received the correction (and does not sue the other adult). Such healthy interactions and relationships are building social capital that benefits both the child and the community. Coleman said that these kinds of close connections between families and schools, and between local communities and schools, could establish relationships that result in better school performance. In other words "social capital" helps in the creation of "academic capital."[4]

Rather than focusing on relations between families and schools, Harvard professor Robert Putnam studied how individuals participate in the broader society through local organizations. He used "social capital" to describe how connections among individuals in formal and informal organizations provide a basis for a healthy participatory democracy. Think of a citizens' group organizing to fight the construction of a chemical incinerator near their community, or the monthly church potluck dinner where members discuss candidate qualifications in the upcoming school board election. These social interactions can lead to positive outcomes for communities.

Putnam's research into how we come together in these groups follows in the long tradition of the famous French historian Alexis de Tocqueville who traveled across the United States in the 1830s studying the energetic Americans in their young republic. De Tocqueville marveled at the high rate of individual, voluntary participation in American democracy, which he claimed was a unique phenomenon in the entire history of the world. The Frenchman believed that it was this widespread membership in churches, clubs, and other forms of voluntary associations that provided an essential basis to American democracy.[5] Putnam has shown through careful research that the networks of social engagement that so impressed de Tocqueville are in sharp decline in the United States. For example, in his best-selling book *Bowling Alone*, Putnam notes that although Americans continue to bowl for amusement, membership in bowling leagues has decreased drastically.[6] He points out that this decline is symptomatic of a larger withdrawal from community participation, noting also that attendance in public meetings (down 40% from 1973 to 1994), membership in civic and fraternal organizations, voter turnout, and PTA membership have also decreased at alarming rates.

We will not deal here with the specific question of whether or not the overall social capital of the United States is actually declining, though it does seem to be the case.[7] What we would like to show is how social capital in the sense discussed by Coleman is linked to social capital in the sense discussed by Putnam. In other words, family and community connections that promote school achievement are related to participation in formal and informal groups that promote civic engagement. Aggressive school desegregation, as it has been practiced since the 1970s, undermines both of these essential forms of social capital, hurting families, schools, and communities.

FAMILIES, SCHOOLS, AND COMMUNITIES: SOCIAL CAPITAL AND SCHOOL ENVIRONMENTS

Social capital develops from interactions among individuals in groups and organizations. Also, social capital, like monetary capital, is an investment that can lead to advantageous outcomes for both individuals and groups. Social capital can protect a child from delinquent behavior, enhance academic performance in school, and help pass a useful city ordinance. In fact, Putnam argued that social capital was so essential for individual well-being, that if you smoked and participated in no groups, it would be a toss-up as to which would kill you first—your cigarettes or your isolation.[8]

Let us look more closely at four types of interpersonal interactions that create this beneficial elixir called social capital, and show how each boosts school performance. The first type blossoms from the relationship between children and parents in individual families. The second type derives from relationships formed in formal or informal social groups, among sets of adults concerned with children (think PTA). The third type is forged in relations between parents and schools, of which the "room mother" is a variety. The fourth type of social capital develops from the structure of relations among children in schools. This fourth type—school peer networks—turns out to be, we believe, perhaps the most important type of social capital for positive academic outcomes.

SOCIAL CAPITAL IN CHILD AND PARENT INTERACTIONS

Research evidence supports the commonsense view that relations between parents and children affect how children perform in school. Positive parenting styles, reading to children at home, and parents sharing educational cultural activities with their children have all been found to foster academic achievement.[9]

Socioeconomic status, which is closely connected to race and ethnicity in the United States, has been found to be associated with parental styles that promote success. As one group of researchers concluded, "For parents who want their children to do well on tests (which means almost all parents), middle-class parenting practices seem to work."[10] Other researchers have found that the absolute amount of parenting per hour, responsiveness of parents to children, and the quality of parental speech to children were major predictors of performance on IQ tests. Moreover, these elements of parental style were also products of social class. These investigators stressed the importance of middle-class parental styles, concluding that "the major differences associated with differences in IQ were the extensive amount of time, attention, and talking that higher SES parents invest in their children and their active interest in what their children have to say."[11] In an influential book on the black-white test score gap, Christopher Jencks and Meredith Phillips explicitly connect this gap to variations in parenting styles between racial groups.[12]

Researchers have found that reading to young children is significantly related to reading readiness on entering preschool[13] and in kindergarten[14] and to high vocabulary scores.[15] Clearly, reading is associated with the parents' own educational backgrounds, so that members of minority groups with comparatively low levels of parental education are at a disadvantage. As Figure 4.1 shows, there are clear differences among racial and ethnic groups in early childhood reading, and these differences follow the same pattern as differences in educational achievement. Although a majority of parents among all groups did read to their children, the percentages were lowest among the academically disadvantaged groups, blacks and Hispanics.

Exposure to art, music, and literature by parents also appears to be associated with children's academic performance.[16] The reason for this association may be that these kinds of activities develop intellectual abilities, or it may be that the mastery of elite cultural practices gives students the abil-

Figure 4.1
Percentages of White, Asian, Black and Hispanic Children Aged 3–5, Not in Kindergarten Who Were Read to by Parents, 2001

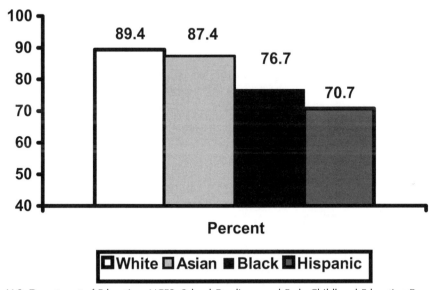

U.S. Department of Education, NCES, School Readiness and Early Childhood Education Program Participation Surveys of the National Household Education Surveys Program (ECPP-NHES: 2001).

ity to express the elite tastes that are considered markers of class distinction.[17] It no doubt helps if students faced with a test question about Van Gogh's art has actually seen it with their own eyes. In any case, such exposure is also tied to social class, which is in turn, once again, closely connected to race.

Although social class seems to play a part in how parents interact with their children, parent-child relationships, of course, transcend class and race. Laurence Steinberg, of Temple University, found that, on average, even inferior parenting styles, which he defined as permissive (too much liberty) and authoritative (too much control), produced better students than disengaged parenting.[18] Along similar lines, James Coleman argued that close relations between parents and children could provide the support and control that would enable young people to flourish in schools.[19] Coleman wrote, "When both parents are present, there will be, if all else is equal, a stronger parent-child relation than when only one parent is present."[20] In other words, just being there counts. Also, more is better. Research shows that single-parent families showed significantly greater conflict and significantly less communication and cohesion than two-parent families.[21] This is logical: two parents can divvy up the myriad of responsibilities in busy American families, reducing workload and stress. Additionally, children with two parents in the home have twice as many opportunities to engage in meaningful interaction with a concerned adult (who is also likely to be less stressed out).

This issue of family structure brings us back to the demographic change that we discussed in Chapter 3. The interactions between Hispanic children and their parents may not generate as much of the social capital that leads to better grades in school because of limited parental socioeconomic status or the language barrier. However, most black children grow up in single-parent families. Therefore, parent-child social capital in black American families tends to be limited not only by social class but also by family structure—and, some might argue, by language.

SOCIAL CAPITAL IN PARENT-TO-PARENT INTERACTIONS

Families do not exist in isolation. The "capital" inherent in any relationship consists of connections among sets of people surrounding the relationship, as well as attachments between the parties in the relationship. When parents maintain close contacts with other adults who affect the lives of their children, for example, this adult network can impose consistent norms and standards to direct the behavior of young people. As pointed out earlier,

Coleman saw networks among parents and other adults as critical to maintaining social capital. In a study of academic achievement among Vietnamese American young people, one of the authors of the present book accounted for this achievement by describing the dense social relations among the parents and other adults who surround these students.[22] In New York's Chinatown, the tight network of family connections that characterize this urban ethnic enclave puts tremendous pressure on school-aged children to do well. Parents often greet each other with such questions as "And how is your child doing in school?" or they may ask a child directly, "What grades did you make on your report card?"[23]

In South Korea, where seven of ten children typically begin their day in a public school, then spend five more hours in a "private academy" in the evening,[24] parent-to-parent interaction plays a key role in maintaining high academic expectations and determining where "the best" private schools are. A Korean educator who was also a student in the first author's graduate class pointed out that Korean students are rank-ordered according to their school grades, and parents often now pry this information—which used to be publicized—from teachers. Parents are very anxious to find out how other students rank, so that they can identify the best students, and then ply these students' parents for information on which private schools, called *Hakwon*, their bright children attend. According to the Korean educator, "Parents ask each other how their respective children are doing in school, what rankings their (the other parents') children have, which private schools they go to, and how their kids study at home and so on."[25] Thus, parental networks in Korea serve as an important conduit for transmitting critical information on quality schooling and of indirectly pressuring parents, in turn, to put pressure on their own children to do well in school. Is it any surprise, then, that Koreans typically have among the highest scores on standardized tests among all Asian students?

Of course, adults in black families and in families of other educationally disadvantaged groups do have networks of social ties. In her classic study *All Our Kin*, Carol Stack described the resilience of black families in a low-income neighborhood and she described how women, in particular, helped each other meet the everyday challenges of life.[26] Strategies for survival, though, are not necessarily the same as methods of encouraging scholastic performance. As M. Patricia Fernandez-Kelly has documented, social relations among adults in urban minority neighborhoods tend to provide support and encouragement to children without giving the children the kinds of direction that would pay off outside those neighborhoods.[27]

SOCIAL CAPITAL IN PARENT AND SCHOOL INTERACTIONS

Another important form of social capital develops when parents become involved in their children's schools. When parents either volunteer in schools or meet with school staff, they contribute to their children's academic performance by creating strong links between the family and the educational institution. Again, think of social capital as an investment. When a parent attends the school's open house and personally meets with his or her child's teachers, this intimate one-on-one contact sends several messages to the teachers. For one, the teachers see that their efforts are being supported at home and are therefore more likely to bear fruit than efforts expended on an uninterested and defiant student whose parent would not even show up at a suspension hearing. (Or if they do come to the hearing, blame the teacher and the school for their child's misbehavior.) After all, teachers are only human, and like all humans they want to believe that their hard work is not in vain. In fact, research has found that the teacher of a student with involved parents is likely to invest more time and effort in this particular child than a child with uninvolved parents.[28] Second, the parents and teachers can share information that will allow them to better tailor their efforts to benefit the child. Third, the child receives the message that the parent takes schooling seriously. Fourth, the child knows that the teachers are aware of the support they have in the child's home, reducing misbehavior on the child's part. One of the authors found it very useful to point out to misbehaving students that he had a good rapport with the child's parent—and wouldn't hesitate to re-open the dialogue if necessary.

Beyond even these four benefits, though, parent voluntarism helps to make good schools. Parents groups can raise large sums of money to fund school activities, funnel donated computers and technology to under-equipped schools, and provide a pool of chaperones to accompany school field trips. All pupils, not just the children of volunteer parents, benefit from having adults contribute time, resources, and attention. Unfortunately, the data indicate that as minority representation in schools grows, schools generally enjoy less of the family engagement type of social capital.

A survey that we distributed among teachers in a school district in 1996 (the results of which we reported in an earlier book[29]) showed that teachers felt that parental involvement was essential to maintaining a constructive social environment. One teacher volunteered the observation that "discipline problems in my school stem from the fact that parents just aren't involved."[30] In the midst of desegregation related chaos four years later, a guidance counselor in the same school district wrote a revealing letter to the editor of the local daily newspaper expressing the same viewpoint. She connected the lack of parental involvement to the racial composition of schools:

> Will this [school desegregation] get the minority parents involved in the schools? This is the real problem. I've been in at-risk schools for 23 years. The problem is the same now as it was then. Parental involvement is the real problem. Put the blame where it belongs. Can federal judges drag parents to school and make them become more involved in their child's education? This would be interesting to see. Parent involvement is the main reason for poor test scores and discipline problems.[31]

Lest the author of this letter be accused of passing a biased judgment, it appears that minority parents really are, for whatever reason, less involved in schools. In another survey we conducted a year after forced busing began in this same district, the teachers of bused low-SES African American students supported this guidance counselor's point of view that lack of African American parental involvement in the desegregating schools was undermining the success of the experiment.[32]

Figure 4.2 shows two measures of active parental involvement for white, black, and Hispanic families. Taken from data for the National Center for Educational Statistics, this shows us percentages of parents in 1999 who had attended an event and done volunteer or committee work in a child's school during the previous year. Clear differences among the groups show that 72 percent of white parents had attended a school event, compared to 54 percent of black parents, and only 51 percent of Hispanic parents. Doing volunteer work in a school or serving on a school committee shows a greater level of involvement than merely attending an event, so the percentages for this second measure are understandably smaller than those for the first. A little under half (43%) of white parents had done some kind of service work in schools. By contrast, though, only slightly over a quarter of black parents and slightly under a quarter of Hispanic parents had been volunteers.

We want to stress that this should not necessarily be taken as a reflection on the commitment of minority parents to their children's lives and educations. There may be many reasons for comparatively low parental activity in schools. Work schedules that leave no time for other things parents would like to do, unfamiliarity with the school environment, lack of information, language problems (as is the case for many Hispanic parents), and other obstacles can all stand in the way of parental activity in schools.[33] Since black children are much more likely to live in single-parent families, these single

Figure 4.2
Active Parental Involvement in Schools, by Race and Ethnicity, 1999

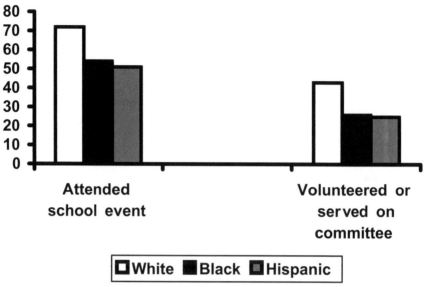

National Center for Education Statistics, The Condition of Education, Societal Support for Learning, Table 54-1.

parents may simply have more on their plate than two-parent families have, and consequently single parents have less time to become involved in their child's school. One obstacle to school involvement frequently mentioned by teachers in one of our surveys was that black parents simply could not get to their child's new suburban white school because of its distance from their urban neighborhoods and lack of ground transportation.[34] Whatever the causes of differences in school involvement by adults across racial and ethnic groups, though, these differences do exist and they have consequences.

By definition, if minority parents are, on average, less active in schools, then the pool of parental volunteers will necessarily grow smaller as the minority population of the school grows larger. Figure 4.3 presents the average percentages of parents who volunteer in schools by the racial composition of schools. Readers may note that in schools in which Hispanic students make up large proportions of minority school populations, percentages of active parents would decline even more steeply, since Hispanic parents tend to be the least involved in schooling of all the categories.

However, the relative academic disengagement among African American parents is not just class based. John Ogbu's recent study of the black middle-class suburban community of Shaker Heights, Ohio, uncovered less black parental involvement in the schooling of their children than among either white parents or even black immigrant parents.[35] Ogbu suggested that African American culture in general, and African American families in particular, place less emphasis on formal education than other ethnic and racial groups do. This relative lack of interest could certainly explain lower black parental involvement in schools, as well as lower black grades, discussed next. Black children benefit academically from the social capital generated by parental involvement in schools just as children from other racial and ethnic groups do. Roger Goddard, a University of Michigan researcher, studied forty-five predominantly low-SES African American elementary schools in a large midwestern city. He found that there was a strong positive relationship between his measure of social capital—which incorporated relational networks, norms, and trust—and success on standardized math and writing tests. In fact, he found that controlling for school social capital, school socioeconomic status had no effect on students' test outcomes.[36] In other words, a school's social capital boosted black academic achievement and counteracted the negative influence of the disadvantaged students' backgrounds.

Figure 4.3
Average Percentages of Parents Who Volunteer in Schools, by Percentages of Black Students, 1999

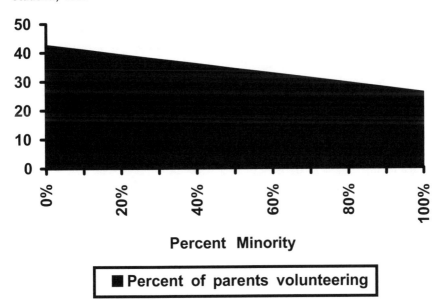

Percent Minority

■ **Percent of parents volunteering**

SOCIAL CAPITAL IN STUDENT-TO-STUDENT INTERACTIONS

The final type of social capital may be found in the social ties among the students themselves. We devote the most discussion to this type of social capital because we believe it has perhaps the most important influence on academic outcomes, especially among teenagers. In his early book *The Adolescent Society*,[37] James Coleman examined how school outcomes are consequences of the social groups and cultures that exist within schools. In an age-segregated society such as our own, where we concentrate many children together in groups (grades) of the same chronological age, attitudes and practices are largely shaped by other pupils, and not the teachers or administration. But even before the age of megalithic 3,000-student high schools, Ralph Waldo Emerson observed in the nineteen century, "You send your child to the schoolmaster, but 'tis the schoolboys who educate him."[38] Today's schools and classrooms are much larger than the cozy one-room schoolhouse of Emerson's time, and as a consequence students today are virtually swallowed by their peer groups. While still influential, teachers in twenty-first-century America do not have the control and authority over students that yesteryear's "school marm" had, for she could swat a recalcitrant child—and then hug him—with total parental support and no fear of a lawsuit.

One of the authors was led to think about the role of students as educators several years ago while working as a substitute teacher in a New Orleans high school. The school, which had good physical facilities and resources, stood in the center of a fairly affluent, middle-class black neighborhood. Still, despite the attractiveness of the surrounding homes, the institution was a troubled one. Some of the students showed interest and worked hard, but there were frequent behavior problems and the general attitude among young people was complete alienation from the whole project of education.

A long-time teacher explained what he believed had happened. He maintained that in the past, when the school had drawn its students almost exclusively from the comfortable homes in the immediate vicinity, the educational climate in the school had been quite good. The school board, though, had decided that young people who lived in public housing could benefit from contact with the middle-class adolescents. Accordingly, the board redrew the zone boundaries so that some of those who would have gone to this school went off to another one, and many of the pupils from public housing took their place.

From that time on, the teacher said, there had been a steady deterioration in the quality of the school. Whether the low-income students learned from the middle-class was uncertain, but the reverse had definitely been the case. Even students from prosperous homes, with parents who had high educational aspirations for children, began to take on the norms and values of their least-advantaged classmates. Laurence Steinberg's extensive study of families, schools, and peer groups found the same thing: the power of a child's peer group can undo much good parenting. Indeed, Steinberg found that, on average, African American students from homes with the most effective parenting earned lower grades than Asian students from homes with completely disengaged parents (the worst home environments)! Further research into this anomaly revealed the cause of this substantial ethnic achievement gap. Steinberg found that black and Latino peer groups tended to demean academic achievement, equating doing well in school with "selling out one's cultural identity."[39] For Asian peer groups, however, doing well in school was valued, and the social capital of Asian peer networking tended to counter negative influences on education that might come from some dysfunctional Asian home environments.

THE POWER OF SCHOOL PEER CULTURES

This perspective helps us to understand not only the dynamics in the predominately black New Orleans school that began receiving students from low-income housing but also what happens in all schools. Students bring with them to schools the social capital they have acquired from their homes and neighborhoods. Thus, their relationships with their families and communities are being invested not only in their own outcomes but also in the entire school. Students who come from families that have studied and planned their children's education, whose parents and communities have high expectations for them, and who have the advantage of two parents bring all these background characteristics with them to the school. Conversely, students who come from families with parents who have completed relatively little formal education, whose communities contain few examples of success, and who live with one, struggling parent also bring their own backgrounds with them. African American students, regardless their social class, also tended to bring with them to school a general distrust and distaste for learning. Out of the backgrounds brought by all students comes the school's social climate for order and achievement.

This, we think, offers an excellent example of how the fourth type of social capital works. In the "supercharged" school climates created from students' collective backgrounds, students influence each other as much as or even more than they are influenced by school inputs (e.g., the teachers and curriculum) and, ultimately, even family inputs.[40] In these largely peer-created school social milieus, there is a "transference" of the various forms of capital between students in their multitude of on- and off-campus contacts, or "dense networks of social interaction," to use Putnam and Goss's expression.[41] School peer groups develop their own expectations for group members that "influence individuals' behavior because the actions of group members . . . are judged by group members relative to group norms."[42] If doing well in school is considered "un-cool" in your group of sixteen-year-old friends, then you are very unlikely to be motivated to get good grades and in fact may consciously or unconsciously do poorly.

This fourth kind of social capital explains the observations of Signithia Fordham, a black sociologist at the University of Rochester, of the relative lack of academic enthusiasm among even middle-class black students in a Washington, D.C., high school. At "Capital High," Fordham noted the existence of a norm among black students that associated doing well in school with "acting white."[43] Such was the pressure on black students to disengage from academics, that those black students wishing to do well in school often hid their academic accomplishments from their friends rather than risk being accused of "acting white." In this case, any social capital a student brought from home was being eroded in Capital High's peer networks where other students sneered at high grades. The more integrated and accepted a student is in a peer group with such a corrosive attitude toward high academic achievement, the worse a student is likely to do academically.

Acknowledging that there may be a prevalent "anti academic" attitude among African Americans is not a popular position to take—regardless its truth. In his book *Losing the Race: Self Sabotage in Black America*, John McWhorter, a black linguistics professor at UC Berkeley and current fellow at the Manhattan Institute for Policy Studies, gave many examples from his personal experience to substantiate the existence of black underachievement among middle-class blacks that cannot be blamed on white racism or discrimination. In fact, he claims just the opposite, saying that blacks admitted to elite universities under affirmative action programs do not take education as seriously as students from other racial and ethnic groups. Moreover, McWhorter also contends that urban black communities are disintegrating, not because of white racism, but because of attitudes tied up in the rise of "the rap culture." He believes this violent dimension of hip hop has helped supplant the more optimistic black culture that used to permeate the inner-city black experience. According to McWhorter:

The rise of nihilistic rap has mirrored the breakdown of community norms among inner-city youth over the last couple of decades. It was just as gangsta rap hit its stride that neighborhood elders began really to notice that they'd lost control of young black men, who were frequently drifting into lives of gang violence and drug dealing. Well into the seventies, the ghetto was a shabby part of town, where, despite unemployment and rising illegitimacy, a healthy number of people were doing their best to "keep their heads above water," as the theme song of the old black sitcom *Good Times* put it. By the eighties, the ghetto had become a ruleless war zone, where black people were their own worst enemies.[44]

Many of his black colleagues have roundly accused McWhorter of selling out. However, at least some of the criticism leveled at the linguist seems unjustified. An experience the first author had at a national educational conference in 2001 hints at this. I attended a session on multicultural education, and immediately after the last presentation I approached a black graduate student whose nametag identified his school as UC Berkeley. Having just read McWhorter's controversial book, I introduced myself and asked the graduate student how McWhorter's ideas were going over on his home campus. The student frowned, and then claimed that the book was unscientific and biased. However, when I asked the earnest young man if he'd read *Losing the Race*, the grad student sheepishly admitted that he had not, but he hurriedly added that he'd "heard all about it."

According to the respected black syndicated columnist Clarence Page, who writes for the *Chicago Tribune*, there is a norm in the black community he calls BPC—Black Political Correctness. He says blacks violate BPC when they "hang out our dirty laundry" in public.[45] Bill Cosby, the black entertainment father-figure (with an educational doctorate), also apparently violated the unspoken dictates of BPC when he criticized lower-SES blacks for "not holding up their end in this deal" at a speech in honor of the fiftieth anniversary of the *Brown* decision. "They are buying things for kids—$500 sneakers for what? And won't spend $200 for 'Hooked on Phonics.' " Kweisi Mfume, the former president of the NAACP, was in attendance at the speech. Afterward, he told Page that he agreed with what the famous black entertainer said.[46] Contrast Cosby's comments with parental involvement in Korea, where 12.7 percent of an average household's expenditures are on private tutors or private schools,[47] and we begin to have some inkling of why such a huge achievement gap exists between Asians and African Americans (which we explore in more detail in Chapter 7).

In a spoof on "police brutality" that showcased an unhelpful inner-city black attitude toward cops that he claims amounts to self-sabotage, the Chris Rock TV comedy show featured an "educational video" entitled *How Not to Get Your A—— Kicked by the Police.* The "video," a spoof of a public service announcement, shows several "how to" and "how not to" scenarios to respond to police officers. In one "how not to" scenario, a black male in a car with booming rap music is pulled over by the police. The driver jumps out the car and yells at the cops, "What the f—— you want mother f——er!?!" The police promptly beat him. The video suggests a more helpful "how to" alternative approach: turning down the music and asking the policeman in a pleasant voice, "Is there a problem officer?" Though, of course, not all black drivers respond in the way the belligerent characters in Rock's skits do, the comedian is highlighting an attitude that seems to be more prevalent in the black community than elsewhere. Attitudes, social capital theory indicates, are contagious.

Since blacks are many times more likely than whites to be suspended or expelled from school for infractions disproportionately related to "disrespect," black defiance of authority truly does seem to be a problem that is working against the best interests of individuals in the black community not only on the street but in the classroom as well. This is not to say that there is not genuine, unjustifiable police discrimination and brutality against minorities—because there certainly is. What Rock's "public service announcement" suggests is that black males play a part in provoking some of this violent police reaction.

So we see that among influential academics, entertainers, journalists, political leaders, and educators in the African American community, there seems to be some agreement that certain elements of black American culture do not encourage high academic achievement. And that they may, in fact, counter it. These elements have become part of the normative structure, or "expectations," of some black peer groups, exerting pressure on everyone in the group to "get with the program." Unfortunately, the program seldom seems to include striving for the honor roll.

The observations of both the New Orleans teacher, cited earlier, and Signithia Fordham's study of "Capital High" point to a kind of Gresham's law of adolescent interpersonal influence at work in schools. The economist Gresham stated, "Bad money drives out the good." The "bad investments" in social resources, such as ridicule for "acting white" and defiance of authority, tend to drive out the good—the hard work of parents and teachers trying to interest children in academics. As any parent, teacher, or psychologist will testify, during the high school years young people generally want to establish their independence and to distinguish themselves from their elders. Adolescents are therefore particularly susceptible to influences that oppose the established structures and regulations of teachers, principals—and the police. For this reason, the fourth kind of social capital, the pooling and transference of characteristics brought into schools from homes and communities, is extremely sensitive to investments that do not lead to productive school environments or to individual accomplishments.

Peer cultures are tenacious, and they punish individuals who do not conform to their established norms. Peer influence explains the student who hides her homework activity from her peers. It also explains the attraction of gangs, drugs, violence, skipping school . . . and dropping out. Peer cultures also set tastes in clothes and music, not the home. How many high school sophomores prefer their parents' style of dress and music? Such a "goody goody" student would no doubt be targeted for scorn and ridicule by his or her classmates. Moreover, rather than the individual student bringing the positive influences of his or her family background to bear on the peer culture of the school, especially middle and high school, the school's peer culture is more likely to determine how the adolescent behaves at home. Adolescent psychologists refer to the peer pressure that children sense when away from their peers, a peer pressure that makes them self-conscious of their actions, as "the imaginary audience."[48] The adolescent "imagines" that he or she is "on stage." This explains, for example, why a sixteen-year-old is impervious to a parent's pleas to lower the volume on the punk rock or rap (often with lyrics raging against established authority, from groups with names like Rage Against the Machine) that is rattling the light fixtures downstairs. For bilingual adolescents, even the choice of which language to speak, beyond the hearing of peers, is dictated by the school peer group, not the family environment.[49]

The Positive Power of Peers

There is, fortunately, a positive dimension to the theory of peer group–generated social capital. When students come from homes where academic achievement is stressed, and these students form tight-knit communities on school campuses, peer networking within these cohesive units supports doing well in school. We can see this dynamic working in insulated and isolated school gifted and honors programs that concentrate high-achieving students, and among the previously discussed Asian ethnic peer groups, who are, by the way, disproportionately represented in gifted and honors programs. Steinberg found that Asian peer groups in his ten-year longitudinal study were much more academically oriented than whites, blacks, or Latinos.

There was much more peer pressure within Asian groups than among other ethnic groups to do well in school. According to Steinberg, "Asian students benefit tremendously from the network of academically oriented peers. Indeed, one of the striking features of Asian student friendships is how frequently they turn to each other for academic assistance and consultation."[50] A daughter of one of the authors attended a school for the academically gifted and observed that "all the Asian students [more than other students] constantly compare grades and ask each other how they do on tests and what grades they make on their report cards."[51]

DISRUPTIVE SCHOOL CLIMATES

In Chapter 7 we will focus more closely on the academic consequences of school racial desegregation. Here, we focus on the fact that students bring their varying backgrounds with them to schools, where they are combined with other students' backgrounds to create the school's unique social and academic environments. We have already seen that minority race is strongly associated with poverty and with the likelihood of coming from a single-parent family. Moreover, we have seen that leading academics have identified a prevalent anti-academic orientation among black youth. Thus, the examples just cited suggest that minority students who come from disadvantaged backgrounds, especially blacks, are more likely to exhibit the behaviors that create problems in schools. The evidence supports this point of view.

Figure 4.4 shows percentages of black, Hispanic, Asian, and white students in grades 7 through 12 suspended or expelled from school in 1999. There are clear differences among them. Only 13 percent of Asians and 15 percent of whites had received these penalties. By contrast, 20 percent of Hispanic and 35 percent of black students had either been suspended or expelled in 1999. To the extent that these higher figures represent actual student misbehavior, rather than discriminatory enforcement of discipline, these figures indicate that schools with large proportions of Hispanic or black students are less focused academically than schools with small proportions of these students. After all, if harried teachers are distracted from doing the job they were hired to do by disciplining students, they are not engaging the other students in positive intellectual ways.

Constantly disciplining unruly students is an emotionally, mentally, and physically exhausting experience, which saps the teacher's vitality that could otherwise be focused on actually helping students to learn the subject matter. Both authors could recount literally hundreds of examples they have heard of teachers burning out in inner-city schools (and even in suburban

Figure 4.4
Percent of Students in Grades 7–12 Who Have Been Suspended or Expelled, by Race, 1999

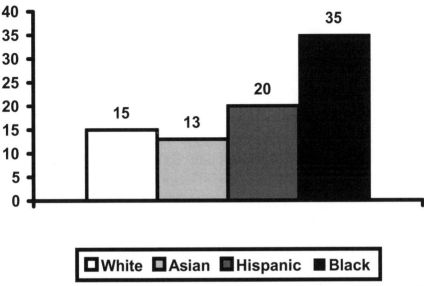

U.S. Department of Education, National Center for Education Statistics, National Household Education Survey (NHES), 1999 (Parent Interview Component).

middle-class schools) because of the drain of constantly having to discipline unwilling and belligerent students, some of whom have violently assaulted these teachers. Many of these educators quit (sometimes after only one day), transfer to middle-class or private schools, change professions, or retire as a consequence of burning out from dealing with defiant students all day long. The first author considers his experiences teaching in secondary schools as one of the most rewarding experiences in his life. However, having taught for six and a half years in high-poverty at-risk schools, I recall that one of the most onerous and time-consuming dimensions to disciplining students was simply documenting their misbehavior in writing. In one high school, teachers were required to fill out a disciplinary form in quadruplicate listing teacher and student name, period, time, and date of infraction, a detailed description of the infraction (which usually bled onto another page); sign the document; and distribute the copies to the appropriate administrators (who may or may not have followed up). In my lowest-level classes, which were often nearly 100 percent minority, I may have had to "write up" several students a day—all taking time better spent preparing lessons, grading papers, meeting with parents, or counseling students. At the more dramatic extreme, I have chased students across campuses, tripping and tearing up my knee on one occasion, been hit breaking up fights between students much larger than me, been "flipped the bird," verbally insulted, cursed, and threatened, and had personal items stolen. And I felt I was one of the more popular teachers. One of my less fortunate colleagues, who could maintain no semblance of control in his classes, would regularly have his classroom lights turned out and desks thrown at him. His wall was full of holes where desks and chairs had been hurled.

One of my ninth grade students, who when he occasionally came to class usually reeked of pot, was convicted of staking out and murdering a narcotics officer with a few of his buddies. A few years later, I met another student (a white) at the Louisiana Department of Education—dressed in prison garb and pushing a mop on my floor. He was doing time for armed robbery. Understand that I genuinely liked most of my students, including the troublemakers (sometimes *especially* the troublemakers). For example, when he was in my ninth grade civics class, the student who eventually did time for armed robbery had begged me to allow him to come on my regularly scheduled field trip to a New Orleans prison with my senior sociology students. His friendly charm won me over, and I set about getting permission from his five other teachers to allow him to take the trip, which he very much seemed to enjoy. I guess he enjoyed it a little too much. In any event, all my formal secondary teaching experiences occurred in the 1980s. Almost to a teacher, I am told that student misbehavior is worse, if not much worse, today. Also, I am often told, the mandates of the No Child Left Behind Act, as laudable as they may be, have increased teacher paperwork exponentially. It is difficult to imagine.

But can we discount some or even most of these suspensions and expulsions of minority students as reflections of biased teachers and administrators? It seems we cannot. Major research studies find no evidence to support the so-called prejudiced teacher hypothesis as an explanation for overall differences in ethnic grades or disciplinary actions.[52] Indeed, substantial evidence confirms that misbehavior on the part of minority students is actually greater than indicated by most statistics. A recent study of the issue has concluded, "In many school systems black students are less likely to be suspended for the same offense as a white student. Moreover, the greater the discretion given administrators in suspension decisions, the fewer the black students suspended."[53] It does indeed look very unlikely that the high suspension and expulsion rates of minority students are produced by biased enforcement.

School safety has become an increasingly serious, literally life-or-death issue. Figure 4.5 considers percentages of white, black, and Hispanic students in 1999 who felt too unsafe to go to school in the previous year, who were threatened with a weapon, and who were in fights in school. In some respects, Hispanics were the most disadvantaged of the three groups. Over 11 percent of Hispanics felt that their schools were unsafe places, compared to 6 percent of blacks and fewer than 4 percent of whites. Also, one in ten Hispanics was threatened with a weapon in school, compared to about 8 percent of blacks and 7 percent of whites. We saw in the previous chapter that there are indications of rising hyper segregation in the growing Hispanic school population. If Hispanic students are going to schools where about one in ten is threatened with weapons and feels too unsafe to attend, is it difficult to understand why other groups, including some Hispanics themselves, seek to avoid those schools? The first author could certainly understand why parents might avoid putting their children in the high school at which he taught. After he left, the student population became even poorer and more heavily minority, ironically, as a consequence of an onerous desegregation order that we document in one of our books.[54] Since the author's tenure at this high school, one student violently stabbed another in the lunch line, murdering her.

Figure 4.5
Percent of Students Reporting Violence on School Grounds, by Race and Ethnicity, 1999

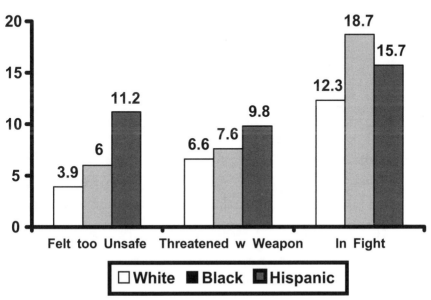

U.S. Department of Education, National Center for Education Statistics.

On a somewhat less serious but probably much more common measure of school disorder, black students report the most problems. One out of every five black students (19%) reports having been in a fight in the previous year. Hispanics are not too far behind, since 16 percent were in fights. By contrast, 12 percent of white students reported having been in a fight. Thus, it stands to reason that if there are more incidents of problematic behavior among minority students, then schools with large minority populations will have more incidents. Figure 4.6 bears this out. Here, we show reports of principals of behavioral problems in schools by the racial makeup of schools. Nearly 60 percent of principals in schools with minority student populations under 5 percent reported that they had only moderate behavior problems or no problems at all. In contrast, over 70 percent of principals in schools that were over half minority students reported moderate to serious problems, and nearly one-fourth of those principals reported that their schools had serious prob-

Figure 4.6
Percent of Principals Reporting Discipline Problems in Schools, by Percentage of Minority Students in Schools, 1996–1997

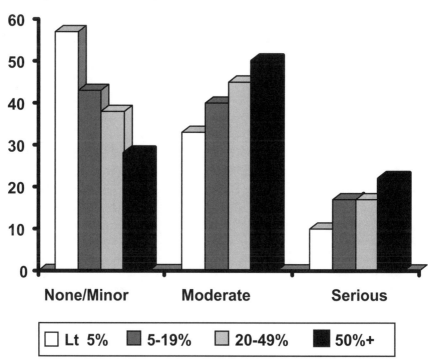

U.S. Department of Education, National Center for Education Statistics.

lems. The greater the proportion of minority students, the greater was the probability of disorder. Once again, we have evidence of diminished social capital in majority minority schools.

Disruptive students not only distract a teacher from teaching but also present unhelpful models for the rest of the class. In terms of social capital, this means that having several disruptive students in a classroom erodes the positive home influences that the other students have brought with them to school. Student-to-student interactions may now consist less of constructive academic learning, sharing, and positive modeling, and more cutting up, teasing, and intimidation. In short, social order is replaced with rising levels of social disorder. In one of our surveys, we found that teachers in majority white middle-class schools that had been receiving bused disadvantaged minority students for a year reported that the school environment in general had become less orderly. In a typical comment, one teacher observed, "I find that many of our [previously zoned, middle-class] students, perhaps those who were on the 'edge,' are emulating the behavior and disrespectfulness that many of the transferred students brought with them."[55] Indeed, a greater percentage of teachers in our survey indicated that the mostly middle-class students were worse off as a result of having the low-SES African American students bused in to their school than indicated that the bused students were better off as a result of being placed in a middle-class school. Again, we see the principle of negative peer influences counteracting the positive. Still, 60 percent of the teachers felt that the bused students were better off in their new middle-class schools—suggesting the magnitude of the problems in their former schools.

Somewhat sadly, the first author heard teachers from the receiving middle-class schools expressing pity for the better students who now had to waste much of their time watching the teacher disciplining the bused students. I conducted an extensive interview with a dynamic fourth grade Caucasian teacher in this district of 1,500 teachers. She was assigned primarily to teach the bused black students and explained to me that she spent more time teaching these students fundamental social skills than academics. She felt that by the end of the first year she had finally taught her students such basics as how to respect one another and say "thank you," but that when these same students moved on to the fifth grade, negative peer influences countered much of her hard work. Two years later this same teacher was assigned to teach the more accelerated, high-SES students zoned for her school. She said she taught these zoned students more in the first six weeks than she was able to teach her bused students in a whole year. Rather than bitterness or resentment, however, the interviewer sensed this teacher's deep empathy and compassion for the bused students she taught. Indeed, she was chosen by the family of one of her bused students to give the eulogy after he died in a tragic fire, and in 2004 she was chosen as a finalist for teacher of the year in the school district.[56] During our interview she made the touching comment that teaching her disadvantaged students left her so drained at the end of each day, that she had to spend much time in prayer to recharge her batteries. She could not understand how a nonbeliever in God could deal effectively with the multitude of troubles these children brought with them to school.

Student discipline problems do seem to be worse among low-SES minorities. Early voluntary busing programs in Los Angeles experienced relatively little difficulty when only the "black elite" were using the programs to send their children to schools in the mostly white West Side. However, once mandatory desegregation began moving the least advantaged into the West Side, conflict and complications followed. By 1982, one principal in a receiving school characterized the incoming students under mandatory desegregation as "perpetual troublemakers." He explained, "Some ethnic groups and some parents value education more than others. They push their children more. And the behavior of their children is different. For example, the kids here (white kids from Bel-Air) fight with their mouths. They can say some pretty mean things. The Queen Anne kids [bused in from a low-income minority neighborhood] fight with their fists."[57] A few years earlier, in Inglewood, California, the change in school racial population led to such a dramatic decline in school environments that the black parents who had initially sued the district to begin desegregation began looking for ways to leave the district. Police reported that crime and vandalism had increased in Inglewood schools. Mrs. Marsha Flaggs, one of the nine black parents who had successfully sued the district, said that she was pulling her daughter out of the public school system: "Public schools have become a place where bad things happen. I can't just let my children be buried there."[58]

We have seen some of the ways in which dysfunctional relationships between parents and children in individual families, between parents and schools, and among students within schools put minority students at an educational disadvantage. These disadvantages mean that schools with large minority populations enjoy less social capital than those with relatively small minority populations. Problems in families become problems in neighborhoods, and problems in neighborhoods tend to become problems in schools. School desegregation was a strategy for remedying the disadvantages of minority students by mixing them in with more advantaged middle-class white students. However, the middle-class schools that receive disadvantaged students can easily fall into the same chaos that plagued the schools that sent those students. After giving a desegregation presentation at a national educational conference, one of the authors was approached by a researcher who had studied the effects of the voucher system in Milwaukee. She shared with the author statistics that showed middle-class flight from the Milwaukee private schools that had been receiving voucher students from the city's lower-performing public schools. She believed that the same dynamic was at work in Milwaukee's private schools as in public schools that receive large infusions of disadvantaged students.

SCHOOLS AND THE CREATION OF COMMUNITY SOCIAL CAPITAL

We have seen how families and communities make investments in schools, a dynamic first popularized in *The Coleman Report*. We have also seen how these investments can be eroded. There is yet another dynamic through which social capital is created. Schools are not just places where we make investments—they are themselves investments in the surrounding community. Harvard professor Robert Putnam described how schools are central institutions for neighborhoods. By weakening the links between schools and communities—and reducing a very useful kind of social capital—centrally planned desegregation has also weakened vital sources of civic engagement in minority neighborhoods, as well as in white neighborhoods. Let us not lose sight of an important question: If school desegregation was supposed to strengthen inner-city black communities, why are these communities now more distressed than ever? The short answer is that the plan obviously did not work, for this second kind of social capital was seriously depleted by our misguided social engineering.

Schools are created out of communities. Communities that are plagued by fragmented families, joblessness, crime, and poverty will produce troubled schools. This does not mean that schools cannot contribute to solving the problems that surround them, however. Healthy communities are created by highly involved citizens actively participating in local associations, organizations, and institutions. From a bottom-up perspective, the neighborhood schools that suffered so severely during the era of judicially mandated desegregation could once again become centerpieces of strong communities, including minority communities. There is still hope.

As mentioned at the beginning of this chapter, Robert Putnam, like Alexis de Tocqueville before him in the 1830s, sees American civil society as built on the foundation of active engagement by citizens in voluntary associations. On the subject of schools, Putnam writes, "The parent-teacher association

Figure 4.7
Memberships of Parents in Voluntary Associations

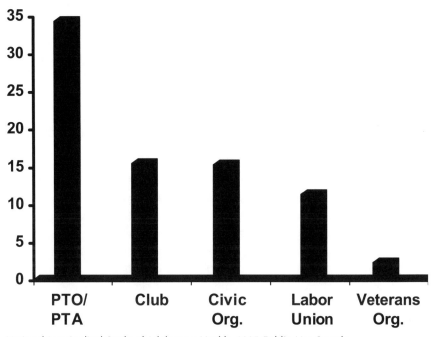

National Longitudinal Study of Adolescent Health, 1995 Public Use Sample.

(PTA) has been an especially important form of civic engagement in twentieth-century America because parental involvement in the educational process represents a particularly productive form of social capital."[59]

In fact, parent-teacher groups appear to be one of the most common types of voluntary associations. Figure 4.7 uses data from the National Longitudinal Study of Adolescent Health to show the reported memberships of parents. More than one-third of people who have children belong to these school associations, a much higher proportion than those who belong to sports or hobby clubs, civic groups, labor unions, or veterans' organizations. Further, people who are involved in parent-teacher organizations are more likely to be involved with other kinds of organizations. These two observations are logical. Since the first concern of most parents is their children, the organizations concerned with the well-being of children are the types of organizations to which parents are most likely to give their time and energy. Second, joining one organization makes it more likely one will join yet another. Moreover, simply joining an organization also increases the likelihood that one will participate in other civic activities. In sharing results of his research on social capital, Robert Putnam reported, "Members of associations are much more likely than nonmembers to participate in politics, to spend time with neighbors, to express social trust, and so on.[60]

Figure 4.8 supports the view that the various forms of social capital are correlated, and it suggests that parental involvement in schools is central to public engagement of other sorts. Not only are parent organizations the most common source of membership among people who have children, those who take part in these organizations are much more likely than those who do not to join in associations of all other sorts. We note that the connection of PTO or PTA membership with civic organizations is particularly strong. School involvement is a form of participation that lies at the heart of any healthy local community. This involvement promotes contacts and cooperation among neighbors and it gives people a very good reason to take an active roll in local politics. After all, school taxes are among the highest we pay, and both sales and property taxes for education are largely levied through local political processes, so PTO and PTA meetings are logical places for like-minded citizens to discuss the high taxes they are paying for their schools (indeed, they are

Figure 4.8
Membership of Parent-Teacher Members and Non-Members in Other Organizations

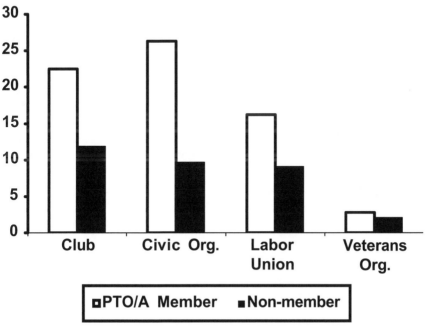

National Longitudinal Study of Adolescent Health, 1995 Public Use Sample.

usually meeting in venues paid for by their taxes) and organize for change if they think change is necessary. Anyone concerned with the well-being of local American communities should view with great misgiving policies that tend to loosen these traditionally close ties between communities and schools.

Too often in our research we have seen where desegregation measures have alienated citizens from schools they used to call their own. One of the saddest stories we heard was from a former high school football player in Baton Rouge comparing the crowds in a rival school's stadium before and after forced busing. About a game in which he played before the court order, he said, "When we broke through the banners in the end zone, the stands were filled and there was standing room only." Only one year after busing began, he returned to view a game between the same two teams and noted: "I was in shock . . . the fan base had gone from standing room only to almost total abandonment."[61] Schools are local institutions that have the potential to deeply involve citizens in their own communities and to lure them into the political processes that run those communities. As former Speaker of the House of Representatives Tip O'Neill wisely noted, "All politics is local."[62]

In Chapter 3, we argued that school desegregation efforts have been undercut by demographic changes beyond the control of social planners. We suggested that schools will be desperate, disorganized places to the extent that the schools draw their students from desperate, disorganized neighborhoods. Schools, though, can play an important part in neighborhood organization and cohesion. When parents and neighbors work together in their local schools, they do not simply contribute to education. They also form bonds with each other, creating useful social capital. Think, for example, of the many ways parents connect with each other through a school's sporting and music programs. "Soccer moms" are continually interfacing with each other, sharing important civic information at the most elemental grassroots level. These informal groups as well as formal associations provide a basis for a strong democratic society. Moreover, they are formed from the bottom up by active engagement in an institution at the heart of a community—not by top-down government planners in a distant city who may have never even visited the schools they are demographically manipulating on paper. (And, our experiences suggest, the social planners rarely put their children in the schools they are "desegregating.")

The researcher Laurence Steinberg was able to tease out of his data those neighborhood factors that create a positive social environment for children. He discovered that the healthiest neighborhoods were characterized by "high parental involvement in the local schools, a high level of parental participation in organized activities serving children (sports programs, arts programs, etc.), and a high level of parental monitoring and supervision of children."[63] Indeed, he found that even children from disadvantaged home environments who lived in these healthy communities benefited from contacts with children from more stable and nurturing home environments.

DESEGREGATION AND THE DESTRUCTION OF COMMUNITY SOCIAL CAPITAL

Disrupting or destroying such a key institution as the public school in one of these socially vibrant communities can diminish the fund of political social capital, leaving once vibrant communities looking like Baton Rouge. Nationally recognized desegregation expert Christine Rossell of Boston University, who studied literally dozens of desegregating districts, including Boston, declared of Baton Rouge, a system that white flight has devastated, "I do not believe I have ever been in a school system where the schools were in such poor condition as a result of taxpayer non-support."[64] The methods of desegregation all tend to disrupt the school as a place for voluntary engagement and involvement. Tearing down racially identifiable schools, consolidating schools, rezoning school districts, and busing children out of their communities all tend to weaken the ties between neighborhoods and schools. More than that, though, the takeover of a school system by a judge removes local control and alienates adults from schools.

So-called white academies or segregationist academies sprang out across the South in the 1960s and 1970s in response to court-ordered desegregation. Although racism undoubtedly played a part in the creation of some of these academies, the desire to maintain local control over schools also drove the establishment of these schools. In a national newspaper investigation of southern white academies in 1982, the reporter concluded, "There is strong feeling within the Southern communities that maintaining local control over these schools is essential. Many of the residents said they do not want tax exemptions if it means that the federal government will be allowed to tell them how to conduct school business."[65]

As federal control of schools through desegregation has increased, families that have remained in public school systems have frequently seen schools that they considered their own taken away from them. In our earlier research on desegregating school districts, we reported the case of Glade Elementary, in a semirural area of Louisiana. Glade had been originally developed as a neighborhood school, with the intention of maximizing parental involvement and student and family attachment by keeping children in Glade throughout their elementary school years. Parental dedication was such that in the two years before a new desegregation plan began moving students around to achieve racial balances, parents had raised over $10,000 to buy school equipment and resources. When a federal plan mandated shifting neighborhood students out of Glade and other students in, parents felt they had lost the investment of their time and commitment, as well as the investment of their funds. They felt they had lost their school and, with it, a part of their community.[66]

Black communities have generally been the hardest hit by attempting to move students around to achieve abstract, racial ratios. Lamenting the loss of a local school closed to achieve a court-ordered racial balance, a retired principal in a small town in Louisiana exclaimed, "The whole community revolves around Woodland school. Why are they so particular not to close the neighborhood schools in the white areas and they're so quick to close the schools in the black areas?"[67] In 2000, we conducted three surveys of middle- to upper-middle-class black community members in a desegregating district that closed two black neighborhood elementary schools and bused the displaced children to five predominantly white schools. Though respondents in our first survey were initially optimistic that the court order, which at that time had yet to be implemented, would at last bring a measure of social justice, after two months of busing 67 percent of the middle- to upper-middle-class African Americans whom we surveyed disagreed with the plan to close the black schools.[68]

The suspicions of this African American community were justified. After four years of busing black students out of their communities, only about 51 percent of these displaced pupils were still on grade level. By contrast, in a nearby black neighborhood school that the judge had not yet ordered closed (but soon would), about 92 percent of students were still on grade level after the same four-year period. In addition, their standardized test scores had been rising dramatically, since the school had become the focus of many educational resources.[69] In an ironic twist to the story, many in the African American community, led by the NAACP, were now actively protesting against the possibility that the judge would order this relatively successful black neighborhood school closed and the black students bused to distant schools in white communities.[70] Their protests fell on deaf ears. The neighborhood school was closed in fall 2004 and its students bused out of their community to distant majority white schools.

We are slow learners. Even at a relatively early stage in the period of judicially mandated desegregation, a study of black high schools in North Carolina found that the closing of black schools and the consolidation of schools to bring together pupils from different, segregated neighborhoods had been devastating for community cohesion. After a comparison of black high schools in the 1962–1963 school year with high schools in 1972–1973, Frederick A. Rogers concluded:

> The desegregation of public high schools in North Carolina destroyed "community" within the schools for the black student specifically, and ultimately this change is likely to contribute to the destruction or at the very least, a radically altered direction for the black community in general. Destruction of community within the black high schools is, in part, related to the loss of black influence and control over the shape, kind, and extent of educational experiences black youth are to have. In addition, the desegregation of public high schools in North Carolina proved to be *school consolidation* [italics in the original] and, as such, reduced the number of high schools (attendance units) in the state by almost one half and increased dramatically the student population in each attendance unit.[71]

Rogers found that although black high schools in North Carolina had been chronically short on funds and materials during Jim Crow, these schools did enjoy the participation of the adults around them. More than that, in North Carolina, as in Louisiana, local social activities revolved around the schools. With sharp sociological insight, Rogers noted that

> the black high school played a crucial role in defining, directing, and creating major social functions in the black community. Black communities would have been unable to carry on many activities critical to their development, and they would not have been exposed to ideas and issues that enabled their members to take advantage of existing opportunities or enabled them to pursue newly created opportunities. The black community needed the black high school to carry out its social functions. In that sense, the black community was almost entirely defined by the scope of the black high school.[72]

In this description of the impact of desegregation, one can see that social capital moves in two directions. As parents and other adults become more involved in a school, the school as a whole benefits. This involvement also benefits the society that surrounds the school, though. Groups such as the PTA help provide the organizational basis for community life and connect with

other associations to tie the members of a locality together in webs of belonging and activity.

Rogers wrote near the beginning of the era of judicial desegregation. Three
decades later, the destructive effects of removing educational institutions
from their immediate social settings were also clear to Vivian Gunn Morris
and Curtis L. Morris in their detailed examination of desegregation's impact
on the small town of Tuscumbia, Alabama.[73] The Morrises' book does not ro-
manticize the segregated schools of the Jim Crow era. Trenholm, the black
high school in their study, was consistently shortchanged in instructional resources, physical plant, and technology. But it occupied the central place in
local black society. It was a focal point of adult involvement. Although desegregation meant that students moved to a better physical structure with
more materials, it also meant that this central place for forming commitments
and voluntary associations was destroyed. Morris and Morris recount that
students and adults were in shock when the school was torn down. The col-
ors and other symbols of the school "were important socially and emotionally to the students and to the African American community. It was around
these symbols that the school community rallied."[74] Asa G. Hilliard III, in a
foreword to the Morrises' study, summarizes the authors' findings on the impact of desegregation: "The demands of the African community were hi-
jacked in the court system and among supporters who saw the solutions to
our problems as the breakdown of communities by sending children to be integrated into predominantly White schools."[75]

In Topeka, Kansas, the school district where the desegregation era was
born, the former black superintendent blamed the continuing poor academic
performance of black students on . . . desegregation! On the fiftieth anniversary of the *Brown* decision, he told *Time* magazine that "the closing of black
neighborhood schools—with their traditions, yearbooks, mottoes, fight songs
and halls of fame—ripped the centerpiece out of those communities."[76]

Moreover, in the early days of desegregation, blacks were often bused out
of their schools simply because these schools were black—and not because
the facilities were substandard. Almost thirty years after an all-black high
school in Lafayette, Louisiana, was closed, the man who was its black principal at the time reflected wryly, "There was nothing deficient about the
school, except there were blacks there."[77] This school, too, had been a central
part of the black community before its closing. A black state representative
who graduated from this same high school in the early 1960s lamented, "I
think one of the things we lost was the closeness—the Friday night football
games, the family ties . . . there is a resentment, usually that it is the black
schools that were closed."[78]

UNDERSTANDING THE IMPORTANCE OF COMMUNITY

In arguing that schools are central institutions for communities, especially minority communities, we are not arguing for a policy of resegregation or for racial separatism. Race-based schools can have definite disadvantages. In our research, we have found that mixed-race schools are generally associated with relatively higher test scores for minority students.[79] At the same time, we have found that mixed-race schools can often be difficult to maintain if race is at all connected to social or economic advantage because the sharing of advantages must also imply the sharing of disadvantages—and parents know this. However, school racial composition is only one of many determinants of student performance, and individual student performance is only one of the matters that should concern us in thinking about the role schools play in strengthening communities. The school is a foundation for an active, engaged citizenry. When tinkering with community schools in the name of racial engineering disrupts community social networks, we should all be alarmed.

Communities are often based on race or ethnicity. Race became a defining quality for black communities because black Americans were so long excluded from many of the other sources of collective identity, from unions and clubs that were not based on race and from neighborhoods based on freely chosen location. Recall that a community is a set of individuals connected to each other within definite associations and institutions and, as such, is a basic source of vitality for a society. We have already established that schools occupy a key place within a community. Therefore, communities based on race, and racially identifiable schools within these communities, can contribute to a strong civil society. The several Chinatowns, the Cajun heartland, Little Italy, South Boston, Harlem, and East Los Angeles are all thriving communities with a strong unifying ethnic element.

While generally positive, we also recognize that race and ethnicity can pose dangers as bases for communities and schools. Exclusively black or Hispanic schools and neighborhoods are, all too often, cut off from the social connections, knowledge, experience, and financial resources of the majority population. Balkanization and discrimination are always threats when race or ethnicity becomes the main determinant of identity and interaction for people.

Multiracial neighborhoods and schools are desirable because they can provide social ties across racial lines. We hope that with enforcement of laws against discrimination in housing and with economic opportunities for all citizens, more multiracial neighborhoods will grow on the American landscape. But the government cannot create these neighborhoods by moving black and white Americans around metropolitan areas in order to follow a blueprint for population design. This would not only be contrary to American ideals of personal freedom but would also do enormous damage to the civil society of localities across the nation. De Tocqueville and Putnam were right: A democratic society rests on voluntary associations, not on compulsion. Racially identifiable communities, like racially identifiable schools, may have problems, but the answer to these problems is not the destruction of existing communities. Rather, the solution lies in strengthening communities—a central role of the neighborhood school.

Trying to design school populations by racial blueprints is not as radical as trying to tell people where to live in order to create mixed-race neighborhoods. Still, either project ignores the ways in which people form strong social networks. Individuals form voluntary, cooperative bonds with others. The most basic of these bonds is the family. Beyond the family, individuals form associations to further their own ends. Becoming part of associations with others leads people to develop collective ends and shared goals. Voluntary associations, both formal and informal, take place within localities such as neighborhoods, and within institutions, such as schools, places of employment, and local government. Social capital moves in two directions: in the direction described by Coleman and in the direction described by Putnam. Involvement in associations like the PTO and PTA, and in the connection with fellow citizens these organizations foster, strengthens both the institutions (e.g., the school) and the communities in which they exist (the neighborhood). Plus, simply being involved in these organizations and institutions encourages yet more involvement.

In Chapter 3, we pointed out that the new poverty in American society poses a serious problem for school desegregation. As we described it, the new poverty is not just a lack of money; it is also a problem of social organization. Concentrated disadvantage, joblessness, fatherless homes, and violence are among its chief characteristics. The new poverty, moreover, affects minority group members much more than it does whites and Asians. This makes it difficult to bring about a true desegregation of schools because members of the middle class, which is still predominantly white in most parts of the country, will seek to avoid having their own children in chaotic schools dominated by children from poor, jobless, fatherless families. As we have sought to demonstrate, schools with large minority populations often have relatively low parental involvement and relatively high levels of campus disorder. At the same time, though, by disconnecting black families and neighborhoods from community schools, the program of coercive desegregation has exacerbated the problem of social organization. One cannot promote parental involvement in schools by closing local institutions and moving the students away. One cannot use schools to promote the building of desperately needed cooperative associations by detaching minority neighborhoods from their schools.

In our view, social capital flows from communities to schools, and then from schools to surrounding communities. By weakening the links between families, schools, and communities, centrally planned desegregation has also weakened vital sources of civic engagement in minority neighborhoods, perhaps even more than in white neighborhoods. It should be clear to readers that we attach a great deal of importance to local control, which we see as essential to the bottom-up creation and maintenance of healthy civic institutions. In the next chapter, we consider this issue of control in the larger context of what gives value to education in the first place. We argue that what makes schooling valuable is in part determined by who shares it with us.

CHAPTER 5

The Political Economy of Education and Equality of Educational Opportunity

WHY SEEK EQUALITY OF OPPORTUNITY IN EDUCATION?

If one were to ask people why we have public education and why students should enjoy equal access to public education, one would receive a number of answers.[1] Some respondents would point out that we need trained workers for our economy, and that the amount of training required of workers is continually rising. Therefore, we need to educate all potential workers, including those from families unable to bear the costs of schooling for their own children. Other people would say that public instruction has "spillover" benefits (or "externalities," in economic jargon) beyond the purely economic. The "schools, not jails" slogan is based on the view that schooling can lessen juvenile delinquency and divert people from criminal careers, precisely because it places them in socially useful jobs. Further, communities with good schools can attract business investment and people who can afford to be homeowners, so that even residents who have no children will indirectly benefit from the availability of high-quality, public education.[2] Still others would answer that a democratic society cannot be successful without an educated citizenry because it takes knowledgeable citizens to choose wise government leaders and participate in the processes of government.[3] Thomas Jefferson was an ardent proponent of the necessity of a broadly educated citizenry for the survival of the young American republic.

None of these responses, not even Jefferson's, really addresses the question of equality, though. If we are training future employees, then we need job-focused variety in the training, not equality. An economy needs people with different skills who would receive differing levels of financial rewards even if the distribution of wealth and income were more equal than it is today. Some critics of the American educational system have attacked it for perpetuating the inequality of a capitalist society.[4] However, these critics ignore an indisputable, if not uncomfortable, fact: if we have public education in order to put people into existing jobs, then sorting people into unequal economic positions is exactly what public schools are supposed to do.

The response that education benefits the surrounding community also provides no support for providing the same level of education to all students or to all communities. During the term of President Richard M. Nixon, the president's education commissioner, Sidney Marland, Jr., appeared before the U.S. Congress to argue that what he saw as social disorder and alienation among American youth resulted from an educational system that was not closely linked to vocational and career training.[5] For Marland, the externality of social order would be a consequence of schools doing an efficient job of placing young people into appropriate jobs.

The view that education contributes to communities by attracting businesses and desirable residents not only provides no support for equality in education but also implies that educational systems are part of the competition among communities and are therefore necessarily unequal. As the economist Charles Tiebout recognized, localities vie with each other for businesses and people.[6] Although general prosperity can increase, at any given time a firm can choose to move either to one place or another; it cannot set up shop everywhere. Similarly, people who are valued local citizens can own a finite number of homes, and for every place someone buys a home, there is another where that person will not buy a home. Many of the externalities of schooling, then, are matters of some districts having better schools than others.

To be an informed citizen, one must be able to read well, to think critically, and to discuss public issues. It may also be the case that citizens of a democracy need to have some common set of values, and that public education can be an effective way of instilling these values.[7] This would only be a claim that all citizens should share some basic educational foundation, though. A good education for all citizens is highly desirable, if it can be achieved, but there is no reason that all citizens need to be educated to the same level or in the same way.

An answer that most of us would give, and which would be much more relevant to the issue of equality in education, would be that education is an essential source of economic opportunity. It is, in other words, a resource that enables young people to compete for unequal positions in a market economy.

This means that an education is, first, an economic good that people can use to obtain other economic goods. Second, education is a right of individuals, rather than a service to society as a whole.

The idea that education is an individual right to a basic social good has led to a long series of attempts at equalization in funding of schools over the course of the past half-century. If each American has a right to an education that will put all at the same starting point in a competitive economy, then it seems unjust and unreasonable that spending on some students is only a fraction of spending on others. Even if, as we have argued in this book, school achievement is influenced more by the characteristics students bring from their neighborhoods and families to schools than it is by the books, buildings, and equipment of schools, this should not be an excuse for financially short-changing the schools of the disadvantaged. Money is never irrelevant. But money is not everything, either, especially with regards to producing positive academic outcomes.

The heritage of locally supported schools means that schools rely heavily on local tax revenues for their funding, primarily in the form of property taxes. School districts located in relatively well-to-do communities can raise more tax dollars for schools than poorer communities can. Thus, locally controlled and supported schools in the United States have been highly unequal in the amount of money they spend on students.

Seeing education in terms of the civil rights of individuals has led proponents of equalization of spending to pursue their goals through the court system, maintaining that students in districts that have relatively small revenues suffer a violation of legal rights. For example, plaintiffs in the *San Antonio v. Rodriguez* case in 1973 attempted to have the Texas system of financing schools declared unconstitutional. Attorneys arguing against the Texas system of education financing claimed that different levels of funding for different school districts violated the Fourteenth Amendment's guarantee of equal protection under the law. However, the U.S. Supreme Court threw out the lower court's decision that the Texas system was unconstitutional, on the grounds that the U.S. Constitution offers no guarantees of education.

At the state level attempts to equalize spending have been somewhat more successful, and several state courts limited inequality in spending among their districts. Among the most notable was the *Serrano v. Priest* decision in California in 1971. In this case, the California Supreme Court ruled that spending among California school districts could not differ by more than $100 per student. Critics of court-ordered equalization have argued that such decisions led to a lowering of support for public schools, particularly among wealthier families, who removed their children from public school systems altogether.

In eloquent, persuasive, and moving terms, the author and educational critic Jonathan Kozol has linked the isolation of African American students in *de facto* segregated schools to the unequal distribution of funds across district lines. Describing the gap between predominantly white suburbs and predominantly black central cities in locations across the country, he points out that average per pupil spending in New York City in 1987 came to about $5,500, whereas some New York suburban areas spent over $11,000 per student. Kozol noted that in 1988 Detroit spent $3,600 yearly on each student, whereas nearby suburbs spent well over $6,000 on each of their pupils. In pages that everyone concerned about contemporary education should read, Kozol gives us vignettes of the desperately poor neighborhoods surrounding inner-city schools, the lamentable conditions in those schools, and the struggles and aspirations of disadvantaged students and their families. Kozol expresses frustration that

> the rigging of the game and the acceptance, which is nearly universal, of uneven playing fields reflect a dark unspoken sense that other people's children are of less inherent value than our own. Now and then, in private, affluent suburbanites concede that certain aspects of the game may be a trifle rigged to their advantage. "Sure, it's a bit unjust," they may concede, "but that's reality and that's the way the game is played."[8]

We share this frustration, and we agree that there is a deep contradiction between the belief that all Americans should be competing on an equal footing in a market economy that rewards the hardest-working and most talented individuals, and the reality that people in our nation really do begin this competition with dramatically unequal preparation. It is even more frustrating and disturbing, given our centuries of slavery and legal discrimination, that the unequal starting points should be so closely associated with race.

Clearly, attempts to create equal opportunities through redistributing school funding are motivated by many of the same goals as attempts to equalize opportunities by distributing students among schools. Both are motivated by the belief that the benefits of public education, whether produced by the allocation of tax revenues or by the socioeconomic settings of schools, should be available, as a fundamental right, to all those preparing for life in our society. Despite our discomfort with inequality of opportunity, though, we think that there may be a problem with seeing education as a "game" consisting of individual players who are all supposed to begin with the same chips, but that has been unfairly rigged in favor of some. In order to describe to readers why we believe this is a misleading picture of the way the political economy of education actually works, we want to begin with an examination of how the chips acquire their value, and then look at the nature of the game itself.

By looking closely at just what kind of economic good a public education really is, we can begin to understand what schools are selling and what makes this "educational good" so desirable. Thinking about education in this light can help us see how redistributing students by race or by social class affects the value of what schools have to offer. In turn, we can see whether school desegregation, which is motivated by the same goals as equalization of funding, does actually make a desirable education more widely available.

WHAT MAKES AN EDUCATION VALUABLE?

In classical economic theory, goods are frequently assumed to have a relatively fixed utility for consumers. However, the market value of those goods can vary because supply and demand can affect "marginal utility"—the amount of satisfaction derived from each additional quantity of the good. As demand goes up, even though the utility remains the same, the marginal utility increases because there are more potential consumers desiring the good. However, some economists recognize that utility may not be fixed and that utility, and not just marginal utility, may be created by consumption. The more people who want Tickle Me Elmo or color Game Boy, the more people there are who want these things precisely because other people want them.

The utility of a good can also be established not simply by how many people want it, but by which people want it. This is the exclusivity factor, an economic fact pointed out by Thorstein Veblen, who coined the term "conspicuous consumption."[9] Exclusivity can create utility in two ways: First, the "snob appeal" of a good can contribute to its utility. Second, some types of goods are substantially shaped by their consumption. An example of this would be the neighborhood as a commodity. Arguably, one of the reasons that wealthy neighborhoods are nice places to live is that people who live in them (the consumers) have the money to make them nice places to live. The other customers are a big part of what is being sold.

We propose that schools may be seen as commodities that depend heavily on who consumes them (the students) for their utility—their quality of intrinsic desirability. The implication is that it is difficult to redistribute or equalize educational experiences because some degree of exclusivity is part of the value of those experiences. Thus, we have the essential paradox of "educational opportunity for all."

Higher achievement scores and higher socioeconomic status of student bodies raise the "marginal utility" of an educational institution—lower scores and lower-status students lower the "marginal utility." Thus, schools populated by low-achieving, low-SES students have lower "value" for consumers who are "shopping" for educational value. And consumers of education do indeed shop. There is more than a grain of truth in the following description by humorist and Pulitzer Prize winner Dave Barry about education-obsessed New Yorkers' search for the best possible schools for their children:

> Serious parents start obsessing about Harvard before their child is, technically, born. They spend their evenings shouting the algebraic equations in the general direction of the womb so the child will have an edge during the intensely competitive process of applying for New York City's exclusive private preschools—yes, PREschools—where tuition can run—and I am not making this figure up—well over $15,000 a year.[10]

MORE THAN MONEY

What makes a preschool worth $15,000 a year? It is probably not the building that houses the program, regardless of how ritzy it is. Rather, we believe, this price includes the privilege of attending school with the sons and daughters of New York City's most socioeconomically advantaged students. This view, that the students create the value of their education for each other, is a logical extension of ideas that are widely accepted among educational economists. Eric Hanushek, in one of the most widely cited studies of the influences on student performances, concluded in 1986 that "there appears to be no strong or systematic relationship between school expenditures and student performance."[11] We can take student performance as an indicator of what students have learned and the skills that they have acquired—in other words, an indicator of the "utility" of education. Although Hanushek's findings became "the prevailing view among economists who study school resources and academic achievement,"[12] they have been questioned by school administrators and others who have maintained that spending on education can be an important part of improving education.

The issue of how much money matters and how it can be spent most effectively is an important one. Certainly no one, including Eric Hanushek, has claimed that educational spending is completely irrelevant and that we should spend nothing at all on schooling. Yet even those who maintain that current forms of spending have a significant effect on educational perfor-

mance rarely argue that spending is the only influence on academic achievement. The questions of how much money should be invested in schools and
how the money should be spent are important ones from the perspective of
a public official. But if we look at the matter from the point of view of a consumer of education—a family making decisions about its own children—the
issue is not whether money makes any difference at all, but what makes the
most difference in determining whether a school is "good."

As a rule, much more federal money is targeted to predominately minority than predominantly white schools. Yet, these billions of dollars have in
general not made these schools significantly more attractive to middle-class
students. The case of the two newest and most technologically advanced
schools in Lafayette, Louisiana, is typical. One is a 90 percent African American school, populated almost entirely with at-risk, high-poverty students and
located in a new, modern facility incorporating all the most modern educational and technological innovations available. The school has also been well
known for its disorder, unsatisfied faculty, and abysmally low student performance. Rather than breaking down the doors to get their children in, parents are looking elsewhere; the school has a problem filling its classrooms to
capacity. In the same district in an even newer, more technologically advanced majority black school ordered built by a judge in the name of desegregation (though the school could not attract a 50% white student body), so
many resources flooded into the school that teachers and administrators did
not know what to do with them all.[13] These resources included a room full of
brand new pianos, a dance studio, and a cutting edge computer lab.

In a few desegregation cases, the amount spent has been nothing short of
phenomenal—though it still was not enough to attract middle-class students.
For example, as a consequence of the 1996 court-approved consent degree in
East Baton Rouge Parish, Louisiana, $27 million was subsequently spent on
desegregation efforts, including the establishment of "equity" accounts for
historically black schools. So much money was flowing into these schools that
the superintendent at the time declared, "The principals are telling me they're
finding it difficult to decide what else they need beyond what they've already
bought."[14] Even the spending did not slow down the white exodus from the
school system.

As much money as the Baton Rouge equity spending seemed to be, it pales
in comparison to the funds ordered spent in the desegregating Kansas City,
Missouri, School District (KCMSD) to help close the black-white achievement
gap and attract white students. In *Jenkins v. Missouri*,[15] the district court
judge's directive to the KCMSD to spend $2 billion over a twelve-year period
was upheld by the U.S. Supreme Court.[16] Since the local district was virtu-

ally bankrupt as a result of white flight and the failure of voters to pass school tax increases, the federal judge held the state partially liable for both the segregated school system and the cost to fix it. He also ordered the local property taxes doubled and an income tax surcharge on all those working in Kansas City but living elsewhere. The high court ruled that such draconian measures were constitutional and necessary to overcome state-sponsored segregation. According to a very thorough Kato Institute policy analysis of the KSMSD desegregation spending program,

> Kansas City spent as much as $11,700 per pupil—more money per pupil, on a cost of living adjusted basis, than any other of the 280 largest districts in the country. The money bought higher teachers' salaries, 15 new schools, and such amenities as an Olympic-sized swimming pool with an underwater viewing room, television and animation studios, a robotics lab, a 25-acre wildlife sanctuary, a zoo, a model United Nations with simultaneous translation capability, and field trips to Mexico and Senegal. The student-teacher ratio was 12 or 13 to 1, the lowest of any major school district in the country.[17]

In the ensuing twelve years, white flight continued, black achievement was little better, and the black-white achievement gap had not been reduced. Even the original federal court judge on the case had to admit that the massive spending had made little difference in school achievement, and that the district had done everything in its power to undo vestiges of past *de jure* segregation.[18] In *Missouri v. Jenkins II* the U.S. Supreme Court ultimately restricted the federal court's far-reaching powers in the case, questioning the efficacy of spending almost $200 million per year on desegregation remedies in a district with less than 45,000 students. The high court, in a pragmatically inspired decision, ruled it was unconstitutional to use state funds to raise KSMSD teacher salaries to higher levels than those in the surrounding districts.[19]

Jenkins II also ruled that the district did not have to raise minority achievement scores to the national average to meet the "quality of education" desegregation target; it had only to undo that part of the black-white achievement gap caused by previous *de jure* segregation. The Supreme Court reiterated the criteria it established in its 1971 *Swann* decision that any desegregation remedy "must be designed as nearly as possible to restore the victims of discriminatory conduct to the position they would have occupied in the absence of such conduct." It is certainly beyond the realm of science how one could ever calculate the number of points on a nationally normed test pre-*Brown* discrimination cost blacks in KSMSD. Doing so is apparently not beyond the legal realm, though. The system was declared unitary in 2003 after the new judge on the case ruled that the black-white achievement gap had been sufficiently reduced to finally undo all vestiges of past *de jure* segregation.[20] The exorbitant spending in the KCMSD was aimed not just at raising black achievement levels but also at stemming white flight by making the schools more attractive. The Kato Institute estimated that it cost Kansas City about $500,000 in spending for each white student it attracted. What we see in Kansas City is an experiment in just how much of a difference almost unlimited governmental funding can make on both raising student achievement levels of low-SES students and selling an educational system to the more socioeconomically advantaged. The answer seems to be that the astronomical spending boosted achievement a little bit but utterly failed to attract middle-class students.

Contrast the above scenarios with the case of Ben Franklin High School in New Orleans. The school for gifted students was housed for years in an old, dilapidated building with no air conditioning (it has since moved to a much better building). Yet, while housed in its decaying urban digs, Ben Franklin traditionally produced either the highest- or very nearly the highest-performing students in the entire state of Louisiana, with parents clamoring to get their children admitted. Clearly, exorbitant spending did not help in making the Kansas City, Missouri, school district more attractive to the middle class, and a substandard building did not deter parents from fighting to get their children into Ben Franklin. What about Ben Franklin High, then, made it so attractive?

IT IS THE CLIENTELE

The view that stretches back at least to James S. Coleman's pioneering work on academic achievement in the 1960s, which we have cited earlier in this book, is that the socioeconomic makeup of the school is what makes the most difference. Our own research has supported this view.[21] We think that commonsense, as well as research, supports such an argument. Education is a social process, not just information that books and teachers pour into the heads of students. Students learn from those they interact with all day long, and the people they are around most are other students. If the other students come from homes with well-educated parents who place a premium on books that they read to their children, then these students bring these educational assets with them to school. The more students in a school who bring such assets, the better the school can educate all students.

Parents make choices about the education of their children. They choose some public schools over others by moving into neighborhoods they believe have good schools. They choose magnet programs or schools with special offerings by seeking out these opportunities within public schools. If they believe it is in the best interest of their children and they can afford to do so, they choose private schools, as do the wealthy New York parents who will spend $15,000 a year on their preschoolers.

When parents make choices about education, they are taking part in an educational economy. As one writer on educational economy has observed, "Economic agents are utility maximisers. Every time we make a choice, we select the alternative that yields the greatest utility, subject to the resources available. . . . Education exists because it provides utility. If it did not, there would be no demand for it."[22]

Regardless of how great or little a part funding for schools plays in the quality of education, if schoolmates with educational advantages are the most important influence on educational quality, then when parents try to put their children into the best schools they can afford, whether they realize it or not, they are placing their children with the most-advantaged schoolmates they can afford. As we have pointed out previously, the American history of racial and ethnic inequality has left us with a substantial achievement gap between whites and minority students. This means that the racial composition of a school is, unfortunately, still a big part of what determines the utility of the school.

Now, the reader will note that in the passage of the educational economist we just cited there are two influences on choice: "the greatest utility" and "resources available." Without governmental attempts at redistribution, those who have the greatest resources can obtain the best educations. Since the financial resources of families are closely related to the individual educational advantages of children (children from fairly well-to-do families are the most likely to have college-educated parents and high educational aspirations), this means that those who can afford good educations will send their children to school with children from other families that can afford good educations. Of course, although financial resources and educational advantages are related, they are not the same thing. Most college towns have good schools where faculty, comfortable but rarely wealthy, concentrate their own children. In this case, though, the "resources" consist of being in a location with many educationally advantaged people.

Why do schools with educationally advantaged students also tend to be better funded than schools with the less advantaged? People put their money where they put their children. In a sense, other people's children *are* of less inherent value than our own, at least to us. If we valued all children as much as we value our own, we would treat our own exactly as we treat every other child ("Sorry, Mary, no college fund for you. We're distributing all our savings equally among all children in our county.") Whether this is the way people should behave is debatable. We argue that those who give no preference to their own wards or offspring are, to put it bluntly, bad parents. Even if we are wrong about this, though, most people do put their efforts, their emotions, and their money into the well-being of their own families.

But we suspect we are not wrong. Many years ago the economist Adam Smith recognized the utility of individual self-interest for the larger good of society.[23] Whereas twisted self-interest run amuck can lead to selfish actions that hurt others, it would seem that Smith's "invisible hand" principle is particularly germane to parental self-interest in rearing well-educated children. It is difficult to disagree that, all things being equal, contributing well-educated children to society is more beneficial to us all than contributing poorly educated offspring.

One might argue that this tendency for families to invest in their children, more than in the children of others, is a good reason to try to redistribute students. By putting children of privilege in schools with children of those who have suffered historical deprivation and discrimination, we not only spread the assets of educational preparation more widely but also encourage those who can invest in education to put their resources into schools that serve students from all backgrounds. It might work this way if school systems were monopolies. The reality is that school systems are complex competitive marketplaces that can exercise the least control over the choices of those with the greatest available resources.

THE EDUCATIONAL MARKETPLACE

The greatest problem for any controlled economy is the existence of alternative markets. If there are two neighboring cities and one limits the profits of property owners through controlled rents, whereas the other allows property owners to maximize their profits by charging whatever the market will bear, then those who can readily transfer their funds will tend to shift investment out of the controlled market and into the uncontrolled one. This may be offset by special cultural characteristics of the one with controlled rents or by the difficulty in moving money from one place to another. So, although there is a tendency to move investment out of the controlled economy, the strength of the tendency does vary.

The city with the controlled rents would have the advantage of relatively cheap rents. These may not be attractive to investors, but they would certainly be attractive to renters, especially renters with limited incomes. With little investment and plenty of low-income inhabitants, housing would be tight and unappealing to upper-income residents, who would be better able to afford the higher-rent costs in the uncontrolled city. One of our two cities would eventually consist of deteriorating neighborhoods inhabited by the poor; the other would become a bastion of affluence and upper-end employment.

Of course, reality is more complex than this. If the city with controls did have some especially desirable qualities, the controls might simply encourage people to transform rental housing into owner-occupied housing, driving out those who could not afford to buy their own homes. Or, the city might develop into pockets of comfortable owner-occupied neighborhoods and clusters of low-rent neighborhoods. In looking at possible consequences of attempts to control an economy, we always have to understand how people with differing abilities to choose will respond to those attempts in varied settings.

Turning from the example of cities to schools, we can ask what kinds of educational alternatives are available to families. To begin with, the United States has both public and private systems of education. Neither of these is free. Public education is funded through local property and sales taxes, state money, and federal money. The greatest share for most districts comes from the local taxes that voters impose on themselves. One relevant question is why some localities will tax themselves at higher rates than others, and we will discuss this (and what it means) shortly. But if public education is not free, its costs are at least relatively widespread and all property owners pay these costs, whether or not they have children in public schools. So why would parents choose to pay tuition for a private school? Quite simply, they must be getting something they believe they will not get in a public school, and this something must be worth the additional cost to them—indeed, huge costs of as much as $15,000 a year per child for preschool alone.

There is a substantial literature that indicates that private schools do a better job of educating students than public schools do.[24] Although this finding is not accepted by all researchers, "research has consistently found that, even after controlling for selection effects, private-school students are more likely to graduate high school, attend college, attend a selective college, and graduate from college."[25] In addition, many parents may choose parochial or other religious schools because these teach or reinforce the beliefs and values they want their children to receive.

So, the question now becomes this: Why don't all parents send their children to private schools? If these are apparently better than public schools, and if all parents want to give the best possible education to their children, then why don't families abandon public schools altogether? Going back to the example of the two cities, one of the reasons people might choose to live in the controlled city, apart from the cheap rents, could be some special cultural characteristic of that city. Similarly, many parents will avoid religiously affiliated private schools precisely because they do not share the schools' beliefs and do not want those taught to their children.

Another reason families choose public schools is that sometimes these might really be the best choices. Private schools may, on average, show better results than public schools, but this does not mean that all private schools are better than all public schools. In many places, the local public school may be the best educational institution around, like the aforementioned Ben Franklin gifted high school in New Orleans or the much sought after Bronx High School of Science in New York. Even when a private school does appear to be a somewhat better choice than the public, the family needs to consider whether it is worth the extra expenditure, given the other demands on income and long-range plans for children. The more affluent the family is, the less of a sacrifice it will have to make for even small added benefits from private schooling. Additionally, parents who are highly educated are likely to place a great deal of value on any extra educational advantages and will be more willing to make sacrifices to obtain those advantages.

It is not at all surprising, then, that studies have consistently found that the affluent and well-educated parents are the most likely to send their children to private schools.[26] The children from upper-middle-class or affluent families who had incomes at least three times greater than the poverty level made up almost two-thirds of the children in private schools in 2000, although just 42 percent of schoolchildren lived in these families. By contrast, children from families below the poverty line made up only 8 percent of all the students in private schools, including parochial schools intended to serve low-income neighborhoods.[27] Not only were the well-to-do more likely to spend their money on private education, but also private schools where they spent their money were good places to find other children from equally advantageous economic backgrounds.

In addition, given the connection between socioeconomic status and race in our country, it is also not surprising that most private school students are white. Our estimates from the 2000 census indicate that 77 percent of the nation's private school students were white at the opening of the new century, despite the fact that this group made up just 64 percent of all the American children enrolled in kindergarten through twelfth grade, and only 62 percent of public school students. Hispanic students, who made up 15 percent of all pupils, were 8 percent of nonpublic school students. Non-Hispanic blacks, who made up 14 percent of American students, constituted just under 8 percent of those in private schools.[28] Keeping in mind, again, that these percentages include parochial schools established in minority neighborhoods, we see that nonpublic schools in our country are overwhelmingly white and upper middle class.

Could these figures be just a reflection of the fact that people who have more money can afford to send their children to more expensive schools, and whites tend to have more money? Even wealthy people have to decide that it is better to spend their money in one way than in another, and their decisions may change as settings and opportunities change. Figure 5.1 shows that the proportion of white and relatively affluent students (which we define as those coming from homes with incomes at least three times higher than the poverty level, or roughly $65,000 in 2000) in public and private schools has

Figure 5.1
Proportion of White and Middle-to-Upper Income Students Enrolled in Private Schools, 1970 and 2000

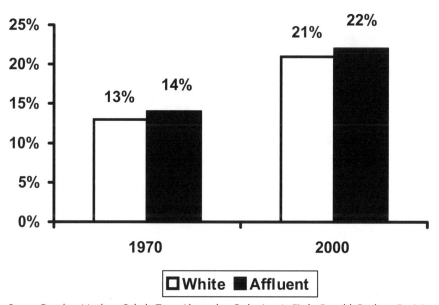

Steven Ruggles, Matthew Sobek, Trent Alexander, Catherine A. Fitch, Ronald Goeken, Patricia Kelly Hall, Miriam King, and Chad Ronnander. *Integrated Public Use Microdata Series: Version 3.0* (Machine-readable database). Minneapolis: Minnesota Population Center (producer and distributor), 2004.

changed over time. During the period 1970 to 2000, from around the beginning of the nation's massive campaigns to redistribute students by race to the end of the twentieth century, the proportion of white students choosing private schools, rather than public schools, increased from 13 percent to 21 percent. During these same years, the percentage of middle-class to upper-class students in private schools went up from 14 percent to 22 percent. By contrast, minorities and the poor continued to be heavily concentrated in public institutions. In 1970, 96 percent of black non-Hispanic students, 92 percent of Hispanic students, and 95 percent of students below the poverty level were in public schools. Thirty years later, over 92 percent of black non-Hispanic pupils, 93 percent of Hispanics, and 94 percent of low-income pupils were attending schools in the public sector.

The loss of more than one out of every five white and affluent pupils from the public school system has serious implications for equality of opportunity, as we will discuss. It also means, though, that the competitive advantage of private schools had, for some reason, increased relative to public schools. It would be perfectly reasonable to maintain that the growing appeal of non-public education had nothing to do with busing, or closing racially identifiable schools, or changing public school demographics. One could plausibly argue that the shift was a consequence of growing dissatisfaction with state-run institutions or of an increase in the appeal of religious schools. To find evidence on this issue, we will have to turn to an examination of the histories of specific school districts, which we will do in the following chapter. For now, though, it should suffice to observe that this movement to private schools was not the same in all places in the United States.

Figure 5.2 shows that in 1970 and in 2000, the racial makeup of places seems to have made a great deal of difference in whether or not white and well-to-do students chose private schools. In 1970, 13 percent of white students and 15 percent of relatively affluent students were in private schools in metropolitan areas in which fewer than 30 percent of public school students were black or Hispanic. But 18 percent of the white and 22 percent of the affluent pupils were in private schools in the metropolitan areas in which more than 30 percent of the public school pupils were of these two minority groups. After three decades, the distribution of white and affluent students looked similar, but the greatest increase was among white students in metropolitan areas with large minority public school populations.

In order to understand why there might have been an overall growth in the private school population over the last part of the twentieth century, we need to consider the demographic changes pointed out earlier in this book. The nation's minority population grew dramatically, especially in the school-

Figure 5.2
Proportion of White and Middle-to-Upper Income Students in Private Schools, by Percentage of Minority Students in Metropolitan Areas, 1970 and 2000

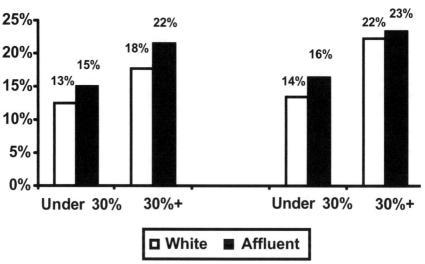

Steven Ruggles, Matthew Sobek, Trent Alexander, Catherine A. Fitch, Ronald Goeken, Patricia Kelly Hall, Miriam King, and Chad Ronnander. *Integrated Public Use Microdata Series: Version 3.0* (Machine-readable database). Minneapolis: Minnesota Population Center (producer and distributor), 2004.

aged population. As a result, more American young people were in places that contained many students from historically disadvantaged minority groups. As shown in Figure 5.3, in 1970 only about 3 percent of either white or relatively affluent students lived in metropolitan areas in which black or Hispanic students made up more than 30 percent of public schools. By 2000, though, 29 percent of white students and 43 percent of middle- to upper-class students lived in metropolitan areas with large minority populations.

Apparently, the increase in private school enrollment was connected to the increase in minority enrollment in public schools, with the greatest growth in white students in private schools in metropolitan areas with large minority public school populations. Again, to fully understand this, we will need to look at what actually happened in particular school districts, but thinking about schools as marketplaces can give us a way of thinking about why this happened. In the example of the two cities that we gave earlier, we can consider what would happen as the low-income population of one expands in response to affordable rents. The residents with higher incomes could respond by buying property in special gated communities that, in essence,

Figure 5.3
Percentage of White and Middle-to-Upper Income Students in Metropolitan Areas
with More than 30 Percent Black and Hispanic Public School Enrollment

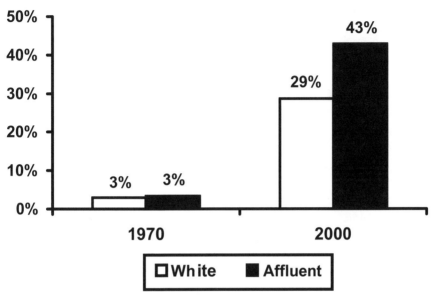

Steven Ruggles, Matthew Sobek, Trent Alexander, Catherine A. Fitch, Ronald Goeken, Patricia Kelly Hall, Miriam King, and Chad Ronnander. *Integrated Public Use Microdata Series: Version 3.0* (Machine-readable database). Minneapolis: Minnesota Population Center (producer and distributor), 2004.

charge a membership fee for moving in. Some might choose such communities in any case, but more would be willing to pay these higher costs as the neighborhoods around them become more undesirable. But why would the cheaper neighborhoods become undesirable? Because, to a large extent, neighborhoods are goods whose value is established by their exclusivity. To put it simply, most people do not want to live in low-income neighborhoods. Aside from the social problems generally associated with poverty, poor people do not have the money for the upkeep of homes and neighborhoods.

Turning back to schools as commodities, like homes, we can see why having large numbers of minority students as consumers of public schooling might put public schools at a competitive disadvantage. There is a large racial and ethnic achievement gap, which we examine in much more detail in Chapter 7. The desirability of a school is, in large part, a product of its general level of achievement. Therefore, as minority enrollments go up, average achievement levels go down. We are not suggesting that every single school with high minority enrollments will have low achievement levels. We are also not minimizing the accomplishments of minority students who overcome the odds and surpass all others, including those who have much greater opportunities. We are observing that an achievement gap associated with race or ethnicity necessarily means that heavy minority enrollments do lead to lower overall performance of schools. It is axiomatic: When the overall performance of public schools goes down, the incentive to pay extra costs for private schools goes up.

Private schools are not the only competitors of public school systems, however. Each public school district also competes with other districts. We Americans often think of our system of public education as simply serving those who happen to live in a place. But we are a highly mobile people, constantly moving and constantly searching for new and better homes. Even when an American family moves to a location for a job, the automobile means that mothers and fathers do not have to live where they work. It has become routine for middle-class people, with children, who are newly arrived in a city or town to inquire first about the quality of schools in different areas before deciding where to settle. A parent in Scottsdale, Arizona, objecting to a school board plan to change attendance zones, put it succinctly in a letter to a local newspaper: "No family moves into a neighborhood without inquiring about the schools."[29] Any real estate agent will also attest to the fact that schools are the first consideration of home-seekers with children.

Competition among schools, then, can be competition between private and public schools for students, but it can also be competition among communities around school districts. This is the reason that researchers have found that housing prices are higher in public school districts that have reported high levels of student achievement.[30] A high-quality school tends to draw home-seekers with children into its boundaries, driving up home prices. In effect, those who purchase or rent homes in order to be in a desirable school district are paying tuition in the form of higher mortgages or rents than they would pay if they lived elsewhere.

Many residents pay a second type of hidden tuition, in addition to housing costs in good school districts. The automobile has made it possible to live farther from one's place of employment, but distance also means expenditure of time and money on travel. If all schools in all places were of equal value, then a big motivation for commuting would be removed. In the course of our research, we spoke with one parent in the New Orleans area who had chosen to live across Louisiana's broad Lake Pontchartrain, away from his place of employment, and spent at least an hour in traffic each day. Echoing the sentiments of many other commuters, he lamented:

I'd have to say that the schools were the number one factor in why we bought our house out here. I wish I didn't have to commute all the way across the bridge [the twenty-four-mile causeway] to go to work every day. But the schools in New Orleans are a nightmare. I couldn't put my kids in one of those places.[31]

At this point, we come very close to our example of the two cities. When the value of one location goes down, those who can afford to do so look for other places to live. If artificially low rents or subsidized housing draw the poor into one community, then the members of the middle class will be willing to pay higher costs to live elsewhere. The city may have previously had a great deal of economic inequality, divided into rich and poor neighborhoods. When controls are introduced to allow the poor to live wherever they choose, this may appear to be a good way to create equity. The problem, though, is that those who are not poor will simply move farther away. Rather than creating equality, controlled housing costs will simply have resulted in poverty being spread over a wider geographic area.

Given that students create the achievement level of schools, parents who are looking for good schools tend to settle in districts that have high-achieving students. Again, since a clear and widely recognized achievement gap exists between white students and those of the largest minority groups, those who can afford to choose where they live will tend not to live in areas that have large minority student populations. When numbers of relatively low-performing students enter a school, the families of higher-performing students begin to move away. Instead of creating equality of educational opportunity, redistributing historically disadvantaged students can simply spread educational disadvantage over a wider geographic area, much as government subsidized housing can distribute poverty.

So every public school must compete with private schools and all other public schools that law and distance would allow prospective students to attend. What influences the choices that families make among these competing possibilities? The first answer, of course, remains the quality of education available in any one institution or system. The quality of education, it should be remembered, is largely a function of the other students, so that those who can make choices will always tend to choose to move away from the educationally disadvantaged and toward the advantaged. As in the case of private versus public schools, though, cost is still an issue. The greater the benefit a family gains from moving or paying a high mortgage or paying tuition, the more it will be willing to make the sacrifice. If we think of cost as what a family has to give up, then it is clear that a big mortgage payment costs a high-income family much less as a share of its total resources than it costs a relatively low-income family. The availability of alternatives is also a part of the calculation. If a region has few highly regarded private schools, then settling in a neighborhood with a good public school may look desirable. If a family lives in a small city surrounded by comparatively deprived rural schools, then it can either accept the local public schools as they are or take whatever private schools may be available (or home-school the children, an increasingly popular option).

From the economic perspective that we are suggesting, a claim that "desegregation causes white flight" may be true, but it is overly simplistic. Instead, one should see the quality of education provided by a school as largely the consequence of the educational advantages that students bring to a school. Since white and middle-class students bring more advantages to schools, schools that contain relatively few underprivileged minority students tend to be better schools. Each family chooses the best education available that it can afford. Where there are educationally exclusive public school areas, those who can afford to do so will move into those areas. When these public schools can compete effectively with private institutions, private schools tend to attract a relatively small proportion of those who can exercise choices, unless religious belief or some other cultural preference gives the edge to a private school.

The existence of private and competing public schools makes it difficult to establish monopolistic control over any school system. But the complexity of the educational marketplace encompasses more than these two forms of competition. Choices inside of schools also exist. According to the National Center for Education Statistics, at the beginning of the 1990s, 92 percent of large school districts and 82 percent of medium school districts had advanced placement programs. In urban areas, 74 percent of school districts offered honors programs, and these were offered in 56 percent of suburban districts. Gifted and talented programs, the most elite and exclusive of all, could be found in 99 percent of southeastern districts, 82 percent of western districts, 80 percent of central districts, and 72 percent of northeastern districts.[32] In some states, over one out of every ten students was classified as gifted or talented. The remarkably talented states of Michigan and Wisconsin, for example, enrolled 14 and 15 percent, respectively, of their elementary and secondary students in these programs in the early to mid-1990s.[33]

All these special programs provide opportunities for an elite, exclusive education within public schools. They also tend to be highly segregated by race and class. A study of eighth graders based on the 1988 *National Educational Longitudinal Study* found that white students made up 82 percent of the students classified as gifted, although they made up only 71 percent of the total student population at the time of the study.[34] Since the classification of students as "advanced placement," "honors," or "gifted and talented" is based largely on achievement measured through test scores, the test score gap between white and disadvantaged minority students means that classroom segregation inside of schools is generally a result of such programs.

We should consider, then, how attempts at desegregation tend to affect the educational marketplace, considering that the "product" is the quality of education. First, the effect of redistributing students depends on how many students will be redistributed and on how great the gap is between the advantaged and the disadvantaged. If there is no achievement gap at all between students from different racial groups, redistribution will not affect the product at all. If this were the case, though, there would be no reason for desegregation in the first place. If only a few students from historically disadvantaged groups enter schools with members of advantaged groups, this should have a fairly small impact on the quality of education. Districts with large minority populations who have much greater educational disadvantages than students from the national majority pose the greatest problem. Thinking about our imperfect example of the city, if controls, subsidies, or other means of housing assistance bring a single low-income family into a neighborhood, this may have relatively little impact on the community. If the city consists almost entirely of middle- to upper-income people (admittedly an unlikely scenario), then it may be possible to scatter all the disadvantaged in good neighborhoods without much of a change. If, however, the city consists primarily of the economically disadvantaged surrounding small pockets of affluence, then the quality of life in affluent neighborhoods will be seriously threatened by their opening to the poor.

Next, if we consider how desegregation affects choices, this depends on the resources of those making the choices. The most well-to-do families have the least difficulty in moving to private schools if there is any decline in the desirability of public schools. If public schooling declines greatly, perhaps as a result of the entry of large numbers of students with significant educational disadvantages into previously elite institutions, then middle-class families will be willing to move or make other sacrifices in order to find high-quality schooling.

Finally, the choices that families make depend on what choices are available to them in addition to their resources. If there is a well-established set of private schools or a parochial school system, this is an ever-present possibility to which those with reasonable resources can turn if the quality of education declines in their public schools. If there are suburbs within driving distance, then resettlement in the suburbs may be an option. When the decline in overall school quality is not so serious that the educationally advantaged want to avoid desegregating schools altogether, special programs inside of schools, which offer exclusive schooling within apparently egalitarian settings, may become attractive.

One clear implication of this economic perspective on educational quality is that the tendency of schools to "sort" themselves according to race and socioeconomic status is not just "a 'taste for dissociation,' or the desire to be apart from people of a different race."[35] If it is true, as has been observed, that states with racially diverse populations have more school districts than states with little diversity,[36] this is only partly a result of desires of people to associate with people like themselves or of prejudice against people different from themselves. More important, the sorting is produced by each family's search for the best available schooling it can afford.

As we look in the following chapter at events in a wide sampling of desegregating school districts, readers should pay attention to how this model of schools as educational marketplaces can be used to understand what has happened in different districts around the country. Before looking at these school districts, though, let us briefly consider what this model means for equality of opportunity through schools.

WHAT DOES THIS MEAN FOR EQUALITY OF OPPORTUNITY?

The most important investment in education made by any family is the investment of its children. The school that receives a child also receives all the years of socialization and attention that the parents have been able to give him or her. The school receives the parents' own education and knowledge that has been communicated to the child and which the child then spreads throughout the school in his or her interactions with students and faculty. Schools chosen by educationally advantaged parents, who generally also have the economic ability to make choices, have concentrations of the best-prepared students. Since these students make their schools desirable to others, the socioeconomic sorting becomes a trend of exclusivity, with educational elites drawn to schools that contain those like themselves.

The inequality of schools is then reinforced by the ongoing actions of parents. As pointed out previously, parental involvement in schooling is closely associated with race and social class, with white parents and middle- to upper-class parents showing much higher levels of involvement than the parents of black and Hispanic children. To recognize this is not to blame minority parents. Their lower involvement may well be the consequence of more limited time and lack of familiarity with the educational system. Where minority students are bused from their neighborhoods, their parents' lack of participation may be a consequence of long distances to travel. In any event, acknowledging a documented fact, as uncomfortable as it is, is not the same as making a moral judgment.

Parental involvement contributes to the quality of a school in many ways that are not strictly financial in character. It is also a major source of the financial resources of schools. As one work on educational economy pointed out, PTOs "raise significant funds in a variety of ways: product sales, auctions, competitions, galas, and other fundraising drives. Traditional product fundraising generates an average of $13,000 per school. Nationwide, almost $2 billion is raised each school year by parent and teacher organizations."[37]

In addition to fundraising, parents also contribute to schools through volunteer work. "Nationally one survey estimates that almost 3.4 million public school volunteers logged approximately 109 million work hours in 2000. This was reported to be roughly equivalent to 52,000 full-time staff in 2000."[38]

Schools that offer good educations by providing students with well-prepared, reasonably motivated schoolmates, then, also end up having an edge in the availability of parental labor and in the financing produced by parents. Whereas the amount that resources can contribute to school quality is a point of debate, few researchers would argue that parental involvement in schools is unimportant. Schools become a way that middle-class parents can help to find places for their children in the middle class:

> Schools in socio-economically middle and upper class neighborhoods thus receive more resources than schools in disadvantaged neighborhoods: the latter typically lack volunteers or as many volunteers as the former. This could be regarded as exacerbating equity problems, which would not necessarily be resolved by the presence of parent volunteers in the schools without them. After all, differences in the quality of volunteer help might still leave us with an inequity.[39]

Few parents will engage in active fundraising or will volunteer hours of service in schools that do not serve their own children. To do so would be to take scarce time away from their own offspring. Similarly, every dollar a family gives to a school its own children do not attend is a dollar the family cannot give to the school its children do attend. Parents not only tend to give time and money directly to the schools that educate their children but also support property taxes when their children are in the schools that receive the benefits of those taxes.

When parents choose to place their children in private schools, they remove their own participation, as well as the academic skills of their children, from public schools.[40] Moreover, they give themselves an incentive to be reluctant to raise property taxes for public schools. Although they may agree with the proposition that all children have the right to an equal education, they are paying higher taxes on top of their tuition payments takes funds away from their children.

Moving into public school districts where there are few economically disadvantaged children is in the best interest of their own children, but it deprives the districts where disadvantaged minorities are concentrated of middle-class engagement. Since property values tend to rise with high test scores, as noted earlier, they also tend to fall with low test scores. Therefore, the racial test score gap means that the concentration of white families outside of minority areas hits those areas twice. It removes higher-scoring students, making test scores go down, driving property values and potential tax revenues down. The absence of white families also means that many who have the revenues to pay property taxes are lost to minority school districts.

The third primary alternative for those seeking the best opportunities for their children, elite programs or rigorous tracking within schools, is in many ways preferable to the other two, from the point of view of maximizing the opportunities of the disadvantaged. Advanced placement tracks and gifted classes can provide payoffs to those in them while helping to ensure that the schools that contain them receive the tax support and involvement of historically advantaged groups. Such within-school stratification do not promote equality of opportunity, though. By definition, those in the non-elite tracks will enjoy fewer opportunities than those in the elite tracks.

Our economic model suggests that when people are prevented from seeking the self-interest of their children in one way, this simply pushes them toward other alternatives. If, for example, students are redistributed throughout a school district, the general level of school quality will go down, but the quality of special advanced placement tracks may go up, as educationally advantaged parents desperately seek to have their children enter these tracks. At the same time, other parents of relatively high performing groups will have their children move out to other school districts or to nonpublic schools. As the proportion of disadvantaged minority students increases with these departures, educational quality in general goes down even further and competition for the few top schools or programs becomes even more intense. Ironically, a school system that in general shows deplorable achievement may end up with small pockets of outstanding performance—like Ben Franklin High gifted in the abysmally low achieving New Orleans school district.

In the following chapter, we will turn to consider brief histories of desegregation in school districts across the United States. We encourage readers to keep our sketch of the economy of educational opportunity in mind and to think about whether this sketch does seem to describe the patterns of occurrences in those districts. Before we look at these districts, though, it might be worthwhile to consider the implications of our model for school vouchers as well as a provision in the No Child Left Behind (NCLB) Act to move children from low-performing to high-performing schools. Both of these school reform measures have a great deal in common with school desegregation. Like school desegregation, most voucher programs and the NCLB Act aim at the redistribution of opportunity. Unlike command and control approaches to school desegregation, vouchers and NCLB emphasize freedom of choice of individual families, an emphasis that appeals to the fundamental political values of many Americans. However, our description of the educational marketplace leads us to be skeptical of vouchers or the NCLB Act for truly equalizing educational opportunities.

If education is an exclusive good, with a value established by its consumers, then the redistribution of advantaged and disadvantaged students always tends to lower the educational quality enjoyed by the advantaged. If low-performing students in failing public schools are allowed to transfer wholesale to the highest-performing public schools per NCLB guidelines, then academic levels at these receiver schools will necessarily fall. Elite private schools maintain their value by being selective. Even if the state were to subsidize the tuition payments of those who would not otherwise be able to pay, those elite schools would quickly become non-elite if they were to adopt open admissions policies, and their top-notch students would begin to leave. If they continued their selectivity, a few, bright, hardworking minority children would be able to enter with vouchers, but this would make little impact on racial and ethnic inequality of educational opportunity in general. In addition, if the best private (or public) schools were to be selective only on educational performance, with subsidies removing the barriers of paying tuition or a high mortgage, then the best schools would become even more intensely competitive academically, and other schools would be left as the default for those who failed in the academic competition. The result of academic standards would probably be greater educational inequality, not less. In addition, given the continuing achievement gap in race and ethnicity, much of that inequality would be along racial and ethnic lines.

These brief reflections on the consequences of vouchers and NCLB are logical extensions of our economic model of education, but there is still insufficient evidence on voucher programs or the NCLB Act to determine if the reflections are correct. The nation does have several decades of evidence on redistribution of students through school desegregation, though. At this point, we turn to examine that evidence by looking at the history of desegregation in districts throughout the nation.

CHAPTER 6

Rational Self-interest versus Irrational Government Policy

In the previous chapter we described schools as markets of exclusivity. The value of an education is largely established by the students in the classrooms on the basis of the assets they bring with them from their families and communities. Unfortunately, the long history of racial and ethnic inequality in the United States means that black, Hispanic, and white pupils on average bring different and unequal assets to the classroom. Therefore, faced with governmental attempts to redistribute educational opportunities by redistributing public school students, families who want to hang on to their advantages will attempt to turn to one of the four following strategies.

If other public school systems are available, parents may move or even falsify an address so they can go to a market that offers a higher-quality product. If there are private schools or if they can create private schools, they may leave the public system altogether. If good educational stores exist inside generally worsening markets, they will go to the good internal stores. In other words, if middle-class families can concentrate their children in magnet schools or gifted programs, they may seek the internal option. Finally, if none of the above options is affordable, available, or palatable and parents can arrange to opt out of formal schooling altogether, they may pull their child from an untenable educational situation and home-school their offspring.

Each of these strategies is, of course, a form of racial and economic segregation, undercutting governmental efforts to control the market through desegregation. Which strategy a family takes depends on which alternative is the most readily available, given the family's abilities to bear the costs. A low-income family, whether black, Hispanic, or white, may want to get out of an impoverished inner-city public school but have little chance to do so. Middle-class families, disproportionately white in our nation, have more options available to them. The most common choice is probably to avoid schools that are redistributing students—the classic white flight. If there are no other desirable school districts in a desegregating area and a family with choices must live there, though, then private schools may be desirable. Private schools can be costly, however, so magnet programs, offering a kind of private school experience inside of public schools, may be a family's best choice. Though still the least chosen option of the four, simply opting out of formal schooling altogether is the choice of an increasing number of Americans.

These different strategies suggest that governmental attempts to restructure the educational economy simply will not work. Education can never be a true monopoly, so racial and economic segregation as an expression of white middle-class self-interest tends to continually subvert such efforts.

At this point, the reader might answer: well, I suppose this gloomy view might make some theoretical sense, but reality is a good deal more complicated than theory. Surely there is a chance that we can create a more just and equitable society through our schools? Our answer is to look at what has actually happened in American schools over the history of desegregation to see if the patterns of events have matched our picture of the struggle to redistribute students as a radical, self-defeating process.

Too many large and small school districts have been subject to federal intervention for desegregation for us to look at every one. We have chosen a broad selection of locations—some notorious, some less so—to examine similarities and differences. We do believe that our examples are representative of the histories of other places, and we think that people who live in other parts of the country may well see many of the experiences of their own communities reflected here.

SCHOOL DISTRICTS AROUND THE NATION

Little Rock, Arkansas

Little Rock was one of the earliest and most celebrated of American desegregation cases. It began before governmental attempts to redistribute students, when the goal was still to simply enable black students to enjoy the legal right to enroll in schools near their own homes. After the Supreme Court made its historic decision in *Brown v. Board of Education*, it appeared as if Little Rock schools would quietly follow the orders of the Supreme Court. On May 22, 1954, the Little Rock school board announced that it would comply with the Supreme Court order as soon as the court established a method and a schedule for desegregation. A year later, in May 1955, the Little Rock school board voted to adopt a policy of gradual desegregation to start in 1957. Under the plan devised by school superintendent Virgil Blossom, Little Rock would first integrate the city's Central High School and then gradually integrate lower grades.

The crisis broke out in 1957, the year that the school board had hoped to manage the quiet admission of a few African American pupils into white schools. Seventeen students were selected to be the first to break down the racial lines, but only nine of them decided to go ahead and enroll. Just before the beginning of the school year, on August 27, the Little Rock's Mothers League sought an injunction to halt integration. The injunction was granted by Pulaski County chancellor Murray Reed, but it was rejected three days later by federal district judge Ronald Davies. The enrollment of the African American students might still have proceeded in a relatively peaceful manner if the governor had not used the situation for political advantage. Arkansas governor Orval Faubus was searching for political support to win a third term in office. He decided that he could appeal to whites eager to preserve segregation. Governor Faubus declared that he would not be able to maintain order if Central High School were integrated, and on September 2 he ordered the National Guard to surround the school. His stand drew public attention to the situation and attracted white segregationist mobs into the streets. The next day, Judge Davies ordered that the integration of Central should continue.

The NAACP, under the local leadership of Daisy Bates, organized the African American students slated to enroll in Central High to arrive in a group. They were met by National Guardsmen who turned the students away with bayonets. One of the students arrived after the others and was confronted by screaming segregationists. Television, which occupied a central place in most American homes by 1957, broadcast the scenes from Little Rock around the nation. On September 20, Judge Davies ruled that Governor Faubus had misused the National Guard to prevent integration and forbade the National Guard's employment in this way. Faubus then replaced the National Guard with local police. The nine black students entered Central High School through a side door on September 23. As they made their way into the school, an unruly mob of over one thousand people massed on the streets outside.

President Dwight D. Eisenhower met with Governor Faubus on September 14. Although the president believed that the governor had agreed to allow school integration to continue, it soon became evident that Governor Faubus had no such intention.

Alarmed by the developments in his city, on September 24 Little Rock mayor Woodrow Mann asked President Eisenhower for federal troops to maintain order. Eisenhower responded by sending 1,000 troops of the 101st Airborne and then placing the Arkansas National Guard under federal control. The troops escorted the nine students to the school each day. Some Americans were shocked to see that military protection was needed to guarantee the basic rights of citizens. Others were disturbed at what they believed was a federal military occupation of a state, reviving historical memories of the military occupation of the South during Reconstruction, in the years following the Civil War.

The struggle continued even after the mobs in front of Central returned to their homes and jobs. On February 8, 1958, after several angry confrontations with white students, one of the nine, Minnijean Brown, was suspended for the rest of the year for dumping a bowl of chili on her white antagonists. Shortly after, the school board asked the federal court for a delay of the integration order until the concept of "all deliberate speed" was defined. The delay was granted in June and then reversed in August. In the meantime, the first African American student graduated from Central in May.

At the opening of the 1958–1959 school year, Governor Faubus ordered Little Rock public schools closed, and white students enrolled in private schools or in other districts. On September 27, 1958, Little Rock voters overwhelmingly rejected school integration. However, on June 18, 1959, a federal court declared that Little Rock's public school closing was unconstitutional. Little Rock schools opened a month early for the 1959–1960 school year and enrolled African American and white students.

Eventually, Little Rock calmed down, and Central High School became a story of the success of school integration. After opening its doors to students from all backgrounds, Central went on to become something of a showcase. In 1982, the *Los Angeles Times* proclaimed that Central was the best school in Arkansas, and that it had proved the critics of integration wrong. With a student population that was 53 percent black, it had fourteen National Merit semifinalists, and one of its black students had made the highest score ever recorded in Arkansas on the National Merit examination.[1]

Although there is a great deal of truth to the success story, a realistic view will acknowledge that the success was not quite as clear and unblemished as sometimes claimed. Forty years after the Little Rock crisis, the black student population had continued to grow steadily, making up about two-thirds of Little Rock High's population by the end of the twentieth century. "Despite their overall numbers," observed a national newspaper during President Bill Clinton's visit to the school in 1997, "African Americans occupy just

13 percent of the seats in advanced classes and, in general, they tend to score worse, drop out more often, and draw more discipline than their white classmates."[2]

After the heroic struggles of black citizens to integrate Central in the 1950s, the most satisfying conclusion would be one of unqualified triumph. In a world that rarely follows the plots of good stories, though, the evaluation of events in Little Rock must be more measured. Simply striking down the barriers forbidding black students from enrolling in a local school did give them greater access to educational opportunities. This did not destroy Central as an educational institution, but it also did not create ideal racial balances in the school or eliminate substantial segregation at the classroom level.

Did the desegregating school districts that followed Little Rock, and which generally aimed at explicitly engineering racial balances, meet with better outcomes? A sampling of districts suggests that there were many similarities with the consequences in Little Rock. It also suggests that there were many differences, though, and these differences raise serious questions about the wisdom of trying to manage the demographics of school enrollment.

Beaumont, Texas

Desegregation efforts began in Beaumont in 1962, when the Rev. Edward Brown filed a suit against the Beaumont school district. The Reverend Brown's son, Edward Brown II, had been denied enrollment at Fletcher Elementary, a school near the Brown home. Texas in the early 1960s was not Arkansas in the late 1950s, though, and the Beaumont Independent School District responded to the lawsuit by announcing in 1963 that it would begin integrating all the schools in the district, one grade each year, beginning with the first grade. This did not succeed in redistributing the students of Beaumont's racially concentrated schools, though, and the city went through a period of conflict and oversight by the U.S. Department of Justice through the 1960s and early 1970s. According to a civil rights attorney cited by the *Beaumont Enterprise* newspaper, the district was so tense at this time that it seemed always about to break out in violence.[3] In 1975, the district came up with a desegregation plan that the Department of Justice approved. It combined its two major high schools and redrew the attendance boundaries for all schools.

The wealthier district of South Park was distinct from Beaumont through those years, but it had its own desegregation struggles. The U.S. government ordered South Park to desegregate in 1970, and the district drew up new attendance zones. White reaction was almost immediate. Many white families either put their children in private schools or, even more drastically, sold their homes and moved to other counties. "Within 30 days, the neighborhoods were vacant and virtually every house for sale," said an attorney for the South Park school district.[4] Of the 200 to 300 students assigned to formerly black Hebert High School in 1970, only 100 attended the first day of school and only 10 of those remained by the end of the first month.[5]

In 1981, U.S. district judge Robert Parker came up with his unique "ping-pong" desegregation plan. Families of students drew ping-pong balls for assignment to schools, and then the students were bused all over the district. Two years later, the Beaumont and South Park school districts merged, creating a single large district. In 1994, seeking a way to return to neighborhood schools, members of a biracial coalition of citizens drew up an agreement with the school board that neighborhood schools would be allowed provided all students were guaranteed equal access to superior schools. No one seemed to point out the obvious contradiction between "equality" and "superiority." This ended most of the long-distance busing around the district.

After 1994, though, schools began to resegregate. By 2003, Beaumont's Central High School was 82 percent black and only 3 percent white, while Ozen High School was 92 percent black and only 2 percent white. The white high school students were heavily concentrated in West Brook, which was 55 percent white and 30 percent black. Several of Beaumont's elementary schools were 100 percent black.

Even if the school district had turned back the clock, it would not have been able to find enough white students to bus around by the beginning of the twenty-first century. Whites made up only 22 percent of the students in the Beaumont public school system. After forty years, the Beaumont school system had become one that could not be desegregated. This was not because there were no whites in the geographic area. The population of the city of Beaumont in the 2000 census consisted of 52,239 people listed as black, 53,086 as white, 2,652 as Asian, and 9,126 as Hispanic. Whites made up the largest portion of the population in Beaumont, but they were only a little over one-fifth of the public school students. Still, whites were a distinct minority in Beaumont in one respect: only 9,567 (36%) of the city's 26,546 families with children under age 18 were white. Among the school-aged children (6 through 17), whites made up 6,954 of the 21,002 children, or 33 percent. Even with six years of neighborhood schools, over one-fourth of the first through twelfth grade white students in Beaumont were in private schools in 2000, according to census data. Although it is difficult to establish how much school desegregation influenced the population, we can say that after four decades of desegregation, Beaumont's whites were particularly small in numbers among families with school-aged children. Moreover, the evidence strongly indicates

that the white families with children who were in Beaumont were disproportionately not participating in the public school system. Further, decades
of expensive desegregation and treating children like randomly struck ping-
pong balls had not resulted in any true, lasting racial redistribution at all.

Dallas, Texas

The process of desegregation began in Dallas in 1960, when U.S. district
judge Thomas W. Davidson ordered the integration of Dallas schools in
Borders v. Rippy. Little happened until after a black man brought suit against
the city district in 1970 because his son was not allowed to attend an all-white
school in his neighborhood.[6] The court order that was consequently issued in
1971, and which in part mandated ending the racial achievement gap, was
appealed. In July 1975, the U.S. Court of Appeals for the Fifth Circuit ruled
that Dallas put a desegregation plan into effect by the start of the second se-
mester of the 1975–1976 school year. The following year, in April, a federal
judge handed down an order calling for the division of the Dallas Independent School District into six subdistricts and for busing 17,328 of the district's
141,000 students. The bused students were to come from all racial groups: 51
percent of them would be black, 38 percent would be white, and 11 percent
would be Hispanic. School officials at the time estimated that the busing plan
would cost $26.3 million. At the beginning of the active shuffling of students
around Dallas based on race, there were almost equal numbers of black and
white students, since 44 percent of the district's pupils were black, 41 percent
were white, and 13 percent were Latino.[7]

After two decades of court control, Dallas finally managed to obtain unitary status on July 26, 1994. In the order granting this status, the court criticized the school system for its apparent reluctance to put desegregation
practices into effect over the years, and it required Dallas schools to maintain programs such as majority-to-minority transfers, and to continue other
desegregation strategies. The school system responded by establishing a Desegregation Monitoring division in its Department of Evaluation, Accountability, and Information Systems. By the school year 2000–2001, the
Desegregation Monitoring Division had a budget of $561,538,[8] nearly half of
which went to the salaries of four employees. The division's assistant superintendent received a salary in 2000 of $91,599.[9] The name of the desegrega-
tion Monitoring Division was changed to the "Equity and School Choice
Department" when the Dallas Independent School District was declared unitary in 2003, but it ostensibly still had the same functions.[10] However, as will
be seen, if the functions of the office include those suggested by the name—

providing students with an equal educational opportunity with a genuine choice of high-quality schools in the district—this would seem a very difficult task indeed.

Dallas County, which contains both the Dallas Independent School District and its neighboring districts, in 2000 was 58 percent white, 20 percent African American, and 30 percent Latino (of any race).[11] These calculations do not distinguish Latinos from other races, but if we take all the Latinos as "white," then the overly conservative estimate of the non-Hispanic white portion of the population would be just over 28 percent (51% white − 36% Latino = 15% non-Hispanic white). Within the city of Dallas, the two minority groups were much more heavily represented: 51 percent white, 26 percent African American, and 36 percent Latino (of any race). Again, though, even if we classify all the Latinos as white, the non-Hispanic whites were at least 15 percent of the total population within the Dallas city limits, or double their representation in the public schools. Another way to look at this is that, by a conservative estimate, at least 71 percent of the non-Hispanic whites in Dallas County lived outside the city of Dallas, in one of the county's other sixteen school districts. By contrast, 68 percent of the county's black residents and 64 percent of its Latino residents lived inside of Dallas.

Within the city of Dallas, as within other districts in this chapter, whites were disproportionately in the nonpublic system. Over one third of the non-Hispanic whites in the city were in nonpublic schools, in which they made up 62 percent of the total student population at the systemwide level. Non-Hispanic whites made up approximately 7 percent of Dallas public school students in the 2002–2003, school year. Most of the students were Latino (59%) or black (33%). Any efforts at desegregation made by the well-paid assistant superintendent for desegregation monitoring would have necessarily been aimed at putting Latinos and blacks together because there were too few whites to integrate. Even members of the two minority groups showed a high degree of isolation from each other, though. For example, In 2002–2003, A. Maceo Smith High School was 94 percent black and slightly under 6 percent Latino. Lincoln High School was 96.0 percent black and 3.4 percent Latino. On the other side, Jefferson High School was 87.0 percent Hispanic and 9.4 percent black, and Moises Molina High was 88.0 percent Hispanic and 9.1 percent black. The lower grades were even more racially and ethnically segregated than the high schools.

To summarize this flurry of numbers: There were too few non-Hispanic whites in the Dallas school system for any kind of real desegregation, or "redistribution of advantaged students," because they tended to be either in surrounding, heavily white residential areas or not enrolled in public schools. Consistent with the economic argument we made in the previous chapter, it looks as if white non-Hispanic families had good reason to avoid the Dallas public schools. Mean SAT scores for the class of 2002 came to only 850 for the Dallas Independent School District, compared to 986 for the state. The low score was chiefly a result of the high percentage of minority students, since black students in the district scored only 790 and Latino students scored 858, compared to 1057 for white students. By contrast, students in the mostly white nearby Dallas County district of Highland Park averaged 1194 on the SAT, and those in the Irving district, with a somewhat larger minority population, scored 999.[12] Families who were looking for good schools, as indicated by test results, would reasonably avoid schools or school districts with predominantly minority populations.

The Dallas Independent School District was finally released from all court oversight in 2003, when Judge Barefoot Sanders decreed that "the segregation prohibited by the United States Constitution, the United States Supreme Court and federal statutes no longer exists in the city district."[13] This is a very interesting assessment of what transpired in a district that over the course of thirty-three years of court-ordered desegregation went from 57 percent to only 9 percent white.[14] It is very difficult to imagine how the judge arrived at his conclusion that the district was less racially segregated—whether *de jure* or *de facto*—in 2003 than it was in 1970. The consequences of court-ordered desegregation certainly did not make it any more likely that black parents in Dallas could put their children in a majority white school, nor did it, by a very long shot, reduce inequalities of academic outcomes by race. In other words, the whole experience seems a complete and very expensive failure.

Readers should remember that Dallas is a decentralized, suburban, postautomobile city. It is not, like the older cities of the United States, formed around a decaying industrial inner city, home to minority group members who have been left behind as newer suburbs grow in clusters around the center. Of course, Dallas does have poor neighborhoods (South Dallas), and those who are not poor seek to avoid settling in these neighborhoods or sending their children to school in them. But we cannot explain the failure of desegregation in Dallas by claiming that it would have worked if only whites had not just happened to move out of central city areas for reasons having nothing to do with desegregation itself. As we look at different types of metropolitan areas and school districts, the striking fact is that the judicially mandated redistribution of students did not seem to work well anywhere.

Baton Rouge, Louisiana

By the time it ended in 2003, the case of *Davis et al. v. East Baton Rouge Parish School Board* was said to have been the longest-running desegregation suit in the nation.[15] It began in 1956, when black parents sued the school board for running a dual school system after the Supreme Court had declared this unconstitutional. During the 1960s, the school board attempted to answer the suit by adopting a "freedom of choice" approach to integrating schools, allowing black and white students to attend schools without regard to race. This resulted in little change in the racial configurations of schools, though, and educational institutions in Louisiana's capital remained distinctly black and white.

Despite the long existence of the East Baton Rouge (EBR) suit, active court-ordered desegregation in the district only began in 1981. In that year, federal district judge John Parker decided that the school board had been running a dual school system for the previous twenty years. Judge Parker therefore ordered the closing of fifteen schools and developed pairs or clusters of previously black and white schools that were to exchange students through busing in order to achieve racial balances similar to those of the districtwide demographics.

The response to the 1981 decision was immediate. White families said they would leave the public schools if the mandate were put into effect. The president of the parent-teacher organization at a majority white school, whose daughter was to be transferred to a majority black school in a lower-income neighborhood, declared, "She will not do that. Private schools are starting up every day."[16] Events showed that these were not idle threats. In the first year of court-ordered busing alone, the East Baton Rouge public school system lost 7,000 white students. Private school waiting lists grew long, and new schools started up almost daily. The percentage of white students in the East Baton Rouge school district who attended nonpublic schools had been going down from 1965 until 1980, from just under one-fourth of white students to well under 20 percent just before the judge's decree. From the early 1980s onward, however, this proportion went steadily upward, so that nearly half of the white students in the district were in nonpublic schools by 2000.

In addition to moving from public to private schools, Baton Rouge area white families also either moved out of the East Baton Rouge school district or, if they were new arrivals, settled outside the school district. Before the 1981 decision, settlement in the adjoining Livingston and Ascension Parishes had been growing slowly,[17] but the proportion of the area's white population in these nearby areas began to shoot up rapidly just after the decision. About one-fourth of the region's white public school students were enrolled outside the East Baton Rouge district in 1965. By the end of the 1970s, still only about one-third of these white public school students were in adjoining districts. In the two decades after Judge Parker's 1981 ruling, though, the proportion of white public school students in the Capital City metropolitan area who were enrolled in the Ascension or Livingston districts grew to about two-thirds. A longtime school official in one of the districts outside Baton Rouge told us that the growth of the district's population was "almost exclusively driven by white flight and the initial location of new hires for industry in East Baton Rouge who will not live where they work."[18] Readers should note that this was not a matter of whites leaving some blighted central city for the green lawns of the suburbs. Baton Rouge itself consists almost entirely of suburbs, so this was movement from the suburbs to the suburbs.

Baton Rouge's loss of white students briefly slowed in the late 1980s. A school system central office administrator with whom we spoke attributed this to a brief experiment with "controlled choice."[19] This was explicitly intended to restore the confidence of those who had lost faith in the local public school system. It relied on magnet programs and special curricula. The experiment broke down, however, because of shortages in funding and difficulties in maintaining support from school officials.

By 1996, East Baton Rouge had changed from a majority white to a majority black district. Two-thirds of the public school students in the district were black, although the proportion had been roughly constant at about 40 percent from 1965 until just before the 1981 court order. Largely to stabilize this chaotic, rapidly changing system, the school board and plaintiffs to the *Davis* case, including the NAACP, reached a court-approved consent decree in 1996. This largely ended busing and sought, instead, to pump large infusions of funds into the school system, including generous "equity accounts" for historically black schools. The $2.2 billion program hit a speed bump when it went before taxpayers, though, since voters resoundingly defeated a tax and bond proposal to raise money for continued desegregation efforts. With much of the middle class now out of the local public schools, members of the middle class had little interest in taxing themselves for a system many had fled.

As whites continued to leave the desegregating district, they left the less-advantaged black students behind. Deputy school superintendent Clayton Wilcox observed that "the school system is getting blacker."[20] By the 2002–2003 school year, 73 percent of the public school students in the district were black, and the proportion was a good deal higher in the elementary grades.[21] In attempting to establish desegregated schools, the court had helped to push segregation to the level of the district and into the public-private sector. Meanwhile, a substantial gap in educational outcomes continued to exist. On the math portion of the 1999 Louisiana Graduation Exit Examination, for example, East Baton Rouge's white public schools students answered an average of 72 percent of the questions correctly, whereas black students answered an average of less than 55 percent of these questions correctly. Among schools, the very few that ranked in the state's top categories as "School of Academic Excellence" or "School of Academic Distinction" on the 1999 Louisiana Educational Assessment Program tended to be precisely the schools where the remaining white students were still clustered. The one school in the top category was about 80 percent white, and the four schools in the next highest category averaged about 55 percent white. At the other end, the forty-six schools in the next to lowest "Academically Below Average" category averaged 87 percent black, and the three "Academically Unacceptable" schools averaged 94 percent black.

In summer 2003, the court finally ended the desegregation suit that had lasted almost half a century. Most observers agreed that nothing had been achieved, other than the reshaping of the school district into one that had been initially majority white into one that had too few whites for any kind of desegregation and little public support for school funding.

Charlotte, North Carolina

Charlotte offers an important and interesting case for any survey of desegregating school districts. As we have pointed out earlier, the Charlotte-Mecklenburg school system was historically significant because it began the national move to judicially mandated busing as a means of achieving desegregation. The district is even more worthy of a brief examination, though, because Charlotte acquired the reputation as "The City That Made It Work," and it was held up as a model for efforts at student redistribution throughout the nation.[22] If, in fact, Charlotte was as successful as often suggested, we should look carefully at it to see why. Even if this were a case with a relatively positive outcome, though, it would be wise to be skeptical of claims that these outcomes could be repeated in other locations. Good public policy does not assume that exceptions can become the general rule.

The Charlotte-Mecklenburg school system dates back to 1959, when the city of Charlotte and Mecklenburg County, which contains it, voted to merge their two school systems. Although the system made some attempts to desegregate following *Brown,* and some black students did attend predominantly white schools in the region in the late 1950s and early 1960s, the schools were still largely segregated by race. In 1965, Darius and Vera Swann sued the school district because their son, James, was not allowed to attend the school nearest his home, which was an all-white school. Ironically, then, from the beginning the case that would help to send hundreds of thousands of students away from their own neighborhood schools, the Swanns wanted only to send their child to a school in their own neighborhood.

The *Swann* case went before federal district judge James B. McMillan. In April 1969, Judge McMillan issued his decision, arguing that neighborhood schools were discriminatory because black residents lived mainly in a single section of the city. Judge McMillan maintained that "as a group Negro students score quite low on achievement tests (the most objective method now in use for measuring educational achievement)"[23] as a consequence of attending all-black schools. The judge ordered the district to employ all means of desegregating, including busing.

The school board appealed Judge McMillan's ruling. The case reached the Supreme Court, and two years later the high court upheld the decision. The result was an explosion of similar desegregation plans. The 1971 school year opened with new plans for assigning students by race in over 100 school districts.[24]

Judge McMillan, the plaintiffs, and the school board came to agree on a plan of action in 1974. The judge declared himself satisfied and removed the school from direct supervision, although the school board would have to continue to follow the 1974 plan. One of the key features of Charlotte's program was the pairing of elementary schools. A school in a majority white neighborhood would be paired with a school in a majority black neighborhood, and enough students would be transported from each to create racial balances. The desired racial mixture could frequently not be created with just two schools, so students were drawn from other locations, known as satellites. Most of the students who came from the satellites were black. This placed greater inconvenience on black students than on white, but most involved parties were convinced that sending white children into mostly low-income, black neighborhoods, would cause whites to leave the public schools.[25] From the beginning, then, those carrying out school desegregation did recognize the possibility of white flight and made serious efforts to avoid it.

The pairing strategy was not used at the junior high or high school levels, which had larger enrollments, so the higher grades drew on larger numbers of satellites. Again, these mainly came from black neighborhoods. There was one important exception, however. White students in the well-to-do neighborhood of Eastover were sent into the formerly black West Charlotte. To make this palatable to whites, though, school authorities had to put new educational programs in West Charlotte. The district also redrew the boundaries of West Charlotte so that these would include more middle-class black families and exclude many of the poor black families previously within the area.

Unlike many of the other cases in this chapter, Charlotte did not lose its white students. In the 1974–1975 school year, the system was 34 percent black. By 2001–2002, it was 42 percent black. Whites made up just under 50 percent of the student population in the latter year, with other students being Asian or Hispanic. Changes in student makeup, then, were gradual and small enough to be attributed almost entirely to demographic shifts having nothing to do with the schools.

At first glance, then, Charlotte does look like the rare success story in school desegregation. It managed to put students of different races together in its schools. It did not cause whites to flee the system. There was no downward spiral in the quality of education in the district. A closer look, though, suggests that Charlotte does bear out the economic model of schooling that we described in the previous chapter.

White families did not leave the system, at least in part, because the district substituted segregated classrooms for segregated schools. Desegregation expert Roslyn Mickelson observed, "The Charlotte-Mecklenburg school system instituted widespread curricular tracking at the secondary level at about the same time that it began to comply with the Supreme Court's *Swann* orders to desegregate. Since the mid-1970s, the top tracks—those with the best teachers and most challenging curricula and pedagogy—have been overwhelmingly white while the lowest tracks have remained disproportionately black."[26]

At the end of the 1970s, the Department of Health, Education, and Welfare (HEW) denied the school district a major grant on the grounds of excessive within-school segregation. By the early 1980s, Charlotte's schools appeared to have student bodies that were highly mixed in race. Beneath this appearance, though, a 1981–1982 survey of tracking in English classes showed that "in this district acclaimed for its desegregation successes, relatively few black students experienced a genuinely desegregated education, even in its showcase high school."[27]

Even with the segregation inside of schools, the institutions themselves tended to move slowly toward more racial separation. In a study of Charlotte schools from 1991 to 1993, the Charlotte League of Women voters concluded, "The system appears to be continuing to drift toward blacker and whiter schools. Across the three year period, with few exceptions, the whitest schools got whiter and the blackest schools got blacker, whether they were elementary, middle, or high schools."[28]

At the beginning of the 1990s, the district largely replaced busing with a magnet school program as a strategy for achieving desegregation. Magnet school enrollments would be kept at 40 percent black and 60 percent white.

This meant that whites, with much higher achievement levels than blacks (as we will see), were limited in their access to magnet schools. White parents therefore sued the district, calling for unitary status and an end to race-conscious enrollment policies. Nearly thirty years after the Charlotte-Mecklenburg system had made desegregation history, Judge Robert Parker ruled in September 1999 that the system had achieved desegregation, and he decreed that race could no longer be considered in school assignments.[29] With the end of judicial control, "the previous twenty year drift toward re-segregation accelerated markedly."[30] Students began to return to schools in their own neighborhoods, which were still largely black or white.

The black-white achievement gap, which had been given by Judge McMillan as his reason for ordering desegregation by any possible means, continued to exist after desegregation had been in effect for nearly a third of a century. On the North Carolina Writing Assessment test for 2004, among Charlotte-Mecklenburg seventh graders 62.3 percent of whites were in the top two levels, compared to 27.5 percent of black students. On the tenth grade portion of this test, 73.6 percent of whites and 41.8 percent of blacks were in the top two levels. On the North Carolina high school comprehensive test for reading in 2004, 82.2 percent of whites and 43.9 percent of blacks were in the top two levels. On the math test, the two top levels contained 84.8 percent of whites and 45.9 percent of blacks.[31]

Among the cases examined here, then, Charlotte-Mecklenburg did indeed have one of the most successful desegregation histories. The redistribution of students did not destroy the system. But neither did it end inequality in educational outcomes. The only way families of children with relatively strong academic performance were willing to place their children into schools filled with children of relatively weak academic performance was through in-school racially segregated classrooms. Yet even then, like a centralized economic authority suppressing market forces, the authorities would have to use continual coercion to suppress individual choices. As soon as the judiciary removed itself from the school system, the schools began to resegregate almost immediately.

Louisville-Jefferson County

In the 1974 Detroit case, the U.S. Supreme Court had refused to allow cross-district busing, apparently closing the door on racially motivated busing between suburbs and urban areas. However, the court found reasons for flexibility on this principle in the situation of Louisville, Kentucky, where 52 percent of the students in the city of Louisville were black. There, a court had ruled that Louisville and surrounding Jefferson County, plus another district, if needed, should be included in a single plan. The Sixth Circuit Court of Appeals successfully got around the Detroit precedent by ruling that both Louisville and Jefferson County had engaged in discriminatory practices together and that a single solution was therefore permitted.

Before the case even reached the national high court, the Kentucky state board of education merged the Louisville and Jefferson County districts. However, the Supreme Court's acceptance of the reasoning of the Sixth Circuit Court made it possible for another small district, Anchorage, to be included in the redistribution of students. Under the plan to be enacted, 11,300 black students would be bused to the suburbs and 11,300 white students would be bused to the city. In the face of bitter local anger by some over the decision, U.S. district judge James F. Gordon ruled in late August 1975 that anyone attempting to tamper with school buses to be used in desegregation would face federal prosecution.

On September 4, 1975, Louisville and surrounding Jefferson County became the first metropolitan area in the United States to carry out busing for desegregation between city and suburbs. At a mass rally at the Kentucky State Fairground the night before, at least 10,000 protestors gathered to denounce Judge Gordon as a tyrant. A boycott by white students cut attendance on that first day to less than half of all students enrolled, and about 2,000 protestors defied the judge's orders against protest. At Fairdale High School, in a working-class white neighborhood in Jefferson County, about 200 demonstrators attempted to block buses leaving the school with black students.

On the second day, violence broke out in the white working-class suburb of Valley Station. Although most of the demonstrations around the metropolitan area were peaceful, about 2,500 demonstrators in Valley Station fought with the police, injuring as many as thirty officers. The police fought back with tear gas, arresting about 75 of the demonstrators. By September 10, the Kentucky National Guard had to be called in to stop the rioting and violence in the Louisville area.

Although the struggle was long and hard, with the Louisville school system frequently accused of not living up to court orders, supporters of forced desegregation were optimistic about the long-term results. The Kentucky Commission on Human Rights issued a report in May 1977 claiming that the two-year busing plan had given families with school-aged children an incentive to end housing segregation. The report maintained that the number of black families of pupils was increasing in the previously all-white suburbs and that in ten years busing could end because it would have achieved its aims.[32]

Within the schools, desegregation brought concerns. A survey of students in 1978 found that 63 percent of white students and 43 percent of black students believed there were racial tensions in their schools. "Discipline problems have soared," observed one reporter. "White parents fear that the quality of education has declined, while black parents fear the loss of their community identity and institutions."[33] Segregation by classroom also continued, with white students in advanced classes acknowledging that they had no black classmates.[34]

By 1979, it was becoming clear that segregation was reappearing at the school level, as well as at the classroom level, because white students were disappearing from the Louisville-Jefferson public school system. This led to efforts to readjust the transfers of students. School officials tried to blame the drop in white numbers on declining white birth rates, but parents, in contact with other parents who were making school decisions, disputed these dismissals. Mrs. Jean Ruffra, a parent of two school-aged children, remarked, "What has happened, and the Central Board of Education knows it, is that we have white flight from the public school system. The figures are proof that it is true, and that is the reason they want to revamp the busing plan. Supposedly at the time, this was the best plan implemented in the country, and if it was such a good plan then, why isn't it anymore?"[35]

When Louisville-Jefferson County was finally declared unitary in 2000, the plaintiffs in the desegregation case were opposed because schools were still segregated at the classroom level; they argued that 53.1 percent of high school classes and 33.6 percent of middle school classes were outside the guidelines that required each school to have no less than 15 percent and no more than 50 percent of members of one race. The court, however, responded that the school-level guidelines did not apply to individual classes.[36] Many white students were not in the public school system at all. School attendance data from the 2000 census show that white students were a minority of 36 percent in Louisville public schools. This was because over one-third of the white students in Louisville were in nearly all-white private schools.

An examination of tract-level data in 2000 shows that Jefferson County was still highly segregated residentially in spite of earlier claims that school desegregation was changing racial housing patterns. Neighborhoods with large black populations tended to have few whites, and vice versa. Since the U.S. Census will not give numbers when there are fewer than fifty members in a group, many Louisville tracts either listed no black residents or no white residents in divisions that ranged from about 4,000 to about 8,000 in numbers of people. Of the 170 census tracts in Jefferson County, 85 reported that there were fewer than fifty black residents and 10 reported fewer than fifty white residents. This residential segregation appears even on a larger geographic scale. Among Jefferson County's eight large county subdivisions, the Jefferson Central region was 76 percent white, Jefferson Northeast was 88 percent white, Jefferson Southeast was 89 percent white, Jefferson Southwest was 91 percent white, Louisville East was 93 percent white, Louisville South was 70 percent white, and Louisville West was 79 percent black: Only Louisville Central, located by the river, with by far the smallest number of residents—about 31,000, or about one-third of the other subdivisions—was approximately equal in black and white residents.

Three decades after the conflict over desegregation, black and white students also continued to show highly unequal performance. The *Kentucky Performance Report* of 2003 showed that 56 percent of white non-Hispanic fourth graders in Jefferson County public schools were ranked as "proficient" in reading and 8 percent ranked as "distinguished," the highest of four levels. By contrast, only 39 percent of African American fourth graders were "proficient" and only 2 percent were "distinguished." Over one out of four (28%) of African American fourth graders were in the lowest level of "novice," compared to 13 percent of non-Hispanic whites. In mathematics, 12 percent of whites were in the highest of the four levels and 34 percent were in the next highest. Only 3 percent of the African American elementary school students were in the top category, and just 17 percent were in the next category. Among tenth graders, 11 percent of whites scored in the highest level in reading and 26 percent scored in the next highest. By comparison, 3 percent of African American students were in the top level and 12 percent were in the second highest. In mathematics, most African American students (59%) were in the bottom achievement category. The "proficient" group contained 7 percent of the African American high school students, and only 1 percent ranked as distinguished. Nearly one out of four white high school pupils (24%) made it into the "proficient" category, and one in every ten was distinguished.[37] Despite all the disruptive desegregation efforts of the 1970s, Louisville and its surrounding suburbs were still separate in residence and unequal in education.

Prince George's County, Maryland

United States district judge Frank A. Kaufman ordered Prince George's County to begin busing students to achieve racial desegregation in December 1972, after black parents and the NAACP filed a lawsuit charging that the district was running a dual school system. At that time, approximately 78 percent of the public school students in the county were white. After this decision, however, the number of white students dwindled rapidly, so that whites were a minority a decade later. By 1985, when 60 percent of the students were black, many of Prince George's schools were segregated again because it was difficult to find enough whites to integrate the schools. Recognizing that busing would only diminish the supply of whites still further, in 1985 the school district sought permission from the court to use magnet programs to draw white students into black schools. The special programs in fifty-three of the county's 180 schools provided resources not available in regular school programs, as well as a specialized curriculum that gave students opportunities to specialize in sixteen different themes, such as French, classical studies, and the arts. In order to use these to pull in whites, though, the school system had to maintain slots specifically for white students in those schools and to limit the numbers of blacks who would be allowed to attend.

Using magnet schools to attract white students, rather than using forced redistribution of pupils seems, in theory, like a good way for schools to achieve racial balance. If, as we have argued here and elsewhere,[38] white avoidance of black schools is largely based on rational self-interest, then magnet schools may be seen as a way to make racially mixed schools attractive to white families. However, there are four big, interconnected problems with magnet schools such as those in Prince George's County. First, if the value of an education is created more by the students in a school than by anything the institution can offer in the way of programs or curricula, then desegregation itself may undercut the value of schools, whether they are magnets or not. Second, to the extent that schools contain largely white magnet programs inside predominantly black institutions, then magnets simply replace segregated schools with segregated classrooms. This may be preferable to having white students outside a system altogether and thus not contributing to it, but it does not mean real desegregation and it raises a third problem. Maintaining places in magnet programs for white students means systematically discriminating against black students and denying places to them. It is therefore a strange way to go about correcting the effects of historical discrimination. Fourth, like most strategies that aim at creating some desired mix of students, it deals poorly with changing demographics. If magnet schools work in attracting white students, then they essentially set a cap on the number of whites in a system. Magnets can retain as many whites as there are reserved seats; the number can go down, to the extent that the strategy does not work perfectly, but it cannot go up.

By 1996, the proportion of white students in Prince George's had dwindled to less than 19 percent, whereas black students made up 72 percent of the county's public school population. The initial court order had mandated that no school could be more than 80 percent black. But this became increasingly difficult to achieve with so few whites available. So, as happened in some other desegregating systems experiencing white flight, like Baton Rouge, the court simply changed the goals. In 1995, the court ordered that elementary schools could be no more than 86.6 percent black, middle schools could be no more than 90.8 percent black, and high schools no more than 90.3 percent black.[39] The magnet schools, meanwhile, had 500 openings for non-black students, but no one was available to fill them; meanwhile 4,100 black pupils were on waiting lists trying to get into the magnets. This led to an effort among some on the Prince George's school board to get the federal court to free the district from the 1985 mandate. As school board member Verna Teasdale realistically observed, "In a school system that is 72 percent African American, we are not going to get enough white children to fill those slots."[40]

Others on the school board, though, disagreed with Teasdale. As the *Washington Post* reported, "Board members admit openly that they fear losing the millions of dollars—between $11 million and $16 million—they receive annually from the state to operate desegregation programs, which include the magnets."[41] These other board members favored continuing to deny access to black students because of dependence on desegregation funds for a school system whose demographics had placed it beyond any possibility of true desegregation.

In June 1996, the Prince George's school board voted by a five-to-four margin to ignore the 1985 court order and fill the magnet school positions with black students. In place of the magnet strategy, the board approved a desegregation strategy that created high achievement neighborhood schools over six years. Extra resources would be given to schools that became one-race schools because of the makeup of their neighborhoods. The school board's attempt to act without judicial approval provoked a response from the NAACP, though, which filed a motion with U.S. district judge Peter J. Messitte, who had been overseeing the case since 1994. Judge Messitte required the school board to apply to him before making any change in the magnet plan.[42] Thus, a black school board elected by mostly black citizens was unable to make decisions on behalf of black students without obtaining the permission of a white judge. This united a usually divided school board, which voted unanimously in late July 1996 to ask Judge Messitte to lift the desegregation order that had been in effect since the early 1970s and instead have the county and state pay for a $346 million program to improve neighborhood schools.[43] Just where this money would be found was unclear, however, especially after county taxpayers voted for limitations on taxes at the end of 1996.[44]

During the summer of 1997, an independent panel appointed by Judge Messitte reported that Prince George's had done all it could to end school segregation. The following October, the school board and the NAACP, which had been at odds on the issue of ending racial quotas in the magnet schools, together drafted a plan to end the long desegregation suit over a three-year period if the county and state would agree to provide $500 million to the school system. In view of the difficult tax situation, many legislators responded that this expensive proposal was unrealistic.[45]

Finally, at the beginning of September 1998, Judge Messitte ordered an end to the twenty-six-year court-supervised desegregation of the district's schools. Over the following six years, busing would be phased out as the district built thirteen new neighborhood schools and upgraded old ones. The settlement required that Prince George's County concentrate on improving the achievement of all students and on closing the gap between black students and others.[46]

The white proportion of Prince George's public school students fell to fewer than 13 percent in 2000. By the 2004 school year, the students in Prince George's County schools were 77.3 percent black, 10.7 percent Hispanic, 8 percent non-Hispanic white, and 3 percent Asian.[47] A large racial and ethnic gap in achievement continued in spite of the 1998 settlement. On the eighth grade 2004 Maryland School Assessment test, over half of the black majority (51.9%) and 60.5 percent of Hispanics scored in the lowest basic level in reading, compared to 29.5 percent of whites. In mathematics, 75.9 percent of black pupils and 77.3 percent of Hispanics were in the basic category, compared to 46.6 percent of whites. At the other end, 30.6 percent of whites scored in the highest, advanced category in reading and 19.3 percent in math. Only 3.2 percent of black students and 4.8 percent of Hispanic students were advanced in mathematics, and just 8.9 percent of blacks and 6.5 percent of Hispanics were advanced in reading.[48] Prince George's long desegregation struggle had helped to drive out most of the district's white students, while leaving behind an intact racial achievement gap.

Indianapolis, Indiana

As in many other school districts, the desegregation fight in Indianapolis began in the late 1960s. In March 1967, the NAACP asked federal agencies to investigate the student assignment system of the Indianapolis public school system. The following year, the U.S. Justice Department sued the system under the Civil Rights Act of 1964. Judge S. Hugh Dillin received the case.

In August 1971, Judge Dillin ruled that Indianapolis was segregated by race, and he ordered school officials to come up with a plan to integrate. Two years later, the judge ordered that black students be transferred from Indianapolis to eighteen schools in the suburbs of Marion County, which contains Indianapolis, and several other counties. The other counties were later taken out of the decision by a court of appeals in Chicago. A two-person committee appointed by Judge Dillin drafted a plan that would involve busing 9,200 students.

With Indianapolis, the U.S. Supreme Court allowed another exception, along with Louisville, to its 1974 Detroit *Milliken* ruling. The Indiana city had merged many of the governmental functions of Indianapolis and Marion County in 1969, leaving the school system as one of the few public services that had not become part of the merger. This led an appeals court to conclude in 1975 that not including the schools gave evidence of an intent to discriminate in the maintenance of districts and that busing between city and suburbs would not therefore be the kind of cross-district busing forbidden by the Supreme Court. The desegregation plan was to be drastic. It would involve immediately transferring 6,500 black Indianapolis students in first through ninth grades to schools in the suburbs. These would be eventually joined by another 3,000 black students bound for the suburbs. Within the Indianapolis system, both white and black students would be bused. The Housing Authority of Indianapolis would be enjoined from building any new housing within the city's school district.

Despite the 1975 conclusion of the appeals court, the busing did not begin until 1981, when 5,600 black students were bused from schools within Indianapolis to the townships of Decatur, Franklin, Lawrence, Perry, Warren, and Wayne. Ten racially identifiable elementary schools and one high school were permanently closed.

For a time in the 1980s, the Indianapolis desegregation plan did create just the kind of racial balances desired by the advocates of redistributing students. However, this state of affairs did not last. As the *Indianapolis Star* has recently observed, "Tens of thousands of students, most of them white, have either moved out of the district, or flocked to private, parochial, or charter schools in the area, disrupting the racial balance."[49] Within the schools, the transporting of students from city to suburb created the appearance of racial mixes at the school level, only to maintain racial segregation at the classroom level. In a report on suburban Broad Ripple, the *Washington Post* observed in early 1998 that "Indianapolis' careful desegregation measures bring a mix of black and white students to Broad Ripple's door every morning, only to resegregate them all over again by the time they sit down for class."[50] Since admission to magnet programs was based on academic skills, the white students were concentrated in the resource-rich magnet program, whereas the black students were in the regular classes.

In 1998, the Indianapolis public schools and the six surrounding townships of Marion County signed an agreement to gradually end busing from the city to the suburbs over a thirteen-year period. As a part of the agreement, the Indianapolis Housing agency would help low-income families resettle in the suburban areas.

After over thirty years of desegregation, millions of dollars spent on litigation, and acknowledged white flight from the public school system, "the city's schools are nearly as segregated as they were in the early 1970's."[51] Even though high schools contain a wider variety of students than schools in the lower grades, because there are fewer of them in each district, the high schools in Indianapolis were still very racially segregated during the 2003–2004 school year. Arlington High was 81 percent black, Broad Ripple was 76 percent black, Arsenal Technical was 68 percent black, and Northwest High was 61 percent black. Emerich, with a school population that was 58 percent white and 32 percent black, was the only high school in Indianapolis that did not have a black majority. In the same year, Franklin Central High, in Franklin Township, was 90 percent white. Some other high schools were nearly as racially concentrated. In Decatur Township, Decatur High was 88 percent white. Perry Township had two high schools—Perry Meridian, which was 84 percent white, and Southport High, which was 82 percent white.[52] The nonpublic school system that observers said had received the white flight during the desegregation years was still flourishing, too. In 2000, one out of every five white students in the area, including the city of Indianapolis and the suburban regions, was in the nonpublic system, which was 82 percent white.

Achievement gaps also remained. Despite the fact that busing had not completely ended, within Indianapolis only 34 percent of the students passed both the math and English sections of the state's ISTEP achievement test. Among the surrounding majority white townships, however, 59 percent passed the test in Decatur, 63 percent in Franklin, 63 percent in Lawrence, 56 percent in Perry, 57 percent in Pike, 56 percent in Washington, 57 percent in Wayne, and 67 percent in Beach Grove. These district-level results were closely related to the racial makeups of the schools in those districts, since clear black-white differences remained in achievement. Within Indianapolis, for example, only 36 percent of black sixth grade students passed the mathematics portion of the ISTEP test, compared to 57 percent of whites. In mostly white Decatur, 45 percent of black students passed the mathematics portion of the test, compared to 73 percent of white students.[53] Whatever had been accomplished in the decades since Judge Dillin began to order the redistribution of students, it did not include any meaningful integration or educational equality.

St. Louis, Missouri

St. Louis, along with Indianapolis and Louisville, was one of the few metropolitan areas where the effort to desegregate schools involved both the cities and the suburbs. It is an important case to consider because it is one of the few that have regularly been pointed out as a "success story" of desegregation history. It began in the early 1970s when a group of black students was reassigned from neighborhood schools to less desirable locations on the grounds that the schools were becoming overcrowded. Noting that the students were treated differently from whites, the families of these students began a grassroots movement and initiated a lawsuit.[54] On December 24, 1975, the case came before Judge James Meredith, who found that St. Louis schools were segregated by race. Judge Meredith issued a consent judgment and decree directing the school district to take action aimed at desegregation. Sensitive to the fact that St. Louis was already losing white citizens to the suburbs, the judge did not order the reassignment of students or busing. Instead, the schools were to try to integrate their faculties by setting minimums for increases in minority teachers and to use magnet schools to integrate student bodies.

Judge Meredith's decision was only an interim measure because the case against the St. Louis school board was still set to go to trial. The plaintiffs enjoyed the support of the federal government after the Justice Department intervened on their behalf in 1977. At the trial in 1979, though, Judge Meredith found in favor of the school board. He concluded that the board had tried to create legally integrated schools by allowing all students to attend neighborhood institutions and that segregation had occurred as a consequence of demographic shifts in housing.

Dissatisfied, the plaintiffs appealed. In March 1980, the Eighth Circuit Court reversed the 1979 ruling. Even though student assignments to schools had been racially neutral since the 1950s, the court found, the school board had failed to correct the results of legally segregated schooling incurred during the first half of the twentieth century. The school board, according to the court, had an obligation to create a school system without racially identifiable schools. The case went back to Judge Meredith, who now approved an $18 million plan for desegregation within the district of St. Louis. A system without racially identifiable schools would be difficult to create solely within St. Louis, though, because only 23 percent of the district's students were white, and they were mainly concentrated in a single section.

Court-appointed desegregation expert Gary Orfield wrote a report pointing out that the suburbs would have to be involved to attempt meaningful desegregation. In the early 1980s, then, the court began moving toward an interdistrict remedy. A St. Louis–St. Louis County interdistrict transfer plan took effect in 1983, with sixteen St. Louis County districts participating. The suburban districts had agreed to become part of this metropolitan solution out of fear that a federal judge would create a single district encompassing the entire region.

The transporting of students from city to suburb lasted for the rest of the century. This finally came to an end in 1999, when the plaintiffs to the lawsuit, the state of Missouri, the Justice Department, the sixteen districts, and the St. Louis Board of Education finally came to an agreement to end the desegregation case. At that time, about 12,000 city students were attending schools in the county, and about 1,400 suburban students were traveling each day to the city. With the end of the case, interdistrict transfers were to continue for another ten years.

Many have celebrated St. Louis and the suburbs as a great success in school desegregation. Speaking before the House of Representatives in 1999, Representative William Clay announced:

> I want to call the attention of my colleagues to the remarkable story of desegregation in St. Louis. St. Louis illustrates the gains that can be made for children even in these times. In St. Louis, a 1983 settlement of a desegregation case brought by the NAACP resulted in the largest voluntary metropolitan school desegregation program in the nation, with 13,000 black students from St. Louis attending school in 16 suburban districts. The program was very successful in increasing the graduation and college-going rates of participating youngsters as was a magnet program in city schools.[55]

An examination of the results of over thirty years of busing sending students across district lines raises some questions about this celebration, though. Economist Joy Kiviat, writing in 2000, observed that eight out of ten students in the city of St. Louis were black, and most of them were attending schools that contained virtually no whites. Although per pupil spending came to $7,564, there was a 62 percent dropout rate and students scored at the bottom on standardized tests. In spite of the existence of the highly praised magnet schools, one-third of the public school teachers in St. Louis chose to send their own children to private schools, and private school attendance was above that of the national average, especially among relatively high-income families.[56]

Data from the Missouri Department of Secondary and Elementary Education support Kiviat's bleak view of St. Louis schools. According to this information, from 2000 through 2004, 81 percent of the students in St. Louis City public schools were black. Whites were a little under 18 percent in 2000 and had gone down to just under 16 percent in 2004. On the 2004 Missouri Assessment Program tests, 30.9 percent of white seventh graders were proficient or advanced in communication arts, compared to just 8 percent of black seventh graders. In mathematics, 21.4 percent of white eighth graders were proficient or higher, but only 2.6 percent of black eighth graders were at this level.[57]

The suburban districts that had been receiving students from St. Louis varied in their racial compositions. The students of Webster Groves, adjoining St. Louis, were between 12 and 22 percent black in 1982.[58] By 2004, Webster Groves still had a white majority, and about 22 percent of its students were black. Black students in Webster Groves did better than their St. Louis counterparts, since 17.1 percent of seventh graders were proficient in communication arts and 7.8 percent of eighth graders were proficient or better in mathematics. However, the racial gap in scores was even greater here than in the city, since 61.4 percent of same-grade whites were at least proficient in communication arts and 44.8 percent were at this level in mathematics. The Rockwood district, farthest from St. Louis, with a black student population under 4 percent in 1982, had become 12 percent black and 84 percent white by 2004. In this still majority white district, the race gap was also great. Only 9.3 percent of its black seventh graders were at least proficient in communication arts, compared to 59.3 percent of whites. In mathematics, only 1.3 percent of black eighth graders were at this point, whereas 25 percent of whites were proficient or better.

The best one can say about the St. Louis success story was that it was not a complete disaster. Since the whites in the suburbs were never forced to send their own children into the inner city, and busing from the city to the suburbs never inundated the latter, white families did not move en masse to private schools or leave the metropolitan area. The minority of black students who did go to school away from their own neighborhoods may have benefited from advantageous socioeconomic settings, although the cursory test results just cited suggest this requires more study. The years of interdistrict busing and billions of dollars in transportation and administrative costs did not accomplish any of the stated goals of the program, however. These years did not do away with racially identifiable schools or racially identifiable school districts. Neither did this Herculean effort eliminate the enormous racial achievement gap in either the city or the suburbs.

Chicago, Illinois

As in so many other desegregation cases, the roots of Chicago's lie in the era of the Civil Rights Movement. In 1961 several Chicago parents filed suit, claiming that the city's schools were segregated by race. Two years later, attempting to avoid court action, the school board responded by appointing a panel of experts to study the situation, although the board did not act on the panel's recommendations. The situation turned more serious in 1965, when the U.S. Commission of Education froze federal funds to the city because of the continuing racial identification of the schools. Political connections temporarily rescued the city, though, because Mayor Richard J. Daley contacted President Lyndon Johnson, and Johnson rescinded the commission's cutoff.

Chicago school superintendent James F. Redmond made some efforts at desegregation, proposing the development of magnet schools and the use of busing in 1967. Still, these types of programs made little headway for the next decade. A new era of pressure from above began in March 1976, when the Illinois State Board of Education told the Chicago Board of Education that the city was not complying with the state's desegregation rules and that the state would shut off all funds. The city board responded by initiating its "Access to Excellence" strategy.

Chicago school officials pitched "Access to Excellence" as a way of relieving overcrowding in the primarily black schools in its central area, although it was clear that much of the motivation for it was the retention of state funds and avoidance of a federal lawsuit. This 1977 plan aimed at the voluntary transfer of 6,573 black students in fifteen overly crowded schools to fifty-one schools in Chicago's nearly all-white sections. Some would be transported by school bus and some would be given tokens to ride public transportation to their new schools. By the beginning of the 1977 school year, though, only 1,000 black students had chosen to participate in the program, reportedly because of threats of white violence.[59]

The U.S. Supreme Court added to the complications of desegregation in Chicago, and elsewhere in the nation, when it ruled at the beginning of 1977 that the affluent, all-white Chicago suburb of Arlington Heights could enact zoning restrictions that would prevent the building of racially integrated housing for people with moderate and low incomes. To be unconstitutional, the zoning would have had to be clearly racially discriminatory in intent, and not just consequence.[60] This had two important implications for desegregation. First, it raised the requirements for demonstrating discrimination in schools and neighborhoods. Second, it meant that high-income neighborhoods could legally keep out lower-income people, making it more difficult to integrate schools by integrating neighborhoods.

The voluntary busing may have been voluntary on the part of those riding the school buses and using public transportation, but it was far from voluntary from the perspective of those in the suburbs who were receiving the transfers from the central city. Opposition to the desegregation plan was particularly strong on Chicago's Southwest Side. The controversy turned violent on September 11, 1977, when whites from that area held a candlelight vigil in protest, and angry blacks drove a car into the crowd.[61] White mothers picketed the schools that were receiving central city students, and as many as 500 white students staged a walkout.[62]

Just two years after the voluntary desegregation program began in Chicago, a report to the state superintendent of education concluded that the $35 million program had had virtually no impact on desegregating the city's schools. According to the report, 90.3 percent of black students in Chicago would have to be reassigned to white schools in order to accomplish desegregation.[63] By October 1979, based on a two-year investigation by the Department of Health, Education, and Welfare's Office of Civil Rights, the federal government accused Chicago of maintaining segregated schools and demanded that local school officials come up with a plan for redistributing the system's 475,000 students, who were at that time 60 percent black, 22 percent white, 15 percent Hispanic, and 2 percent Asian. The board of education rejected the HEW conditions, laying itself open to the lawsuit it had tried to avoid.[64]

For the next year, Chicago and the federal government negotiated. Finally, on September 24, 1980, the Chicago Board of Education, the U.S. Justice Department, and U.S. district judge Milton I. Shadur came to an agreement on citywide desegregation. The agreement established a broad framework for action, but no specific quotas or numbers of students at particular schools. Acknowledging that demographics dictated that many students would remain in segregated schools, the agreement established that students in majority black or Hispanic schools would be given compensatory education programs. Whereas majority black or Hispanic schools were acceptable, though, majority white schools were another matter. According to Drew S. Days III, assistant U.S. attorney for civil rights, "The board would have a very heavy burden to justify majority white schools."[65]

From the point of view of numbers, the reluctance to allow majority white schools made sense. Whites, after all, had gone down to under 19 percent of the school population by the beginning of the 1980 school year. However, given the reluctance of white parents to place their children in schools in which their own racial group was in the minority, this essentially guaranteed that white flight, a fact of life in Chicago for decades, would take on an added speed and volume.

The Chicago Board of Education passed a new desegregation measure in spring 1981, delaying busing until 1983, and limiting white enrollment to 70 percent of any school. Under this measure, schools with too many white students would have to gradually cut down on their white enrollments. Those who did not succeed in getting rid of white students would have special programs imposed on them, such as receiving forced transfers.[66] Given the pressure by the federal government to do away with majority white schools, the school board action was understandable. Still, it was another clear message that in the name of racial mixing, school officials were pushing the school system more quickly toward being entirely black and Hispanic.

Although white avoidance of majority black schools was certainly not the only reason for white movement out of Chicago, the unwillingness of white families to send their children into schools in which the children would be surrounded by economically disadvantaged minority group members helped to eliminate the remaining white neighborhoods in the city. By the time of the 1980 census, Chicago was "a highly segregated city in which an expanding black ghetto is displacing whites at its leading edge and leaving shattered, abandoned areas in its wake."[67]

The public received a glimpse of a small part of the ongoing cost of desegregation in February 1981, when the Chicago Board of Education special counsel for school desegregation, Robert Howard, billed the school board $87,732 for about five months' legal work on the agreement with the federal government.[68] This was not, of course, the final bill, nor was it the major expense in this process. Represented by Mr. Howard, in 1983, the school board asked Judge Shadur to force the federal government to provide funds for the desegregation agreement the board had made with the government in 1980. Over a two-year period, the Chicago school system had paid $93.6 million in its own money to implement the agreement, and it expected to pay another $67 million in 1983–1984. Since the school board was facing a deficit of $200 million, the members did not know where they would come up with the money.[69]

Chicago had difficulty getting the money out of a federal government that had imposed the expensive line of action on the city and then refused to come up with the funds. After Judge Shadur ordered Washington, to pay for part of Chicago's school desegregation efforts, the U.S. Department of Education responded that it did not have the money and the Justice Department appealed the order. Illinois Democratic Representative Sidney Yates tried to step in by introducing a bill in Congress to give Chicago $20 million. After the bill passed, though, President Ronald Reagan vetoed it, saying that Judge Shadur had violated the principle of separation of the powers of the judiciary and legislature by freezing other forms of federal spending in Chicago until Washington supplied money for the Chicago Board of Education.[70] After the Seventh Circuit U.S. Court of Appeals upheld Judge Shadur's order, in September 1983, Chicago did get its $20 million, but this was less than one-fourth of what the board of education was by then actually spending on desegregation efforts.[71]

Eventually, even the federal judiciary came to recognize that it is not possible to redistribute white students a district does not have. U.S. district judge Charles P. Kocoras declared at the beginning of 2003 that the agreement between the federal government and the district of the 1980s was no longer workable. He ordered the district to come up with a new desegregation plan, which was approved by the court in spring 2004. The only integration possible in Chicago schools in 2004 involved mixing black and Hispanic students. The city's public school students were 51 percent black, 36 percent Hispanic, 9 percent white, and 3 percent Asian.[72]

The federal government forced Chicago to spend millions of dollars on programs that had no discernible impact whatsoever. Although the white proportion of the student population probably would have declined even without desegregation, active efforts to make white students into a minority in any schools they would attend virtually guaranteed that their numbers would shrink to insignificance. Most remarkable of all, the mostly black and Hispanic leaders of the school district still had to negotiate "desegregation plans" with the federal government.

Detroit, Michigan

On April 7, 1970, the Detroit Board of Education adopted a voluntary plan of racial desegregation to begin the following fall. Resistance to the plan on the part of the Michigan legislature led the NAACP to file a suit with the U.S. District Court the following August. The complaint maintained that the Michigan legislature and other officials had interfered with the plan for the desegregation of schools. The NAACP further demanded a plan that would erase "the racial identity of every school in the system and maintain now and hereafter a unitary non-racial school system."[73] This was a tall order, since the public school system of Detroit was already composed overwhelmingly of black students in the early 1970s.

In response to the suit, the U.S. District Court and later a court of appeals sought a metropolitan solution. The Detroit desegregation plan would combine the schools in Detroit, which were about 70 percent black, with fifty-three predominantly white districts in two suburban counties. Supporters of the Detroit plan saw that in many urban areas the only way that any kind of racial mix could be created would be by reaching out to take white students from the suburbs. "The outcome of the Detroit case," wrote one editorialist as the case reached the U.S. Supreme Court, "will materially affect school desegregation in other Northern cities. In Philadelphia and Chicago, for instance, there are not enough white pupils within the city limits to provide racial balance, and the neighboring suburbs are the only source of supply."[74]

The federal courts and the advocates for the metropolitan redistribution of students argued that respecting school district boundaries simply made it possible to maintain dual school systems that were separate, as well as highly unequal—and therefore unconstitutional. Further, many pointed out that school district lines were rather arbitrary lines on maps and that therefore there was no need to approach these as the natural order of nature. Opponents of metropolitan transfers objected that school districts were political entities. Within a district, elected officials made educational policy. Moving students to other districts would essentially be placing them under the jurisdiction of school boards for which their own families and neighbors had no vote. Others argued, on practical grounds, that shipping busloads of inner-city pupils out to the suburbs could either lead to greater sprawl, as white families sought to avoid the impact of widening desegregation, or to a wholesale abandonment of suburban school districts.

The Nixon administration inserted itself into the Detroit issue. Early in 1974, U.S. solicitor general Robert H. Bork urged the Supreme Court to return the Detroit case to the U.S. Court of Appeals for the Sixth District for more evidence that there actually had been a violation of the Constitution that required busing across school districts.[75] On July 25, 1974, the Supreme Court rejected city-to-suburb desegregation in Detroit, with Justices Douglas, White, and Marshall dissenting from the majority opinion. The court observed that differing treatment of white and black students had occurred within the city's school system and that therefore it was the city, not its politically separate neighbors, that must come up with a remedy. Further, the high court ruled that the judiciary of the lower courts were taking as their own the power of elected representatives:

It is obvious from the scope of the inter-district remedy itself that absent a complete restructuring of the laws of Michigan relating to school districts the district court will become first, a defacto "legislative authority" to resolve these complex questions, and then the "school superintendent" for the entire area. This is a task which few, if any judges, are qualified to perform and one which would deprive the people of control of schools through their elected representatives.[76]

Critics of the court's decision argued that it meant that desegregation could not be achieved in urban areas with predominantly black residents. Families throughout the districts that had faced the influx of central city students, though, reacted with jubilation. As one observer wrote, "In the suburbs of Detroit there were expressions of joy today, excited calling of friends to tell them that the Supreme Court had ruled that their school children would not be bused into Detroit."[77]

The president of the Detroit school board, C. L. Golightly, realized that there was no way to desegregate a majority black school system. After the Supreme Court ruling, Golightly said that he saw no point in pursuing a desegregation plan for Detroit, since trying to spread the white minority around would simply result in an all-black system.[78] Despite misgivings such as Golightly's, after the U.S. Supreme Court struck down cross-district busing, U.S. district judge Robert E. Masacio put a citywide desegregation order into effect in early 1976. Masacio wanted to avoid provoking white flight from a city that was already losing its white population. Only 21,853 of the city's 247,500 students would be bused. White students, found mainly on the fringes of the city near suburban areas, would not be sent into the inner city; their schools would just exchange students with nearby predominantly black schools. No currently white school would be allowed to become more than 50 percent black.

Although it is difficult to pinpoint the exact role played by racial redistribution in changing the school population, Detroit did lose nearly all of its white students. By the twenty-first century, demographics had made school desegregation impossible in Detroit, as in so many large American cities. Whites made up only 12 percent of all the people and only 7 percent of the school-aged children in Detroit in 2000. Nearly one out of four of the small number of school-aged white children in Detroit was in a private school in 2000, so that white students were a scant 6 percent of the public school enrollees in Detroit.

Milwaukee, Wisconsin

When the Supreme Court handed down the *Brown* decision, citizens of Wisconsin generally regarded the court's action favorably, but they thought that it concerned other places.[79] Wisconsin's laws, like those of several other northern states and in contrast to the laws of the South, prohibited segregated schooling. Several of Milwaukee's schools were about half black and half white, and the city's free transfer system made it possible for black children to enroll in predominantly white schools.[80]

During the 1950s, a boom in manufacturing drew black Americans from the South to Milwaukee at a rapid pace, so that Milwaukee's black population grew at a much more rapid pace than that of other northern cities, including Chicago and Detroit. The recent migrants flowed into the center of the city, creating rapidly expanding black neighborhoods with residents of much more limited educational backgrounds than those of earlier black and white citizens. In order to address the needs of newly arrived children with limited academic skills, Milwaukee schools in the late 1950s developed programs of compensatory education. These programs tended to separate the southern-origin black students from others precisely because compensatory education was intended to address the special requirements of the migrants.

As Milwaukee's black population grew within the city center, so did the number of public schools with mainly black citizens. Whereas there had been only seven predominantly black schools in 1950, there were an estimated twenty-three by 1964.[81] In the decade after *Brown* as the demand grew for schools that were truly integrated, and not simply open to enrollment without racial discrimination, many black citizens began to see the increasing number of mainly black schools as evidence of an educational ghetto. When inner-city schools became overcrowded as a consequence of the rapidly increasing black population, the Milwaukee school board bused students from the crowded schools to other less-crowded schools, but it maintained a practice known as intact busing. This meant that bused black students formed separate classrooms within white schools, a phenomenon that, in retrospect, ironically mirrored later decades' white magnet classes within black schools.

Opponents of racially identifiable schools joined together in the early 1960s under the leadership of civil rights attorney and NAACP president Lloyd Barbee. Barbee and his followers demanded that the school district place desegregation at the top of its agenda, integrate the intact busing students, and develop a comprehensive desegregation plan. When the school board delayed, the NAACP and its associates turned to protests and legal action.

During the mid-1960s, activists joined together to form the Milwaukee United School Integration Committee (MUSIC), demanding integration through marches and boycotts of segregated black schools. Lloyd Barbee, the chairman of MUSIC and by now elected a state legislator, also acted as attorney in the desegregation case of *Amos v. Board*, filed in 1965 and supported in part by funds from the NAACP Legal Defense Fund. Long delayed by school board maneuvering, the case finally went to trial in September 1973.

While the case made its way through the court, there were efforts to resolve the situation by legislative means. Democratic assemblyman Dennis J. Conta proposed, in the spring of 1975, that the state legislature merge suburban and city schools into a single school district. The mainly white suburban districts of Whitefish Bay and Shorewood, just north of the city, would be joined together with Milwaukee. At the high school level, this would make possible transfers among Milwaukee's Lincoln High School (94% black), Milwaukee's Riverside (61% black), Shorewood High (98% white), and Whitefish Bay High (99% white). Conta proposed to use financial incentives to get the white schools to take minority students, and to cap transfer students at 20 percent of each student body in order to avoid white flight.[82] Conta's attempt to move desegregation from the federal court to the legislature received insufficient support from his fellow legislators, though, and this attempt at self-imposed metropolitan desegregation failed.

In January 1976, federal judge John Reynolds ruled that Milwaukee schools were segregated and that the segregation had been intentionally established by the school board. The judge decreed that black enrollments needed to be driven down between 25 to 45 percent in one third of Milwaukee's schools during the 1975–1976 school year and to go down by a similar proportion in the following two years. There was indeed a substantial basis to the declaration that the schools in Milwaukee were racially segregated. In 158 schools, over 100 were made up of more than 90 percent of a single race.[83] Still, there seems to have been some mathematical implausibility to Judge Reynolds's demand. The proportion of black students in the system had been increasing steadily, from 21 percent of students in the district when the suit began to 34 percent by the time of the decision. Projections indicated that black students would make up 50 percent of those in the district by 1980.[84] The judge does not seem to have given serious consideration to the problem of making black enrollments at specific schools go down rapidly when black enrollments overall were rising at such a rate. Nor does he seem to have contemplated the possibility that his own decision might speed up the shrinking of white enrollments.

Following a second desegregation trial in 1978, the Milwaukee school board began to make serious efforts at desegregation. For a time, optimum racial mixes were easier to achieve, since the school system did reach the predicted half-white, half-black composition in the early 1980s. This was largely attributable to the disappearance of whites from the city's public school system, though, so it did not bode well for the future.

Although Assemblyman Conta's attempt at metropolitan transfers failed, the state of Wisconsin did enact legislation to promote voluntary urban-suburban desegregation throughout the state. Adopted in 1976, Wisconsin Chapter 220 law provided extra funding to white suburban schools that would accept black students from majority black districts. This program has met with some criticism because it has been extremely expensive and, while making it possible for some individual black students to have a wider range of educational choices, it has tended to funnel money into already well-heeled schools. For Milwaukee, with the largest black population in the state, the program also did not bring about any kind of desegregation. Even with Milwaukee's Chapter 220 interdistrict transfers, only 17 percent of Milwaukee's public school students were white in the 2004 school year. Black students, at 60 percent, made up the majority. Hispanics, at 18 percent, were slightly more numerous than whites.

Schools are generally judged to be desegregated if relevant racial or ethnic groups are within plus or minus 15 percent of their representation as a whole in the district. For Milwaukee, this means that when Judge Reynolds made his 1976 decision, any desegregated school would have been a majority white school, but at least one in five of its students would have been black. By 2004, though, a Milwaukee school could be considered "desegregated" if only 3 percent of its students were white. These are the paradoxical mathematics of racial redistribution.

Los Angeles, California

The desegregation fight in Los Angeles began with the case of *Crawford v. Board of Education* in 1963, when black parents filed a suit on behalf of black and Latino students to enable minority children to attend then all-white schools.[85] The California district's first desegregation trial was held in 1967, when white students were a majority of 55 percent. On February 11, 1970, superior court judge Alfred Gitelson found that the school board had operated a segregated system and he ordered it to take action to desegregate. The school board appealed, and in March 1975 the court of appeal found in favor of the board. In turn, though, this finding was appealed by the American Civil Liberties Union. At the end of June 1976, the California Supreme Court upheld the 1970 ruling by Judge Gitelson. Although the state high court reversed a part of Judge Gitelson's ruling that defined desegregation in terms of specific percentages of students, it ordered the school board to alleviate all the effects of segregation, regardless of the cause of segregation, and show progress toward that end.

During 1977, the L.A. school board submitted a desegregation plan to the California Supreme Court and began hearings on the plan. In February 1978, Judge Paul Egly issued an order approving the board's plan as a first step toward desegregation. The following year, Egly ordered that mandatory re-assignments of students from current to new schools cover grades 1 through 9 by September 1980, and then include all other grades by 1983.

Judge Egly's order was complicated by many of the characteristics of Los Angeles. It is a huge district, covering 700 square miles, with minority students most heavily concentrated in South Central Los Angeles. This meant that extremely long daily bus rides would be required to redistribute the city's students. Many of the districts where the white students lived were surrounded by other suburban school districts, making white movement to less-threatened school environments relatively easy. Los Angeles was a harbinger of the future in many other metropolitan areas because its ethnic composition was far more complex than a simple division between black and white. Some of these other ethnic groups, such as Mexican Americans, felt that the desegregation program was not in their own interests.[86] The Los Angeles plan did not appear to take any of these complications into consideration. It was an abstract blueprint imposed from above.

Spurred largely by events in Los Angeles, California voters approved Proposition 1 in 1979, amending the state constitution to prohibit any more busing or school transfers than required under the U.S. Constitution. Although this ended mandatory busing in Los Angeles in 1981 after the Court of Appeals upheld the proposition, voluntary busing of students for school desegregation did continue under a plan approved by Judge Robert B. Lopez in September 1981. Thus, the school system bused 57,000 voluntary school transferees in 1985. The local NAACP criticized the program in that year, though, because almost all of those being bused were black students. The civil rights organization maintained that a serious attempt to desegregate Los Angeles schools would require busing white students into South Central Los Angeles. Interestingly, Latino education leaders opposed busing, instead favoring greater spending on neighborhood schools within Latino areas.[87]

Los Angeles also tried to desegregate through the common strategy of magnet schools, offering special educational programs in the hopes of appealing to members of all racial groups. The magnet schools tried to maintain enrollments that were 40 percent white and 60 percent nonwhite, but in the early 1980s, they were already finding it difficult to meet the 40 percent target for white students.[88] In 1982, as many as ten of the district's eighty-four magnet schools contained no white students at all, and eighteen had fewer than 20 percent white students. Only thirty-three were at approximately the target enrollments.[89] Many of the magnet schools were also not providing students with the quality of education promised, and they provided educations that were expensive for taxpayers but failed to achieve "either distinction or integration."[90]

Meanwhile, faced with declining social environments in low-income majority black schools, many concerned black parents began behaving exactly like middle-class whites and engaging in various forms of "black flight." "Some . . . are manipulating the school system to their children's advantage [by using false addresses to enroll their children in other school districts]. Others are busing their children to schools in white neighborhoods, placing them in special programs, or leaving the public school system altogether."[91]

Fight over judicial control of the schools continued, even after the U.S. Supreme Court upheld Proposition 1. In 1985, voters in West San Fernando Valley, the heart of opposition to busing, elected busing critic and academic David Armor to the L.A. school board out of fear that the area would return to a mandatory program of transporting students around the area.[92]

Trying to maintain elusive racial balances became increasingly difficult as the population of Los Angeles changed over the course of the 1980s. In 1987, with numbers of minority students in the district rapidly increasing, the school board voted to increase minority enrollments to 70 percent at forty-eight magnet schools, while still designating the schools as "integrated."[93] The changing of ratios was controversial. Some critics accused the school board of intentionally creating segregated schools. Others, particularly in the Valley, were upset because bringing down the acceptable proportion of white students in magnet schools to 30 percent would lower the number of white students who could get into those schools. School board member Roberta Weintraub, speaking to white parents from the Valley, complained, "I'm really tired of our Valley schools getting shafted. My perception is that we will have a massive pullout of the middle class."[94]

With decreasing opportunities for the white middle-class families, many tried devious maneuvers to place their children in desirable school environments. School officials responded with intensified efforts at control. Child-care transfers became a common strategy. District policy permitted parents to transfer their children out of their designated schools if the schools did not provide before- or afterschool childcare or if the parents had arranged for off-campus childcare near another school. The board found that white parents were using fraudulent child-care claims to transfer their children out of minority dominated schools to predominantly white schools. Thus, in summer 1988 the board began to refuse this type of exemption to white students transferring into schools that were 70 percent or more white.[95] In the name of desegregation, which had originally meant allowing minority students to attend white schools, Los Angeles had begun officially approving schools that were mostly black or Latino while energetically discouraging schools that were mostly white.

By June 1988, the pointlessness of the district's long and expensive desegregation suit had become clear. Judge A. Wallace Tashima granted a conditional dismissal of the case that had begun in 1963, and directed the NAACP and the school district to resolve their differences. According to school district counsel Peter James, the dismissal came from the recognition that little could be done to desegregate a school system that was just 17 percent white.[96] After bitter and difficult negotiations between the two parties, the judge finally dismissed the suit in March 1989, twenty-six years after its beginning. The white proportion of public schools had dropped still further from the previous year, to less than 16 percent. The *Los Angeles Times* reported that there was a wide and persistent gap in academic achievement between the minority students and the small number of whites who were left. "More than 20 years after the Los Angeles Unified School District began its original busing program to integrate schools, the minority pupils in that program are doing little or no better than the students they leave behind in segregated schools and much worse than their white classmates."[97]

Pasadena, California

Pasadena, far from the well-televised civil rights fight in the South, had its own form of segregation in the 1960s. White and black families lived in different neighborhoods, and residential housing patterns maintained segregated schools. In 1970, federal district judge Manuel Real ordered Pasadena to desegregate its schools and to begin transferring students from largely black to largely white institutions. The white proportion of the population had been declining in Pasadena since just after World War II, but in 1970 it began a precipitous drop. In that first year of desegregation alone, about 3,000 students withdrew from the district.[98] Although there were no all-black or all-white schools after 1970, from 1970 to 1973 the percentages of whites in the district fell from 49.6 percent to 43.6 percent in kindergarten through sixth grade and from 58.2 to 50.1 in junior and senior high schools.[99]

The desegregation program imposed by Judge Real was so widely hated that it became a major political issue. In March 1973, voters in Pasadena elected an anti-busing majority to the school board by a wide margin. Henry Mareschi, leader of the anti-busing faction, argued that half the decline in whites was attributable to white flight resulting from busing and that if the situation continued, the school population would be only 10 percent white by 1980.[100]

Though substantial, Mareschi overestimated the white decline. When the court order was finally lifted in 1980, white school enrollment had gone down to 29.1 percent of all students, from 53.7 percent when desegregation began. Neither can all of this drop in white students be attributed to desegregation. More minority students, especially Latinos, entered the public school system. Still, it was undeniable that white flight had occurred. Private school enrollments had grown from 19 percent of Pasadena pupils at the start of the court order up to 26 percent by its conclusion. White families had moved into other school districts in order to remove their children from the contentious system. "It was not only white flight, but bright flight," lamented school board member Katie Nack. "We lost some of our best minority students too, because of fear of what might happen and because of relaxation of educational standards."[101]

The events of the 1970s gave the system a reputation as one to avoid, so that middle-class people, whether white or of other ethnic and racial groups, often did not flee the schools so much as they did not enter them at all. The incoming director of Pasadena's testing program, William A. Bibiani, complained, "When I was looking for a house here, several realtors subtly, or not so subtly, hinted that I ought to consider private schools."[102] Mr. Bibiani rejected the realtors' hints, but many homebuyers without his connection to the public school system would have taken the realtors' suggestions more seriously.

Some busing for purposes of racial redistribution continued after the end of Pasadena's desegregation court order. School officials also tried to draw school attendance boundaries in order to get the greatest possible mix of white, black, Hispanic, and Asian students. Still, the demographics dictated that many schools would be overwhelmingly composed of one ethnic or racial group.

Declines in the white student population continued into the twenty-first century. By 2002, the 23,000-pupil district was 85 percent minority. The families of the relatively few white students who remained in the public school system managed to place their children in classrooms composed largely of other whites. Del Yarborough, the president of the Pasadena NAACP and a long-time teacher and principal in the schools, observed, "We may have had integration in the schools, but segregated classrooms."[103]

The small number of white students in the Pasadena schools was not only a result of the fact that white families had withdrawn from the area. Those who argued for ending busing in the early twenty-first century maintained

that "resegregation is improbable because so many of Pasadena's neighborhoods have become residentially integrated."[104] In reality, racial integration of
the schools was impossible with so few whites left in the public school system. The substantial numbers of whites remaining in the area attended over
thirty private schools.

New York City

During the late 1960s and early 1970s, southern political leaders accused
northerners of hypocrisy for vigorously pursuing desegregation in the South
while schools and other institutions continued to be segregated in the North.
It was true that in the nation's largest urban center, New York, schools were
generally identifiable by race. In the four boroughs of the Bronx, Manhattan,
Brooklyn, and Queens, there were roughly 600 public elementary schools in
1970, and half of these were either 90 percent or more white or 90 percent or
more black.[105] In fact, a New York state anti-busing law passed by the state
legislature in May 1969 sought to avoid judicially mandated racial balancing
by specifying that only elected school boards could assign students to schools.
The New York law, held unconstitutional by a federal court in October 1970,
was widely copied by southern school districts as a strategy for avoiding desegregation.[106]

The New York City boroughs made some efforts on their own to achieve
racial integration through busing and school rezoning. These resulted in a
number of conflicts. Responding to a plan by the Board of Education of
Queens to rezone schools for more even racial combinations, the president of
the Martin Van Buren High School PTA declared, "They're talking about integrated schools. Well, they're going to have segregated schools. Because
people will move out, that's all. Or put their children in private schools or
parochial schools."[107] In spring 1971, episodes of violence broke out between
black and white students at South Shore High School in Brooklyn.[108] A mother
and father of a public school student, who had fled the Soviet Union a few
years earlier, complained about the treatment received by their son in a newly
integrated school:

> Each school year he [the son] received certificates for his achieve-
> ments. . . . This year, after attending school for two days in the sixth
> grade, he refused to go any longer. For participating actively in class,
> he has been called "Jewish faggot" and shot at with paper clips from
> catapults by his black classmates, because he "knows everything." . . .
> No teacher can start anything with students of such different ranges. . . .

They [the black students] scatter the free lunches, preferring to extort food more to their taste—and money too—from their white classmates who are a minority and defenseless.[109]

The parents' characterizations of their son's black classmates were probably unfair generalizations from the behavior of a few, and one should be cautious about taking such reports at face value. The conflicts at South Shore certainly involved members of both racial groups and could have been sparked by white hostility. Still, these events testify to the disruptions of New York's efforts at student redistribution, and concerns about the difficulties of teaching students with a wide range of preparation were well founded.

The earliest federal actions in New York were limited in scope. In January 1974, Judge Jack B. Weinstein directed the city's board of education to devise a rezoning plan to integrate Brooklyn's Mark Twain Junior High. Four months later, Judge John F. Dooling, Jr., criticized the board for allowing racial imbalances, and he ordered the members to redraw the boundaries of Franklin K. Lane School, also in Brooklyn, which was attended mainly by black and Puerto Rican students. A local resident of the Lane school district agreed with the judge's decision, remarking that "over the years the Board has gerrymandered our area into an all black school district." At the same time, though, the same man also observed that "the whites who got zoned in [to the Lane district] stopped sending their children to Franklin K. Lane and either sent them to Catholic schools or got addresses so they could qualify for other districts."[110] He did not, apparently, consider the possibility that rezoning would produce a rapid increase in false addresses and Catholic school applications.

All officials recognized that housing patterns complicated the issue of racial balances in schools. Judge Weinstein tried to tie the desegregation of Mark Twain Junior High to an effort to bring more whites into nearby housing projects. The board of education raised the possibility of reaching into the suburbs for whites. "Given shifting population patterns—the movement of the middle class to the suburbs—and the declining number of 'others' [whites] in the city's public schools," declared the board in a report to the New York State Board of Regents, "the task of achieving meaningful integration within the boundaries of New York City or other large cities becomes increasingly difficult."[111]

Over the following years, desegregation in New York City proceeded largely on a school-by-school basis. To create greater racial diversity at virtually all-black Andrew Jackson High School in Brooklyn, for example, beginning in 1976 the board of education set up a special "choice of admissions" zone to encourage white enrollments and move black students elsewhere. The zone plan gave black children who would otherwise go to Jackson the option of selecting any schools in the city with white enrollments of greater than 50 percent (commonly referred to as majority-to-minority transfers). At the same time, white students within the zone were required to enroll in majority black schools, severely limiting their choices of admissions. White students and their families were not cooperating with the plan. The *New York Times* reported that "many white students in these zones have chosen to attend private or parochial schools in the city or elsewhere."[112]

Federal District Judge John Dooling, recognizing that the zone plan was not working at Jackson, ordered the district to come up with another one in 1979. An appeals court overturned the judge's decision, though, on the grounds that Jackson and other city schools were becoming all-minority because of changing demographics and residential patterns, not because of intentional actions by school officials. An editorial writer, at that time, argued that the real problem was white flight to suburban areas and that New York should pursue a metropolitan solution, reaching into places such as nearly all-white Nassau County. The writer did not say how those pulled in from the suburbs could be restrained from doing precisely what the generally less economically advantaged whites within the city were already doing: leaving the public system.[113]

Meanwhile, the school boards of New York tried to engage in desperate juggling maneuvers to keep schools as integrated as possible, avoid overcrowding, and keep whites, who made up only 30 percent of New York students at the end of the 1970s, from fleeing the area. To relieve enrollment pressures on Intermediate School (I.S.) 231, for example, and to minimize white flight, in 1978 the Queens school board created a new school, drawing students from the mixed-race, middle-class neighborhood of Rosedale. Rosedale had already been losing white residents, but the creation of a new, more middle-class school helped to slow down their departure. The president of the school board in School District 29 of Queens, Dolores Grant, explained that "white students were fleeing. That was a fact of life. It was not hearsay. The annex [the new school] helped turn that around."[114] Federal authorities would have none of the explanations of the Queens school board. On August 29, 1979, the Federal Office for Civil Rights gave the board thirty days to desegregate I.S. 231 or lose $3.5 million in federal education funds.[115]

The redistribution of white students from the mostly white Rosedale annex of I.S. 231 to the mostly black I.S. 231 provoked what may have been New York City's greatest desegregation controversy. During summer 1980, New York City Public School Chancellor Frank J. Macchiarola, pushed by the threat of losing funds, ordered that 450 seventh and eighth graders be transferred from the mostly white annex to the predominantly black main school. The transfer would result in white students becoming a minority of 15 percent in their new school. In taking this action, the chancellor overrode the authority of local School Board 29. The president of the local school board, Joseph Albergo, answered by saying that the transfers would result in overcrowding, as well as racial tensions. "No parent in his right mind will send his child to that school, especially under these conditions."[116] Ironically, the annex was one of the city's more integrated schools, since it contained about 40 black and 330 white children, whereas many of New York's schools consisted solely of minority students.[117] An editorial writer at the time observed:

> The loss of more white students would make district 29 resemble more closely the many community school districts in New York City in which meaningful integration is no longer possible because of a dwindling white enrollment in the public schools, which citywide are now less than one-third white. Meanwhile, parochial and other private schools in the five boroughs, which have a combined enrollment of 312,647 are two-thirds white.[118]

The battle over the Rosedale annex took place in the courts and out. Parents of students in the annex, which was located within the mostly white Public School (P.S.) 138 elementary school of Rosedale, sought to appeal the chancellor's order to the court, only to have the appeal dismissed early in 1981. Macchiarola came under additional pressure from the federal government when, at about the same time as the dismissal of the appeal, the Federal Office of Civil Rights declared that the annex was illegal because it had resulted in the segregation of the main school. Angry parents in majority white Rosedale declared a boycott of majority black I.S. 231.[119]

The parents of students at the forbidden annex occupied the building and staged sit-ins. New York mayor Ed Koch barred their eviction, expressing some sympathy for the protestors and seeking a peaceful resolution to the problem. People in the neighborhood claimed that the closing of their local middle school and the transfer of their children to another neighborhood constituted a fatal assault on their community. Joseph Albergo, the fiery school board head, declared, "They're [the federal authorities and the city government] the ones doing the segregating. All these billions of dollars haven't done a thing, but our community became naturally integrated, and they want to destroy it."[120]

During the first week of February 1981, police officers swooped down on the Rosedale annex, evicted protestors, and arrested the few who refused to leave. As word of the evictions spread throughout the community, about 250 demonstrators gathered in front of the school with homemade signs. Local parents declared that they would continue their boycott and refuse to send their children to I.S. 231.[121]

New York's Mayor Koch and Chancellor Macchiarola both criticized the protesting parents for their disregard of the law. Many black parents and several black officials were offended at the unwillingness of the Rosedale inhabitants to send their children to a school where whites would be a small minority and insisted that the Rosedale parents should follow policies established by the city and the federal government. Dr. Shirley Rose, a black school board member, declared, "If they feel that the public school system cannot satisfy their needs they have the right to go to private schools."[122] Responding to Dr. Rose, an assistant principal at Benjamin Cardozo High School observed:

Unfortunately that [white middle-class movement to private schools] is precisely what will happen. At a time when pressure is being put on Congress to pass laws that will bring about a voucher system and/or tax tuition credits, public education needs all the friends it can get. What is happening in Rosedale is hastening the demise of the public schools. The middle class is being told it is not wanted. How can any system of public education function without the support of the backbone of its community?[123]

The people of the Rosedale neighborhood defended their protest marches and sit-ins as desperate measures, intended to save a community centered around its schools. Rosedale was a small working-class enclave surrounded by poverty and urban deterioration. Mrs. Sandra Petker, an active PTA member, explained that "closing the annex would be the beginning of the end, absolutely. Whites have been staying in Rosedale because of the schools. If the community starts moving because of the closed annex, I'd have to move too."[124]

By the beginning of the 1981–1982 school year, appeals to the courts to reopen the Rosedale annex had been decisively defeated and the boycott had come to an end. Reportedly, 10 to 15 percent of the students who enrolled at I.S. 231 were white, and the racial mixture was judged sufficient to qualify the school for a $300 million federal grant through the Emergency School Act to promote desegregation.[125]

We can never know for certain if retaining neighborhood schools would have stemmed white movement out of the boroughs of New York or out of the city public school system. All the indications suggest that maintaining schools such as the Rosedale annex would have at least slowed the process. This is counterfactual history, though, and there is no way to convince those who prefer to believe otherwise. We do know that attempts to redistribute students for desegregation did not desegregate the schools. The proportion of white students in New York schools had gone down from 30 percent at the end of the 1970s to just 15 percent in the 2002–2003 school year. This was slightly more than the 13 percent who were Asian. Hispanics had displaced black students as the largest category in the city, since 34 percent of those on the New York City public school rolls were black in 2002–2003 and 38 percent were classified as Hispanic. In the formerly white enclave of Rosedale, the Rosedale elementary school was 93.5 percent black and 4.8 percent Hispanic. P.S. 138, where the Rosedale annex had been housed, was 88.9 percent black and 6.8 percent Hispanic. I.S. 231 had become the Magnetech 231 Educational Center, offering special magnet programs. Two decades after it was a center of the desegregation controversy in New York, this middle school was 90.9 percent black and 6.3 percent Hispanic.[126]

WHAT HAPPENED IN THESE DISTRICTS?

We have taken these short case studies from desegregation cases around the nation. Choosing a wide sampling of school districts from the northeastern, southern, midwestern, and western parts of the United States, we made no effort to select cases that would support our argument. In fact, we left out some of the most notorious, such as the Boston struggle that we described in an earlier chapter. Some of the districts included here are in large, old industrial cities. Others, such as Dallas and Baton Rouge, are in postindustrial, mostly suburban metropolitan areas. One is struck, though, by an essential sameness that runs throughout. In none of these districts did desegregation really seem to work out as intended.

Despite the general similarity among the districts, we can identify some patterns. These patterns occurring in history are strikingly similar to what we suggested, in the previous chapter, would result from schools as markets of exclusivity. In a number of the locations, attempts to redistribute students were followed by the near abandonment of entire districts by whites. The huge public school system of New York, the nation's largest classic urban area, became an almost entirely minority school district. Even little pockets of white representation such as Rosedale, ironically more racially integrated than the city as a whole, were wiped out. Chicago and Milwaukee, also old industrial centers, became cities in which white students were extremely rare.

Some may argue that whites left New York, Chicago, and Milwaukee for reasons that had nothing to do with the schools, that this was simply a reflection of white abandonment of the cities for the suburbs. Undoubtedly, schools were not the only cause of movement to the suburbs. However, such a defense of coercive desegregation policies would be strange indeed. Essentially, such a defense maintains that the policies would have worked if only demographic realities had been more cooperative.

The claim that schools had nothing to do with suburbanization rings hollow, though. Repeatedly, parents proclaimed that they were leaving desegregating districts because of their school situations. Later, the same groups of people who said that they were leaving because of desegregation were gone. Surely, one has to consider the possibility that actions had something to do with clearly stated intentions. In addition, the abandonment of desegregating districts was not only a movement from central cities to suburbs. Largely suburban districts, such as Los Angeles, Dallas, and Baton Rouge, also lost their white students.

All the districts that saw whites moving across district lines had at least one characteristic in common: there were other places to go. In this respect, the urban-suburban question was relevant. Moving out of New York or Chicago, or settling in a suburb upon moving to one of these metropolitan areas, meant that the disproportionately middle-class white families could put their relatively well-prepared children into schools with other children who were academically well-prepared. Their children would be surrounded daily by others who saw higher education as a natural next step and who did reasonably well on most measures of academic achievement. Movement from cities to suburbs, though, was only a part of the general search for places with better schools, as well as safer, more comfortable neighborhoods.

Most of these locations did see white movement out of desegregating districts. In many cases, this was also followed by middle-class black movement and "bright flight." In some situations, though, whites and middle-class blacks did remain in school systems. Little Rock's High School, opened to black enrollment before the era of coercive redistribution of students became a majority black school, but it did retain a substantial white student body. Charlotte, a critical district in the history of coercive desegregation, actually retained a large white proportion even with its busing program. Why, then, wasn't there white flight from these places?

Part of the answer is that there were few more desirable places to go. Charlotte was not surrounded by potentially desirable school districts, and it included the school area of Charlotte-Mecklenburg. Districts that did not have competing districts had effective monopolies in which the educational product could be manipulated and customers would still be likely to consume it. This suggests that efforts at metropolitan desegregation were based on a sound approach that would have made good sense to John D. Rockefeller. If there is a challenge to a monopoly, extend the monopoly to include it. The problem with this reasoning is that if the perceived quality of the product deteriorates far enough, the customers who have the mobility and financial resources will travel pretty far for an alternative. In Indianapolis, the historical testimony indicates that whites moved beyond the distant reach of the metropolitan public schools.

A variation on the interdistrict approach might be to keep the educational markets essentially segregated by geography while giving a small number of disadvantaged students access to the better schools. The number has to be kept small, of course, because large influxes of the disadvantaged would change the quality of education in the better schools. This was essentially the kind of metropolitan strategy employed by St. Louis and by Wisconsin's Chapter 220. This is good for giving individual black students who want to attend majority white schools the opportunity to do so. But it does nothing to change racial balances or to redesign American society.

Even when a wide geographic area is included in the educational monopoly, this still does not shut down all alternatives to the mixed schools intended by judicial desegregation. Private and parochial schools continue to compete with the public school system. As the value of public school education goes down with redistribution, those who can make the sacrifices become more willing to pay the costs of private education. The districts we have considered here generally have very high rates of private school attendance. Parents said that they were moving to private schools in order to avoid desegregation. In the case of Baton Rouge, we have been able to document white movement into nonpublic schools, and indeed the creation of nonpublic schools, immediately following a judge's order to redistribute students by race.

Both the shift to private schools and the shift to other public districts have clear financial implications for desegregating districts. Those whose children attend nonpublic schools basically pay for education twice. They pay tuition where their children actually attend, and they pay taxes for the public schools their children do not attend. It is not surprising that areas with high private school enrollments frequently have difficulty raising taxes for school spending. This makes the problem of inequality in school funding even greater. School districts that already have poor schools because they enroll students with limited preparation for schooling are further penalized by restricted funding.

Parents in one district are generally reluctant to have their money shifted to another district. Sermons about the duty to treat all young people equally may induce guilt. But they will rarely succeed in getting people to agree to spend less of their money on the preparation of their own children and more of their money on schools their children cannot attend.

Finally, moving from one public school district to another and enrolling in private schools does not exhaust all the options. The value of an education is established by classmates. Since there is a large and continuing achievement gap between black and white students, under most conditions families will want to look for classes composed mainly of whites, although race would certainly be irrelevant in a class that contained top-notch students from all racial groups. When *de facto* segregation between schools is reduced by redistributing students, then segregation within schools tends to be one of the results.

Magnet programs, gifted and talented programs, and other kinds of elite public school education are often criticized as providing private schools inside of public schools. But if those kinds of special offerings were not available, the students in them would not remain in supposedly desegregated public school systems. In addition, magnet and related programs must be elite in character. They must be restricted to those with high levels of academic achievement in order to attract and hold the best students. If they just offer unusual and interesting areas of instruction, then they will attract a wider range of students and the educational quality will go down.

Magnets that are filled through test scores tend to be mainly white as a result of the test score gap. Thus, Little Rock's Central High, a shrine to the history of school integration, still has segregated classes as a result of tracking. When magnets drop achievement as an entrance requirement and attempt to hold on to white students by guaranteeing them places through quotas, this creates new problems. A supposed tool for desegregation becomes a means of intentionally giving whites access to special resources while systematically denying equal treatment to blacks. Since the quality of the programs is not maintained by restricting entry to the highly qualified, whites can frequently find better educational products elsewhere. As in Prince George's County, school systems end up keeping black students out of magnet classrooms in order to hold open places to attract white students who are not coming.

Behind these stories of districts, then, we can see families making choices about educational products, the value of which is established by exclusivity. If they can, members of a middle-class family will move into a neighborhood with a highly reputed public school, paying a higher mortgage than they may pay elsewhere. It is a good school because it is attended by children from their own neighborhood, all of whom have relatively good preparation and come from families who are actively seeking educational advantages. To say that it is a "good school" is to say that it is better than others, since good is a relative quality and schools are necessarily in competition if they are not to sink into a general mediocrity.

When a judge or other authority begins to redistribute the advantages and disadvantages of schools by redistributing students, the good school is no longer so desirable. The family begins to look for other ways to give children an education that will prepare them for a highly competitive society. As in Beaumont, the family may put its home up for sale and move where there is no forced redistribution. Or, it may do a "virtual" move, entering an educational black market by seeking a false address for school enrollment. Or, it may leave the public system altogether and go to the private sector, where the costs may be greater, but where there is no pretense of equality. Or, instead of moving segregation upward by abandoning a public school district, families may move segregation downward by demanding tracking and honors classes in order to retain its competitive advantages while participating in the illusion of redistribution.

As we discussed in Chapter 4, a major factor that accounts for the "advantage" of middle-class schools is the greater availability of "social capital" that leads to the enhanced academic outcomes of students immersed in these beneficial school environments. On the other hand, schools populated with large proportions of low-SES black and Hispanic students suffer from a lack of social capital and as a consequence are characterized by environments that hurt academic achievement. These disparities, we believe, help explain the continuing racial achievement gap, which we explore in more detail in the next chapter.

CHAPTER 7

School Desegregation and the Racial Achievement Gap

Now, we focus on the very real racial achievement gap in the United States. We pay particularly close attention to the black-white gap in academic outcomes, but we also consider the Hispanic-white gap. Asian academic achievement is examined as well, since this fast-growing racial group constitutes an increasingly important presence in American schools, with implications for school desegregation policy. We consider how school desegregation was supposed to reduce the achievement gap, but why there remains a stubborn difference between the average achievement levels of whites, blacks, and Hispanics after fifty years of concerted public efforts to reduce these differences. We summarize the findings of major research studies that have examined how the racial achievement gap has been influenced by a variety of factors over the years. We try to answer the central questions, "Do blacks perform better in majority white schools?" and "Does white academic performance suffer in majority black schools?" We examine how the racial and socioeconomic composition of classrooms and schools influence individual student achievement.

As we have demonstrated in earlier chapters, school desegregation efforts have been mostly spectacular failures, at least in terms of achieving court-ordered racial ratios. But is there even such a reality as an ideal school racial composition that leads to the enhanced performance of disadvantaged minorities? And if such a magical ratio exists, do the academics of the more advantaged majority students suffer at the expense of the poorer minority students? Finally, we ask what can realistically be done to reduce the racial achievement gap if engineering the racial composition of schools, as we have seen in the previous chapter, is not a viable policy option.

A CONTROVERSIAL TOPIC

Writing about race and its relationship to intelligence and school performance is a difficult enterprise. When these issues have been confronted head-on, they have been controversial. Consider the case of Arthur Jensen, the UC Berkeley professor of psychology who was critical of the effectiveness of the educational programs created in the mid-1960s to raise black achievement levels. Jensen published an article in 1969 suggesting that these programs were not as successful as expected because the IQ gap between whites and blacks was more likely to have a genetic than an environmental basis.[1] His study provoked a firestorm of reaction and has since made him a pariah among certain groups in academia. Indeed, although Jensen was regarded by many as one of the preeminent scholars on the subject of IQ, with well over 400 refereed articles in scientific journals, his highly regarded book *The G Factor* was rejected by ten publishers before Praeger published his work in 1998.[2]

Recall that Jensen's 1969 article was published during the heyday of the Civil Rights Movement, and the moral momentum behind the movement was reaching its apex. The country was focused on crafting social and educational programs and policies to undo centuries of injustices against black Americans. To suggest that some African American academic shortcomings might not be improved by social policy, but were in fact a consequence of genetic makeup, smacked of racism to some people. Still, the issue did not become any less sensitive over time. Fifteen years after Jensen's controversial article, the book *The Bell Curve* by Harvard professors Richard Herrnstein and Charles Murray provoked similar outrage when its authors suggested that ethnic and racial differences in "cognitive ability" were largely genetically based, and these differences accounted for differences in class and social structure in the United States.[3] When *The Bell Curve*'s editor, Erwin Glikes, and the lead author, Herrnstein, died just before the book was published, some pointed out that the book was cursed—ostensibly because its conclusions were so odious.[4]

In fact, it is simply difficult to talk about any dimension of race and its connection to genetics, let alone race and IQ. The lead author experienced this difficulty firsthand when teaching a course on race and education to a very bright, very diverse group of graduate students as a visiting professor at McGill University. As a group, we had an interesting time just trying to obtain general agreement in the classroom that specific, completely separate racial categories of humans exist at all (hint: there's some shifting sand underneath all this). So for now, in order to even proceed with a discussion about a racial achievement gap, we will have to proceed under the general assumption that there are distinct "white" and "black" and "Hispanic" and

"Asian" categories of people. Moreover, we will move forward under the assumption that these groups of people may differ not only physically in appearance in systematically observable ways but also in how they perform academically. The federal government certainly believes this to be the case and, certainly, seems rather obsessed with the notions of race, ethnicity, and academic outcomes. Indeed, one of the mandates of the No Child Left Behind Act is that education authorities track the academic performance of subcategories of students, including racial categories, over time. So, we will apparently be obsessing with race and academic outcomes for some time to come.

There have been a variety of explanations, some of which we have dealt with earlier, for why there continues to be a stubborn gap between how certain racial and ethnic groups perform in school and on achievement tests. This is a very delicate subject, and some of the explanations may make us uncomfortable. However, if as a society we are serious about creating equal educational opportunities for all and reducing or perhaps even eliminating racial and ethnic differences in achievement, then we must first understand why these gaps exist in the first place. In this spirit of intellectual openness, we compare the academic performance of the major racial and ethnic groups in America. We also consider the issue of racial bias in testing and the effects of school racial concentration on individual academic performance. We try to answer the questions, "Are further efforts at school desegregation likely to reduce the racial achievement gap?" and "Are there negative academic consequences associated with trying to reduce the gap through orchestrating the racial populations of schools?"

IS THERE REALLY A GAP?

Yes. There is widespread agreement among academics of all stripes that on just about every measure of academic achievement, students classified as black (or African American) and Hispanic in the United States perform markedly lower than students classified as whites or Asians.[5] There is really only one comprehensive, national, statistically representative test administered in the United States that allows for long-term valid comparisons in achievement between white, black, Hispanic, and Asian grade school students. It is the National Assessment of Education Progress (NAEP). Often referred to as *The Nation's Report Card*, the NAEP has periodically been administered to American students ages 9, 13, and 17 since the early 1970s.[6] The NAEP first began testing students' knowledge of math, reading, and science. Writing was added to the test in 1984. The most recent data publicly available from the long-term version of the NAEP come from 1999.

What do the NAEP results show? Blacks and Hispanics have lagged far behind first whites, and then Asians, from the NAEP's first administration, in every subject area and at every age level tested. The largest gap between blacks and whites since both subgroups first took the test in 1970 is in science, and the smallest gap is in math—though it remains sizable. In general, Hispanics have performed better on the NAEP than have blacks, though the white-Hispanic gap remains a large one. The good news is that though there is still a statistically significant racial gap in all subject areas and age levels on the NAEP, the white-black and white-Hispanic gaps narrowed noticeably between the early 1970s and 1999 for all subjects and ages. The achievement gap between whites and blacks has narrowed most significantly for seventeen-year-olds on the reading test.

Figures 7.1, 7.2, and 7.3 provide a longitudinal picture of white, Hispanic, and black NAEP reading scores for ages 9, 13, and 17. To gain an idea of the magnitude of the differences between whites and blacks on reading scores and have a sense of how much the gap has narrowed, consider that on a 500-point test the average white seventeen-year-old reading score in 1971 was 291, whereas the average black score was 239 (Hispanics were not identified at this time). By 1999, the average white score for seventeen-year-olds in reading had risen only 4 points, to 295, whereas the comparable black score had

Figure 7.1
Age 9 NAEP Scaled Reading Test Scores

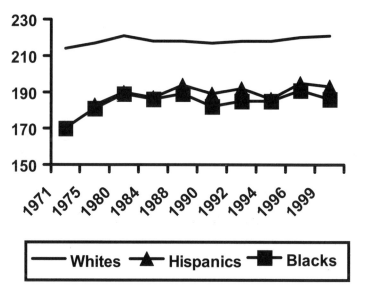

Figure 7.2
Age 13 NAEP Scaled Reading Test Scores

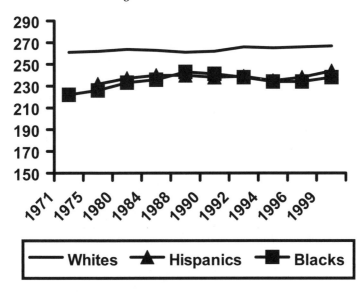

Figure 7.3
Age 17 NAEP Scaled Reading Test Scores

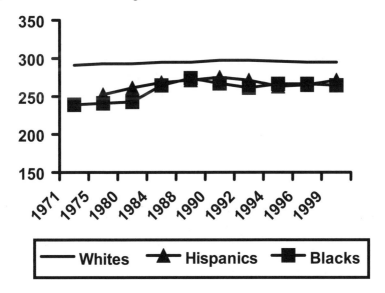

risen much more dramatically, climbing 25 points to 264. Thus, the black-white gap for seventeen-year-olds in reading diminished over this nineteen-year period from 52 to 31 points. This represents a 42 percent reduction in the gap, a significant narrowing by any measure.

In overall terms, though, neither black nor white scores showed much improvement during the 1990s. In fact, in a potentially alarming trend, black scores in reading—arguably the most important foundational academic skill—declined for thirteen- and seventeen-year-olds over the decade of the 1990s. Also, reading scores for seventeen-year-old whites and Hispanics decreased during the 1990s as well. Perhaps more ominous still, during the decade of the 1990s, the black-white gap in math increased at all age levels: 9, 13, and 17. The Hispanic-white gap in math increased at ages 9 and 17 from the 1990 to the 1999 administration of the NAEP. In short, the biggest reductions in the black-white achievement gap took place during the 1970s and 1980s. In reading, over the decade of the 1990s the black-white gap did not narrow at any age, and increased at ages 13 and 17. In science, where we noted the single largest reduction in the black-white gap since 1970, over the 1990s the black-white gap actually increased at every age level tested in this subject.

Thus, we may be seeing a disturbing trend of an increasing black-white achievement gap nationally, at every age level measured, and in every subject area tested by the long-term version of *The Nation's Report Card*. There is also a version of the NAEP that is modified to reflect changes in the curriculum. On this version of the NAEP, the substantial black-white gap has remained roughly unchanged since 1998.[7]

In our own analyses of statewide standardized testing in Louisiana, we determined that, on average, white Louisiana tenth graders scored between 8 and 9 percentage points higher on the state's graduation exit exam than did blacks. Similar racial-ethnic gaps exist in other states' standardized testing programs. For interested readers, these scores can usually be readily accessed online at their state department of education's website. There exists a racial-ethnic gap not only on state and national standardized tests but also in grades awarded by teachers. Based on results of a ten-year study of 10,000 heterogeneously and socioeconomically diverse students, Laurence Steinberg and his team of researchers determined that Asian students had better grades than white students, and black and Latino students do markedly less well than do white students.[8]

THE SAT/ACT GAP

The racial achievement gap is also evident on national standardized tests that assess high school students' preparation for success in higher education.

The SAT I Scholastic Aptitude Test, now known as the Scholastic Assessment Test, is the most-administered test of readiness for college in the United States. Of the 1.4 million high school seniors taking the SAT I for admission to a college or university in 2004, Asians had the highest combined verbal and math scores on the SAT, with an average of 1,084 out of a possible 1,600.[9] The white composite average was 1,059. The SAT does not provide an overall Hispanic average but, rather, reports averages for Mexican Americans, Puerto Ricans, and other Hispanics. Mexican Americans, the largest Hispanic group in the United States, scored slightly lower than their other Hispanic peers, with an average composite of 909. The average black SAT composite score of 857 lagged far behind that of all other ethnic and racial groups (see Figure 7.4).

So we see that Asians score best on the SAT, though only a relatively small 25-point gap exists between Asians and whites. However, the gap between whites and Mexican Americans—the largest Hispanic group in the United States—is a huge 150 points. The black-white gap on the 2004 SAT, though, was an even more staggering 202 points.

More troubling, still, is that the racial achievement gaps on the SAT I between whites and blacks, and especially between whites and Mexican Americans, is growing. Since 1992, the average SAT I score of all racial and ethnic

Figure 7.4
Combined Verbal and Math SAT Composite Averages, 2004

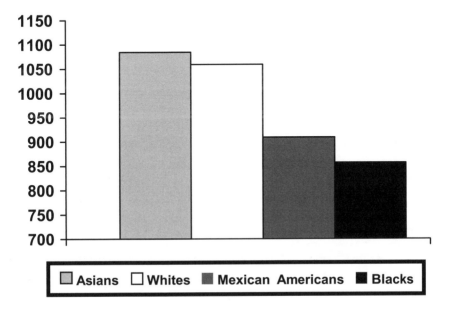

groups has increased. However, the increase has not been the same across all groups of students. Asian SAT scores have grown the most dramatically during the twelve years from 1992 to 2004, increasing an average of 46 points on the 1,600-point test. White scores have increased an average of 25 points. However, black scores have increased only 10 points, and Mexican American scores have risen almost not at all, creeping up only 3 points in twelve years. Thus, not only is there a substantial black-white and Mexican American–white achievement gap on the SAT, the gap has slowly been widening.

On America's second most important test of college readiness, the ACT, we see a similar ethnic and racial pattern as on the SAT. On a test where a perfect score is 36, of the nearly 1.2 million students who took the ACT in 2003, Asian American students earned the highest average ACT composite average of 21.8, followed very closely by whites, who had an average of 21.7. Hispanics scored an average of approximately 18.5. Blacks trailed significantly with an average composite ACT of only 16.9 (see Figure 7.5).[10]

Though blacks lag behind other groups on measures of readiness for college, in terms of high school completion rates, blacks have narrowed the gap considerably in the last three decades. In 1971, only 59 percent of blacks aged 25 to 29 had completed high school compared to 82 percent of whites.[11] By 2001, fully 87 percent of blacks in this age group had completed high school, compared to 93 percent of whites.[12] This represents a 73 percent decrease in

Figure 7.5
Composite ACT Averages, 2003

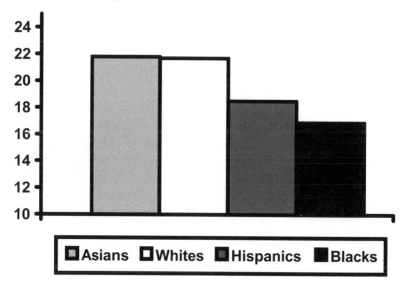

the size of the black-white high school graduation rate gap. Although the high school graduation rate for Hispanics aged 25 to 29 also increased between 1971 and 2001, growing from 48 to 63 percent of all Hispanics aged 25 to 29, Hispanics still trail far behind both blacks and whites on this crucial measure of educational attainment.

In terms of how well students are actually doing in school, though, we see another persistent and growing educational gap. When students sign up to take the SAT, they indicate their high school grade point average (GPA). According to this measure, of SAT takers in 1992, the average Asian GPA was 3.3 on a 4-point scale.[13] The average white GPA was slightly less, at 3.16. The average Mexican American GPA was 3.07. Blacks who took the 1992 SAT indicated that they had lowest GPA of all racial and ethnic groups, averaging 2.82. Ten years later, whites taking the SAT in 2002 indicated that their average high school GPAs had risen to 3.37 (+.21); average Mexican American GPAs had risen to 3.21 (+.14). Average black GPAs had risen the least, climbing to 2.95 (+.13). Thus, we see not only a racial-ethnic achievement gap on average high school GPAs of students taking the SAT, but also a gap that has been widening between whites and blacks, and whites and Mexican Americans. Asian students, though, as on every other measure we looked at, had the highest average GPAs in both 1992 and 2002.

THE HIGHER ED GAP

All racial and ethnic groups tracked by the government have seen significant increases in college attendance and college graduation rates in the last three decades. As can be seen in Figure 7.7, among twenty-five- to twenty-nine-year-olds in 1971, 37 percent of whites, 18 percent of blacks, and 15 percent of Hispanics had attended at least some college (percentages include those who graduated from college as well).[14] College attendance rates soared for whites, and especially for blacks, over the next thirty years. By 2001, fully 65 percent of white adults and 51 percent of black adults had attended at least some college. The gap had narrowed considerably between whites and blacks, but it still remained large. Hispanic college attendance rates increased too, climbing to 32 percent of Hispanic adults aged 25–29. However, the increase was not nearly as great as the increase for blacks, and the black-Hispanic college attendance gap grew almost exponentially, from just 3 percentage points in 1971 to 19 percentage points three decades later.

Still, in the academic year 2001–2002, though blacks constituted about 12 percent of the American population, they received only 8 percent of all postsecondary degrees conferred. Hispanics, who also constituted approximately

Figure 7.6
Adults Aged 25–29 Who Completed High School, 1971 and 2001

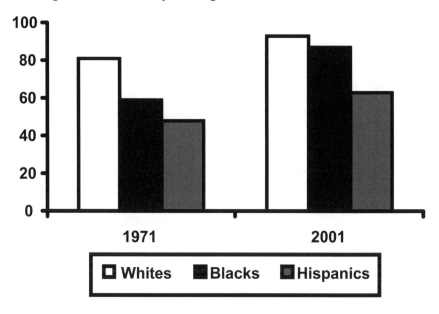

Figure 7.7
Adults Aged 25–29 Who Had Attended at Least Some College

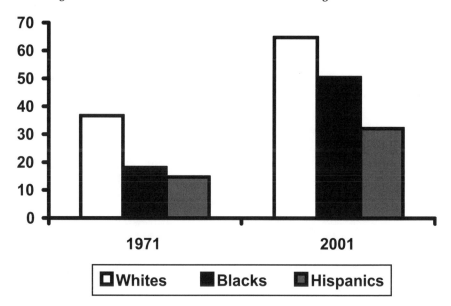

12 percent of the population in 2001, were awarded only 6.5 percent of all postsecondary degrees. Asians, in contrast, who constituted only about 4 percent of the U.S. population in 2002, garnered almost 6 percent of all postsecondary degrees.[15] Nonetheless, racial gaps in higher educational attainment have been steadily narrowing.

So, we see something very interesting, and counterintuitive occurring. Blacks have higher high school completion rates, attend more years of college, and obtain more advanced degrees than do Hispanics. Yet Hispanics in general have higher NAEP scores, higher SAT and ACT scores, and earn better grades (according to some studies) than do blacks. Could this curious disparity relate to differing black and Hispanic attitudes toward school in general? As we will see next, while at school, blacks are not taking the same curriculum as their peers in other racial and ethnic groups.

WHY THE CONTINUING GAP?

In Chapter 4 we delved into the issue of social capital, showing how healthy networks of interactions between children, parents, neighborhoods, and schools boost academic achievement. We also tried to show how white and Asian students are likely benefiting more from these healthy networks than are children from disadvantaged backgrounds—who tend to be disproportionately black and Hispanic in the United States. We want to point out that some scholars believe that diminished black social capital is not at the heart of the achievement gap, but that black social capital is in fact the answer to diminishing the gap (more on this later).[16] Also, in addition to the possibility that diminished social capital is the culprit, other factors in the lives of black and Hispanic children may be hurting their achievement levels more than those of whites and Asians. Some of these factors may relate to diminished social capital, and some may not.

ENVIRONMENTAL HAZARDS AND
EDUCATIONAL ACHIEVEMENT

It is well documented that the physical conditions within which black and Hispanic children live tend to be less safe, and these less-than-ideal conditions can have adverse consequences for academic achievement. According to a very comprehensive Educational Testing Service (ETS) report, blacks and Hispanics are more likely to live in older buildings painted with lead-based paint, a poison that has been linked to lowered IQ and learning problems in children.[17] Also, although it may seem that hunger in the United States is no longer a problem (but that the opposite condition, obesity, is), there are still children who go to bed hungry. According to a 2000 U.S. Department of Agriculture Study, Hispanic and black families are much more likely to report an insecure food supply or hunger than do whites or others,[18] and poor nutrition (not just too few calories) is related to poor academic outcomes.[19] One of these outcomes is low-birth-weight babies. Whatever its causes, black children were nearly twice as likely as white, Hispanic, and Asian children to be born a low-birth-weight baby in 2002.[20] A compilation of research findings by the renowned Child Trends research organization indicates that low-birthweight babies are more likely to suffer impaired social and motor development, be enrolled in special education classes, repeat a grade, or fail than are children of normal birthweight.[21]

The same scholarly study by ETS reported that black children, especially, watch much more television than do their white or Hispanic counterparts. According to data gathered by NAEP, 42 percent of black fourth graders in 2000 reported watching six or more hours of TV per day. This compares to 22 percent of Hispanics and only 13 percent of whites who indicated that they spent so much time parked in front of their set. By any measure, this is an enormous amount of time to be glued to the "flickering blue parent." If we assume eight hours of sleep in a twenty-four-hour period, this equates to almost half of black fourth graders spending more than a third of their waking hours staring at their set! Blacks do not just watch more TV in general, they watch disproportionately more TV in the late night hours, defined as 11:00 PM to 1:00 AM. According to Nielsen Media Research, black youths aged 12–17 watch nearly twice as much late-night TV as all other American teens in this same age group (an average of 194 minutes per week compared to 107 minutes per week).[22] This may suggest that black students are going to bed later at night and are consequently less rested for school that usually begins in the early morning hours.

Whereas our own research on TV watching among Louisiana high school tenth graders suggests that there could be some benefit, albeit a very small one, for black children watching TV, our results were statistically insignificant.[23] Moreover, our research was based on data from 1990. Our opinion (and perhaps yours too) is that the educational quality of much television programming is declining, especially the programming viewed by African Americans. Our research revealed that blacks tended to watch more sitcoms, police dramas, and sports events on TV than other groups. This lineup is not necessarily a recipe for boosting academic performance in school. Moreover, the findings in our own research suggesting why there was a small positive relationship between hours of TV watched and black performance on the Louisiana Graduation Exit exam were not encouraging. Our evidence suggested that the alternatives to watching TV for black children in chaotic home and neighborhood environments may have been even less educationally enriching than TV viewing. If true, this is a very sad commentary.

SCHOOL CURRICULUM

Although blacks may be spending more time in school than their racial and ethnic peers, they are not spending this time taking courses that are as rigorous. According to Richard L. Ferguson, ACT's chief executive officer, "Our research has shown that far too many African American students are not being adequately prepared for college . . . they are less likely than others to take rigorous, college-preparatory courses and they often don't receive the information and guidance they need to properly plan for college."[24] Blacks who took the core college curriculum recommended by the ACT scored 1.7 composite ACT points higher (out of a possible 36) than blacks who did not. The same situation held for black student preparation to take the SAT. A smaller percentage of blacks took physics, precalculus, and calculus courses than did whites, Asians, and all Hispanic groups.[25] So we see that blacks who took the SAT not only reported lower average GPAs than whites, but these lower GPAs are based on an easier curriculum. Thus, simply being in school is not a prerequisite for genuine academic success. One's program of study while in high school, and how well one does in this program, is directly related to success on tests of college readiness.

THE ORIGINS OF THE BLACK-WHITE GAP

Although there is clearly an achievement gap on almost every educational measure between students identifying themselves as "black" or African American and those identifying themselves as "white" or Caucasian, the gap was historically much larger than it is today. Moreover, the history of black education in the United States is uniquely different from the experiences of other racial and ethnic groups in the United States, including Hispanics. Thus, some historical causes of the black-white gap are found in no other ethnic or racial group in the United States. Prior to the Civil War, less than 5 percent of African Americans in the entire country were considered literate—a figure that included slaves and nonslaves alike. In the South, where fears of a slave rebellion steadily increased after about 1840, most states had actually passed laws prohibiting the teaching of slaves.[26] Those blacks in northern, nonslave states who were fortunate enough to receive a formal education were very likely to have been instructed in entirely segregated schools.[27]

Following the end of the Civil War, federally operated Freedman's Bureau schools were opened in the South to impart the bare rudiments of reading, writing, and arithmetic to a few hundred thousand newly freed slaves. Northern religious groups also sent emissaries south to spread literacy along with the gospel to African Americans. With the help of visionaries like the former slave Booker T. Washington, institutions of black education slowly spread throughout the former Confederacy, until by 1910 fully 70 percent of American blacks were considered functionally literate,[28] marking a significant reduction in the educational gap between blacks and whites. Still, public educational facilities for blacks—where they were available—were decrepit, underfunded, and often staffed by teachers who were themselves barely literate. Moreover, in the South, black education was an entirely segregated affair, with the force of law to ensure it stayed that way. So at least through the Civil Rights Movement of the 1960s, much of the black-white achievement gap could be attributed directly to oppression, discrimination, and segregation.

WHY THE NEED FOR SCHOOL RACIAL INTEGRATION?

There was never any serious question about the inferiority of the quality of black schools in general, and black schools in the South in particular. Buildings were often dilapidated, supplies few, and teacher quality not up to par with the quality of teachers in white schools.[29] But beginning with a series of psychological studies dating to 1930s, two researchers studying self-esteem found that black children presented with the choice of a black doll or a white doll tended to choose the white doll.[30] The "doll study" was a catalyst for a growing belief at the time that the separation of black children from the rest of society was causing them to view themselves as inferior. In other words, black self-esteem was apparently suffering in all black schools, and this lowered sense of self-worth was somehow translating into poor school performance. These doll studies were adopted as part of the NAACP's strategy to justify the end of legal school racial segregation. The Supreme Court bought into the social science arguments that separate was inherently unequal in part based on logic similar to the doll study findings. Then, in 1966, *The Coleman Report* added sociological evidence to the psychological evidence supporting the notion that separate black education hurt black students academically. However, Coleman put the blame on black peer pressure, or lack of middle-class white peer influence, rather than lowered self-esteem.

As it turned out, subsequent studies on black self-esteem in the 1960s and 1970s often had contradictory findings to the doll studies.[31] In fact, some research showed that blacks in majority white schools actually had lower self-esteem than blacks in majority black schools.[32] So, one of the initial justifications for reducing the black-white achievement gap through desegregated education was seriously undermined. That left *The Coleman Report*'s findings that blacks suffered academically in majority black schools because of negative peer influences—regardless how dazzling the facilities—as the major scientific justification for continued efforts to desegregate schools. However, as already shown, as low-income black students were bused into majority white schools, academic environments deteriorated and middle-class students of all races fled. Massive white flight in the 1970s even moved Professor Coleman to declare that busing was not working.[33] Even if busing had caused (and is currently causing) white flight, this in and of itself does not undermine Coleman's theory. It just suggests that the ideal racial and socioeconomic student mixture that would bring about a positive educational environment for all is very difficult to "engineer." So, assuming that an ideal mixture of white and black students exists that benefits everyone, what is this ideal mixture? And where this mixture has been achieved, has it led to improved outcomes for blacks? And if blacks have benefited from this mixture, have they done so without hurting the academics of other students?

DO BLACKS ACHIEVE BETTER IN MAJORITY WHITE SCHOOLS?

If the answer to the question "Do blacks achieve better in majority white schools?" were an unequivocal yes, then the most important justification for school racial desegregation would be validated. But the answer is not so clear-cut. Our own research in the state where "separate but equal" became the law of the land in 1896 finds some justification for the rationale that blacks achieve better in majority white schools.[34] We found that the average scores of blacks in majority white schools on Louisiana's Graduation Exit Exam were significantly higher than the average achievement scores of their counterparts in majority black schools. Nevertheless, we found that Louisiana blacks in majority white schools still scored significantly lower than the average white scores.

Wanting teacher input on this important issue, we sought the perceptions of educators in Lafayette Parish, Louisiana. We surveyed all the teachers in five majority white schools one year after these schools received poor, at-risk, inner-city black children whose schools were closed by a federal court order.[35]

Our survey asked the teachers if they thought that these black children had somehow "benefited" by being bused to these majority white schools. A significant number of these teachers (the majority of the teacher corps in these five schools was white) answered this question yes.[36] But when we tried to corroborate the teachers' perceptions by obtaining standardized test scores on these same black students over the next four years, the school board refused to deliver them (we wondered what they were covering up). We were able, however, to determine that only about half of these displaced black students were still on grade level four years later. Therefore, the academic "benefit" of moving these young elementary children from their neighborhood schools to majority white schools seems to have been minimal, if any. Still, keep in mind that the teachers felt there was some benefit to the students being removed from their former inner-city schools—though it may not have been academic.

Nationally, the most statistically rigorous study of the effects of school desegregation on black achievement was conducted in the 1980s.[37] This important study, which factored in the results from all major desegregation research available at the time, concluded that the math scores for blacks in majority white schools were not significantly better than for blacks in majority black schools. The same study found that the reading scores of blacks in majority white schools were only slightly better than scores of blacks in majority black schools.[38] A more recent study found only a very weak relationship between black student performance, and the racial make-up of the school, though the study did find that black performance tended to decline in schools with greater than 90 percent black enrollment.

But even these nonconclusive findings do not undermine the "peer influences," or "student to student," social capital theory. After all, maybe blacks in white schools, even overwhelmingly white schools, may have such strong peer networks that they are simply impervious to the "positive" influences of middle-class students. As pointed out earlier, many schools look on paper as if they are desegregated, but whites, blacks, and Hispanics are mostly tracked in different programs and are not enjoying the same academic experiences.[39] We have seen much evidence to suggest that in-school racial segregation is widespread and rampant. Indeed, we challenge the reader to simply walk across the campus of any large, multiracial American high school during lunchtime and note how students largely segregate themselves by race and ethnicity. Then, after lunch is over, walk down the corridor and peer into the classrooms. You are likely to see the same thing. Such school racial segregation was once seen as evidence for discrimination, whether it was at the classroom or building level. Now, however, a growing number of black academics are asking, in effect, "What's wrong with all black schools?"[40]

IS WHITE ACHIEVEMENT HURT IN MAJORITY BLACK SCHOOLS?

Recall from our discussion on social capital that the most important in-fluence on adolescent school performance seems to be peer pressure. When peer groups are filled with high-achieving students who strive to do well in school, then individuals in these groups—whatever their own backgrounds or race—conform to the group. The converse is also true: a high-achieving student surrounded by peers who have no interest in doing well in school will also tend to conform to this anti-academic orientation of his or her group of friends.

Our own extensive research on tenth grade students in Louisiana supports this theory of student achievement. Since there is a large black-white achieve-ment gap in Louisiana, then white students in majority black schools tend to be surrounded by low-achieving students from backgrounds of poverty and single-parent families. We did indeed discover that white achievement is sig-nificantly lower in majority black schools in Louisiana. Indeed, we found that the average socioeconomic level of a school was a better predictor of a white or black student's score on the Graduation Exit Exam than was his or her own family socioeconomic status. In other words, a high-SES white student tended to score poorly in a low-SES school.

In the same survey we conducted of Lafayette Parish, Louisiana, teachers' perceptions of the effects of busing, we asked a question that indirectly ad-dressed the same issue of whether white academic performance suffered in classrooms with greater numbers of poor black students. We asked the teach-ers if the originally zoned students in their mostly white, middle-class schools benefited as a result of attending school with the displaced at-risk black stu-dents. After all, a powerful academic argument that has gained notoriety and acceptance is that diversity boosts academic achievement.[41] A large majority of our sample of teachers answered no to our question. Based on the teach-ers' responses to an open-ended question on the survey, we were able to de-termine just why they felt that the other students had not benefited from the "diversity" of having poor students sitting beside them in class. Many teach-ers indicated that there were significantly more discipline problems in their school caused by the displaced students. They added that the other students were more likely to imitate the disruptive behavior of the displaced students, than the other way around. Many teachers also noted that they had to slow down the pace of their teaching to accommodate the lower academic levels of the displaced black children. Although our study in one district was nei-ther definitive nor nationally representative, the teachers did provide some useful insights into how stronger students suffer academically when surrounded by students who are more unruly and weaker academically.

ARE STANDARDIZED TESTS CULTURALLY BIASED AGAINST MINORITIES?

A major criticism leveled against the use of standardized tests to compare the academic achievement of different racial and ethnic groups is that these tests are biased against some minority students. Is this true? All the technical evidence suggests that the major standardized tests, such as the ACT, SAT, MCAT, LSAT, and PRAXIS (formerly NTE), are not biased against blacks or other minorities. Psychometrics, the science of test making, has advanced so far in 100 years that there are now very sophisticated statistical procedures for weeding out potentially racially biased items on standardized tests. As a former psychometrician (test specialist) at the Louisiana Department of Education, the lead author used some of these techniques to identify problematic items on Louisiana's Graduation Exit Exam. These procedures involve looking at how racial and ethnic groups perform on each item relative to how they perform on the entire test. An item with possible bias would be an item on which blacks who otherwise performed as well as whites disproportionately answered wrong. These items were thrown out or revised.

In the item creation process, teams of teachers and parents, including minorities, screened items for bias and culled the item bank of all test questions that they felt were questionable. In fact, we were so sensitive to complaints that items could be biased, that when a politician in North Louisiana complained that one of the items on our graduation exit exam reflected badly on politicians, we removed the item from our test bank. If anything, we were overly sensitive to possibly offensive or biased items. All national standardized tests have been through equally if not more rigorous psychometric procedures to ensure that they are free from potential test bias.

Although most standardized tests are carefully scrutinized to ensure they remain free from racial and cultural bias, there is, in fact, a kind of bias that is built into all these tests. We can call this literacy bias. A student may know all the answers to all the test questions, but if the student cannot read the test, the student cannot demonstrate his or her knowledge of the domain being tested. Thus, a seventeen-year-old student who reads on the third grade level and who is attempting to answer history questions on a high school exit exam will likely do poorly on the test. Likewise, a non-English-speaking immigrant child from Mexico will do poorly on word problems in a math test administered in English. Even in these two cases, however, there is a mechanism to help reduce literacy test bias.

In the first case above, a seventeen-year-old whose native language is English and who reads on the third grade level is likely to have a learning handicap covered by section 504 of federal law. These "504 students" can have any number of modifications in the way the test is administered to them, including having the test read directly to them. They can also have extended time to take the test. The first author has even had "504 students" at the university level (future teachers!) to whom he was required to provide special testing arrangements because they were unnecessarily distracted by large groups (incredible, but true). Since English is the native tongue for the vast majority of black Americans, the second case for potential test bias is not really applicable—depending on whether one believes black English qualifies as English. It is true that many blacks are reared speaking a dialect of English, sometimes called Ebonics, that can differ significantly from Standard English. However, these students are attending schools where they are taught the very dialect of English in which the tests are administered. Although it is true that Ebonics differs from Standard English, so does Cajun English, Creole English, Southern English, and Appalachian English. We are not sure that a practical answer to this dimension of literacy bias is to have testing companies write a different version of the test for every nonstandard dialect of English in the United States. To put this in perspective, a study of elementary French immersion students (for whom English was their mother tongue) who were taught most of their academic subjects in French from kindergarten through eighth grade scored higher on standardized tests administered in English than did native English-speaking students who had only ever been taught in English.[42] In other words, there may be something other than literacy bias that is accounting for poor test performance.

Perhaps the more complicated and legitimate issue associated with literacy bias is when students for whom English is not their maternal tongue are tested on subject matter in tests written in English. Indeed, this situation could account for some of the Hispanic-white achievement gap. As we noted in Chapter 2, many Hispanic students who speak little or no English are segregated in schools dominated by other children in the same circumstances. Thus, these students may spend the entire school day in peer groups speaking only Spanish and then return to neighborhoods and homes where the dominant language is Spanish. Even while in school these students may be in bilingual programs where a significant portion of the subject matter is taught in Spanish. School desegregation becomes an issue here because integrating Hispanics into schools where most students speak English would in theory, anyway, help these students to learn English more quickly. And learning English is the key to doing better on tests administered in English. Indeed, the United States is trying to come to terms with how to handle the language education of millions of non-English-speaking immigrants and natives in the United States, on the one hand, while administering standardized tests, on the other. The No Child Left Behind Act does have a stipulation that allows limited English proficient students to be assessed in their own language.[43] However, as long as tests like the SAT and ACT are administered only in English, then students who have not mastered English will be subject to literacy bias.

There is one very important caveat to this discussion of language and achievement: A large proportion of Asian students also speak English as a second language, yet they are scoring better on tests and performing better in schools than every other racial and ethnic group in the United States, including whites. This important fact renders it difficult to make blanket assumptions about the connections between English-language proficiency, on the one hand, and academic achievement in American schools and on American tests, on the other.

THE STUBBORN GAP

Although on many measures of academic achievement the racial achievement gap between whites, blacks, and Hispanics narrowed significantly from the 1960s through the 1980s, the gap persists and may, as we have seen, even be increasing. A variety of policy strategies have been proposed to help reduce this persistent educational gap, including reducing class sizes in majority black and Hispanic schools, increasing funding and resources for majority black and Hispanic schools, and further desegregating schools. Our own research suggests that the latter of these three strategies—specifically reducing black isolation through increased desegregation of majority black schools—shows promise for reducing the black-white achievement gap. We link this finding with Chapter 4's theoretical model connecting the creation of academic capital with the other various forms of social capital that are freely exchanged and magnified on school campuses. In short, majority white schools seem to have a greater abundance of the social capital that is linked to higher achievement and benefits all students in the school regardless of their own backgrounds.

However, as already demonstrated, desegregation is not a zero-sum game. Desegregating majority white schools necessarily means increasing the proportion of African American or Hispanic students in these predominantly middle-class schools. If these black or Hispanic students are high-poverty, low-achieving students, including them in the school also necessarily means introducing into the educational climate any disadvantages that are at the root of their underachievement. As we have already discussed, this strategy can have negative consequences for the achievement of all students in the school.[44] Indeed, if such a phenomenon could be quantified, research indicates that there exists a "tipping point" or "threshold" beyond which the poverty level of a school begins to have an exponentially deleterious effect on all students in the school. According to Dr. Richard Kahlenberg of the Century Institute, who is an expert on socioeconomic integration, this accelerating negative influence occurs when a school's poverty level exceeds approximately 50 percent poor.[45] Our own research suggests that this tipping point could be substantially lower than this.[46] Particularly in majority black schools, where there is often a critical mass of students in poverty, a concentration of children from single-parent families, and an atmosphere permeated with an anti-academic attitude (where doing well is "acting white," and "acting white" is not cool), we see chronic underachievement. Where these disadvantages all come together within the confined space of a school's classroom, we see an immense challenge to a single teacher's efforts to reduce the racial achievement gap.

HOW CAN WE CLOSE THE GAP?

School systems are faced with a paradox. The *ideal* strategies theoretically likely to raise the achievement levels of poor black and Hispanic students could have detrimental consequences for middle-class student achievement. We emphasize *ideal* because the traditional desegregation strategies were precisely that: *idealistic*—and apparently, unrealistic. They look good on paper, but the previous chapter gives evidence that they have been disastrous in practice. If socially engineering ideal school racial concentrations is next to impossible and even counterproductive, then what are feasible strategies for raising black and Hispanic levels of achievement?

Over the years researchers have established a solid base of information on how students learn and how to organize schools to promote learning. Research suggests that smaller, better-equipped classes headed by smart, enthusiastic, and dedicated teachers works. A major problem in poor, urban minority schools is attracting and retaining highly qualified and motivated teachers who want to help high-risk students. Unfortunately, we often as not punish teachers for taking these tough assignments. For example, the No Child Left Behind Act sanctions schools that do not show enough improvement. Teachers are held accountable for how their students do academically as measured on standardized tests. Recall the story in our chapter on social capital about the teacher who said she spent most of her time with high-risk students simply teaching them self-control and manners. She commented that she could teach her middle-class students more in six weeks than she could teach her at-risk students in a whole year. Recall also that this "Teacher of the Year Runner-up" is a living dynamo who devoted herself entirely to her students, praying for them at night, and even delivering eulogies at their funerals. She was essential in the lives of her at-risk students because she was addressing the most pressing needs in their lives before she could move on to academics. In short, she had a "love ethic" for her students. Can anyone seriously question her benefit to society, even if her students' test scores remained below average? Remember also that a majority of teachers who received the at-risk bused students felt these students were better off in the middle-class white schools—even if the students were perhaps not doing better academically.

The NCLB Act does not really recognize why low-achieving students are low achieving in the first place. Teachers in predominantly minority schools are dealing with a plethora of problems, the least of which is low test scores. We believe that these teachers should be rewarded for their courage and the tremendous contribution they are making to society. They certainly should not be threatened or punished. Thus, we would recommend rewarding highly qualified teachers who volunteer to teach the toughest students. Some districts already do this by paying these teachers "combat pay." This is a sound idea. Whereas public school systems have no control over their students' backgrounds, they have a good deal of control over the quality of teachers they place in at-risk schools and how they reward these courageous educators.

We need to recognize that we have, and will continue to have, majority minority schools, including mostly black or all-black schools. Many black educators, researchers, and parents today recognize that racially identifiable schools are unavoidable, and they have been critical of utopian efforts at the redistribution of students.[47] Typical of the sentiment among a growing number of influential black intellectuals was a recent comment in *Time* magazine by Derrick Bell, a New York University law professor and prolific author on race issues. He stated, "The idea that putting black kids together with whites would solve our problems was naïve in the extreme."[48] Other scholars have noted that prior to the 1954 *Brown* decision, many all-black schools were thriving. Before the age of desegregation, blacks tended to view their schools as "good," for they were central to the functioning of black communities.[49]

Is it possible that our stereotyping of all-black schools as inferior schools and our focusing of resources on trying to racially balance these schools has had a corrosive effect on what was once a much more healthy institution? We certainly have devalued the importance of black educators teaching black children. A black teacher and published author with a doctorate, who believed her calling was to work with black high school students, shared with us the following bizarre experience. She went to a majority black high school to apply for an open English position but was told that because she was black, she was unlikely to get the job. The district in which she applied was under a strict court order to racially balance teaching staff, and according to the federal district court judge overseeing the case, there were apparently too many black teachers at this particular school.[50] Another black teacher at a predominately black elementary school told one of the authors that at the end of the school year all the black teachers in her school were assembled in a group and asked to put their names in a hat. Names were to be randomly picked to decide which black teachers would be sent to predominately white schools. She said she was so humiliated that she transferred to an adjoining school system in the fall that was not under a court order. She felt her vocation was to help poor, disadvantaged students, but solely because of her race she was being denied her professional calling.[51] What kind of message do policies like these send to black students, teachers, and administrators? The academic literature is now replete with evidence that suggests that black children benefit from being taught by black teachers.[52] Perhaps Jerome E. Morris, a black associate professor of education at the University of Georgia, offered the best advice on where to find the solution to urban African American problems. Echoing a sentiment voiced more than a century ago by the great black sociologist W.E.B. Du Bois, Morris wrote, "We just might find that the solution resides within the 'souls' of Black people—rather than elsewhere."

It just seems like good sense to allow black community leaders and organizations to decide how to help improve black achievement. The black American community has a vested interest—and the most at stake—in the education of black children. During the Reconstruction era, extremely well educated black leaders like Frederick Douglass were relatively rare, and whites dominated decisions about the destiny of the black American community. The black American community at the turn of the twenty-first century is replete with literally millions of highly trained educators, administrators, physicians, lawyers, architects, politicians, clergy, military leaders, psychologists, university professors, and the like. The talent pool of blacks is more than sufficient to address the issues of black achievement. Real solutions must come from the self-organization of people.

CHAPTER 8

A New Perspective on Race and Schooling: Attaining the Dream

In previous chapters we examined the largely failed efforts to redesign American society through federally imposed school desegregation. We argued that these efforts have been self-defeating because they were based on a flawed view of how schools fit into and strengthen a society. These policies also often ran counter to the individual interests of families. In this final chapter we offer a new, alternative perspective that we maintain is the emerging worldview of how to consider race, school desegregation, and American civil society. We argue that a momentous shift in perspective is taking place regarding how we, as Americans, view race and education.

In academia there is a specialized term that refers to a worldview or dominant perspective, and that is the term "paradigm." The expression "paradigm" was popularized by the philosopher of science Thomas Kuhn, who taught at the UC Berkeley, Princeton, and MIT.[1] A paradigm is a worldview complete with its own assumptions, questions, and understandings of how the world works. The assumptions, questions, and considerations of the now aging worldview on race in America were formed largely during the years of the Civil Rights Movement, which roughly began with the 1954 *Brown* decision. This paradigm worked well to help us understand and make sense of race in the America of the 1960s and 1970s. However, paradigms eventually outlive their usefulness. As time passes, they often become less and less useful in helping us make sense of the world, for their underlying assumptions may no longer line up with the emerging reality. When a paradigm contains too many anomalies that just do not add up and the paradigm no longer provides a realistic understanding of how things actually work, then it is ripe to be overthrown by a new paradigm.

NEW PARADIGMS

Looking back over the course of the last 500 years, we see a very good example of how old paradigms are pushed out of the way and replaced by new, more useful ones. This is precisely what happened during the 1500s to the old paradigm of a geocentric world. During the Renaissance, the Catholic Church continued to insist on the Ptolemaic view that the earth was the center of the universe even as evidence was piling up to contradict this classical and medieval fallacy. At first, just a few visionaries like Copernicus and Galileo dared to question the prevailing ecclesiastical view. After all, one risked being excommunicated—or burned at the stake—for challenging the dominant medieval view of how the universe worked. These two astronomical pioneers were collecting evidence that suggested a universe that did not revolve around the earth. Eventually, the church's paradigm was so out of kilter with the huge body of scientific evidence suggesting it was wrong that even the ordinary man or woman on the street could see how ridiculous it was to believe that all things revolved around the earth. Thus, the geocentric paradigm collapsed upon itself, to be replaced by a worldview that simply made more sense.

We believe that the time is now ripe for just such a revolution in how to think about desegregation and many other racial issues in the United States. Many key assumptions of the old paradigm are increasingly "anomalous," to use the expression of the late professor Thomas Kuhn. In other words, the old civil rights worldview no longer adequately accounts for the new racial reality of twenty-first-century America. Some researchers and activists are still arguing for more government involvement and blame the current trend in the resegregation of American schools on a judicial system that does not have the courage to go all the way, to complete the job it started.[2] These desegregation activists argue that if federal courts had not freed districts from the oversight of federal judges but had, rather, been even stricter in the enforcement of desegregation court orders, then American public schools would be more desegregated than they currently are. These activist positions were shaped by the now aging view of race and school desegregation that developed in the 1940s and 1950s and blossomed with the Civil Rights Movement of the 1960s.

In a sense, those who still cling to the old paradigm are like aging hippies who just can not let go of their colored beads and evolve with the rest of the country. The 1960s was a heady, idealistic time. But like the Victorian Age or the Roaring Twenties, those days are gone. During the heyday of the Civil Rights Movement, the then emerging paradigm was useful. In science, a useful paradigm is one that is at least somewhat predictive. This means that if you do what the paradigm suggests will work, such as tearing down the walls of racial discrimination against blacks in the 1950s and 1960s, then you will get good results—blacks moving up out of poverty and into the mainstream, for example, and a diminishing black-white achievement gap. A successful paradigm also offers a more useful and realistic viewpoint than its competitors. Recall that the civil rights paradigm just made more sense than the competing segregationist paradigm of its time, the one championed by the likes of Trent Lott, Strom Thurmond, and George Wallace. Eventually, the civil rights paradigm triumphed and became the "normal science" of its time. The transition from segregationist to integrationist paradigm is somewhat akin to the transition from the geocentric to the heliocentric view of Copernicus, which put the sun—and not the earth—at the center of our universe, triumphing over the previously dominant view of the Catholic Church. The Copernican and civil rights paradigms were both more useful and closer to the truth than their predecessors. However, neither was perfect, and both have since been eclipsed by even more useful and accurate worldviews in astronomy and social science.

Much has changed in the racial, educational, and legal landscape of the last half-century, rendering the previous research and policy viewpoints on race and desegregation increasingly useless to address the present realities. Some ongoing research on race and education, which is informed by the outmoded thinking of the 1950s and 1960s, is, to use the philosopher of science Kuhn's words, "a strenuous and devoted attempt to force nature into the conceptual boxes supplied by professional education."[3] Desegregation researchers who advocate more government involvement in the desegregation of schools claim that the experiment has failed precisely because we either did not try hard enough or used the wrong tactics. Their complaints made much more sense when they were first voiced in the early days of the Civil Rights Movement when a new, fresh paradigm on race in America was just evolving. As a society, we truly were not doing enough in the 1950s and early 1960s to end discrimination or school segregation. The segregationists of the "old" race paradigm were dragging their heels and using tired arguments to justify keeping black and white schoolchildren separate. Judicial willpower was indeed called for to end what was, in retrospect, blatant racism based on a worldview that was doomed to the trash heap of history—just like the geocentric view of the universe.

Now, however, we have to disagree with the viewpoint that a coercive judiciary and more government intervention and oversight is the answer to racially integrating America's schools or the broader American society. A growing body of research, including some of our own, suggests that after *de jure* school segregation was largely ended by the late 1960s, it was an increasingly activist, federal government that ultimately drove many white and even black middle-class students from desegregating systems in the first place. The body of evidence suggests that had the government been even heavier handed than it was, school systems might well be less integrated today than they currently are. In other words, coercive desegregation was by and large a failure, and the more coercive the means, the more spectacular the failure.[4] In the Charlotte-Mecklenburg, North Carolina, school district (CMS), after approximately forty years of government enforced desegregation, the court order was lifted in 1999. The system began to resegregate almost immediately following the granting of unitary status. Some have suggested that the resegregation of the CMS schools was evidence that the lifting of the court order was premature.[5] Could this outcome not mean something entirely different? Could it not mean that if thirty years of governmental orchestrated student assignment based on race was a failure, then something is fatally flawed with this approach in the first place? After all, if affirmative desegregation was successful, should we not be able to expect that after a generation it would stick?

As we described in our chapter on the political economy of education, parents want the best education they can afford for their children. In its coercive efforts to desegregate schools, the government's vision of an ideal education differed dramatically from the reality of how individuals ascribe value to schooling in the educational marketplace. There have undoubtedly been some white parents who refused to allow their children to be bused to majority black schools because they simply do not like blacks. However, a more realistic interpretation for the failure of coercive desegregation and the massive white flight it caused is that accepting the government's plan for a child often meant accepting an inferior education.

RESISTANCE

As we have discussed throughout our book, one major impediment to moving beyond the old paradigm of school desegregation is the continuing "moral momentum" and mindset lingering from the Civil Rights Movement. That is, it just felt "right" to fight for the ideal of bringing white children, black children, and Hispanic together in schools, whatever the means. There

is also another more practical and less ideological reason for this intransigence, however. Fifty years of desegregation litigation has created a large and
entrenched cottage industry. Experts and lawyers have raked in huge sums
on the desegregation gravy train. The *raison d'être* of entire bureaucratic entities, like the Dallas Desegregation Monitoring Division and its highly paid
administrator, depend on desegregation for their living, even when meaningful school racial desegregation in Dallas schools is numerically impossible. Thus, there is much inertia to maintain the status quo if for no other
reason than many professionals have come to depend on the constant income
stream generated by desegregation program implementation and ongoing
lawsuits or potentially lucrative income from forthcoming new litigation.
Many lawyers, law firms, and college professors have made literally tens of
millions of dollars either litigating for plaintiffs and school boards, testifying
for plaintiffs or school boards, or drawing up desegregation plans.

A striking irony of the desegregation era is that in those cases where the
most public money was spent, the desegregation results were often the least
satisfying. Indeed, in the case of East Baton Rouge Parish (EBRP), Louisiana,
the district went from 65 percent white to less than 25 percent white over a
twenty-year period that cost taxpayers more than $15 million in legal fees
alone. By the time the district was declared unitary in 2003, it was a majority black district in dire financial straits with little public support. With the
declaration of unitary status, lawyers were lining up to be reimbursed. Two
NAACP lawyers were asking $500,000 in legal fees for the last four years of
work they performed on the case, basing their estimate on $150 per hour of
work each.[6] Another lawyer who originally said he would not charge the system for his years of work was threatening to ask for millions. In the year 2001
alone EBRP spent $2.2 million in legal fees. Major national law firms with
reputations for successfully arguing desegregation cases before the Supreme
Court command up to $300 an hour per attorney for their desegregation coun-
sel. Facing such costs, is it any wonder that after negotiating all the exigen-
cies of desegregation court battles many school districts are left flat on their
back and deeply in the red—not to mention more racially segregated than
ever?

SOCIOECONOMIC INTEGRATION

A persuasive argument, made chiefly by Richard Kahlenberg of the Century Foundation, is that government should seek the socioeconomic—and not
racial—desegregation of schools. This latest notion has been proposed as a
remedy to circumvent the growing number of legal prohibitions against the

assignment of students to schools based solely on race.[7] The argument for mixing students from diverse SES backgrounds was first presented by the father of the public school, Horace Mann, almost 200 years ago. It is a compelling argument for the same reasons that the racial desegregation of schools is a compelling argument. After all, students learn from each other, and lower-SES students would benefit by coming in contact with their higher-SES peers and integrating into their social networks and benefiting from their middle-class social capital. Further, the research on social capital supports the idea that this capital is "transferable." The higher-SES group can help raise the educational and social prospects of the lower-SES group. Perhaps most important, SES integration moves away from the much more arbitrary criterion of using a person's skin complexion as a factor in deciding where he or she will go to school. Finally, it just seems like the right thing to do: What a beautiful vision to imagine an educational utopia of happy rich and poor children sitting in classrooms together.

Certainly, moving beyond race in making student assignment decisions is a step in the right direction. However, orchestrating this mixing of diverse SES students is likely to meet with all the same resistance and failure as coercive school desegregation and for precisely the same reasons. In almost all places with large black and Hispanic populations, race and socioeconomic status are closely linked. Students in poverty tend to be black and Hispanic, and black and Hispanic students tend to be the students at or below the poverty level. Indeed, the correlation between the two is so high that desegregating schools based on student socioeconomic status in most places would be almost the same thing as desegregating schools based on race.[8]

Socioeconomic desegregation of schools is a lofty and admirable goal. But so is school racial desegregation. We have no disagreement with either of these idealistic aspirations. Our disagreement is with the means to attaining these ends—top-down social engineering that has until now often resulted in schools and school districts that are less socioeconomically and racially integrated, not more. Surely we do not want to implement policies whose consequences defeat the purpose of the policies in the first place—even if supporting such policies "feels good," "seems like the right thing to do," and is in keeping with "what we've always done." These are simply not logical and defensible positions.

STRATEGIES THAT WORK

We propose several strategies for realistically desegregating schools "to the extent practicable," to quote a famous Supreme Court decision. It is the "prac-

ticable" that has often been overlooked in efforts at school desegregation. Coercive efforts of any kind, even under the guise of so-called schools of choice,
where parents are provided with limited options, have largely failed and
should be abandoned. Coercion, we have shown in previous chapters, turns
school systems into command economies, with all power concentrated in the
hands of central planners, even when lip service is paid to the wishes and
decisions of individual families.

Neighborhood Schools

Returning to the concept of community schools would be a step in the
right direction of slowing down and perhaps even stopping and reversing
the racial resegregation of American schools and school districts. Yes, we acknowledge that many communities are racially identifiable, and returning to
school assignment based on neighborhood attendance zones would therefore
not completely eliminate school racial segregation. However, we believe, that
neighborhood segregation should be seen not as a problem to be solved in
schools but as an issue for the larger society outside of schools—assuming it
should be an issue at all. Moreover, there are successful, noncoercive methods for granting poor minority students, of whatever race, access to majority
white, middle-class schools, should minority parents choose this option.
Majority-to-minority programs offer just such an option to many low-SES minority students. Some magnet programs in majority white schools seek qualified minority students, regardless of their attendance zone. Certain inner-city
school districts like Hartford's have agreements with the surrounding
middle-class suburban districts that offer the opportunity for low-SES minorities to transfer to suburban schools. Of course, let us not overlook the obvious: though not an option for many poor minority students, many
middle-class minority parents can relocate to school districts in which they
want their children to attend school, which is what most middle-class parents have always done. There are laws in place to protect against racial discrimination in housing, and procedures to apply these laws should this
unlawful practice take place.

Admittedly, implementing many of the mentioned policies, or even implementing all the policies together for that matter, would not end school
racial segregation. However, the new paradigm does ask us to face up to the
reality, as uncomfortable as it is, that we will have racially identifiable schools,
at least for the foreseeable future, regardless what actions we take. This frank
acknowledgment, however true, was taboo under the civil rights paradigm.
As we noted in a previous chapter, in a society as affluent as the United States,

parents have many educational options and cannot be forced to make choices about their children's education. If we have learned anything in the last fifty years, we surely should have learned this. Short of forcing people to go to a particular school and live in a particular neighborhood at the point of a gun, the United States is very likely to have some racially segregated school and neighborhood regardless what the government does. We are also likely to continue to have communities that are socioeconomically segregated. This state of affairs is not the ideal. We simply do not see a short-term government solution to this problem.

Strengthening Communities

The new vision of school and race that we propose does not suggest that we just throw up our hands in defeat and lament that there will be racially segregated schools whatever we do. The new paradigm recognizes, rather, that there are benefits to allowing neighborhood schools, whatever the racial or socioeconomic characteristics of the neighborhood. Indeed, the case for the function of neighborhood schools in strengthening society by more thoroughly involving individuals in the life of their community is well documented.[9] Unfortunately, many school desegregation policies have had the unintended side effect of destroying the communities in which the target schools were located. We know that neighborhood schools strengthen communities and that strong communities in turn strengthen schools. The mechanism by which this dynamic works is through social capital. Social capital, like economic capital, can be invested to return large dividends. Social capital is generated in the rich interactions built up between parents and children, and between networks of parents interacting with other parents at their children's school and during school functions. This capital, which is generated in the home as well as in the school, benefits the whole community by establishing strong networks through which information flows freely. A healthy democracy needs as its foundation a well-informed, well-integrated citizenry.

Schools, too, benefit by being situated in communities rich in social capital. Strong parental networks can ensure that the school has ample political, financial, and moral support. Children also benefit by being in an institution that is an extension of a well-integrated community. The seamless relationship between neighborhood and school provides a real measure of security, comfort, and connectedness for a child. The normative pressures of a healthy neighborhood block provide children with boundaries, such as when a parent on one end of the street feels free to correct the behavior of a child who lives ten houses away. This sense of connectedness transfers to schools, and children feel it. This sense of belonging to a broader community that is looking after a child's best interests is psychologically and socially beneficial for the child. Moreover, we propose that these kinds of social capital can be just as prevalent in poor as in rich communities, and in black as in white communities.

Schools populated mostly with minority students—if they are neighborhood schools—result in more and healthier contacts between parents, teachers, and administrators than is presently acknowledged by most scholars. These increased home-school contacts can, in turn, enhance the social capital that facilitates success in school.[10] The protection and creation of neighborhood minority schools takes on even more importance in light of research that suggests that minority students in particular depend upon social capital to do well in school.[11] Understanding why this is might be the case is not difficult, either. In minority homes ravaged by poverty, drugs, or violence, the community outside an at-risk child's home becomes an even more important resource for the child.

PUBLIC SUPPORT FOR PUBLIC EDUCATION

Parents who like their children's neighborhood schools and are not worried that they will be closed or that their children will be moved elsewhere are more likely to generously support the school and the school system. These satisfied "customers" are more likely to vote for tax increases for improved public school facilities and teacher pay raises and to make their voices heard at local school board meetings. They are also more likely to remain in urban areas than to move to surrounding suburbs if they are content with the quality of their children's urban schooling. Their remaining in cities means that their property taxes and sales taxes, which are the primary local sources of public educational funding, also remain in the cities, which are so often strapped for educational dollars. Local urban systems with neighborhood schools that are filled to capacity can then build newer facilities, upgrade deteriorating school plants, reduce class sizes, and raise teacher pay to attract and keep the best teachers.

All this is not just good for the middle-class white families who stay in urban systems; it is also good for the minority families whose children often have no choice but to attend an inner-city school. Even if the minority urban child's school is not completely racially balanced, his or her school could at least provide an enhanced learning environment with highly paid professionals. Research indicates that one input factor over which school systems have control, and which positively influences learning more than facilities do, is the quality of the teacher.[12] And like anything else, a district largely gets what it pays for in teacher quality, though we have heard educators claim some school districts could not pay them enough to teach there. If funds were available to significantly upgrade these deteriorating urban schools, however, in order to lower student-teacher ratios, to provide extra pay for working in high poverty schools, and to increase base salaries, perhaps some of our star teachers would reconsider working with poor minority youth.

LOCAL CONTROL IN MINORITY COMMUNITIES

The new paradigm of race and schooling asks questions that have been off-limits in the civil rights paradigm. One such question is, "Why do black children have to sit next to white children to learn anyway?" Among the black American intelligentsia is a growing sense that problems in the black community might best be solved by the black community itself. This is not a new idea. Both Frederick Douglass in the nineteenth century and W.E.B. Du Bois and Malcolm X in the twentieth echoed the same sentiment. This growing sense that blacks have the tools to solve even the most seemingly intractable problems of the black community is spreading in concert with increasing resentment among African Americans toward the paternalism of the federal government. The black American community of the twenty-first century is in some ways light years removed from the community of newly freed slaves wandering the Southern countryside during Reconstruction. Although there remains a black-white achievement gap, it is in no way comparable to the huge gulf in learning that existed between whites and blacks immediately following the Civil War. Moreover, the differences between these two eras are largely attributable to education. On the eve of the Civil War, possibly fewer than 5 percent of all American blacks were literate (and an even smaller percentage of slaves). In 2000, black American literacy rates were comparable to white rates. Whereas leaders like Booker T. Washington stood out in the 1800s, there are so many distinguished African Americans in 2004 that it would be ridiculous and demeaning to try to list them all here. The African American community of the early twentieth-first century has produced literally millions of doctors, engineers, military leaders, politicians, lawyers, teachers, and every other kind of highly trained professional. The black middle class has grown exponentially since Linda Brown first challenged her segregated schooling in Topeka, Kansas. Arguably, W.E.B. Du Bois's 1903 vision of the "Talented Tenth" has come to pass:

The Negro race, like all races, is going to be saved by its exceptional men. The problem of education, then, among Negroes must first of all deal with the Talented Tenth; it is the problem of developing the Best of this race that they may guide the Mass away from the contamination and death of the Worst, in their own and other races.[13]

Du Bois's "Talented Tenth" has been developed. The "Best" are leading not only their own but also "other races" of humanity as well. With Du Bois's prophetic words in mind, why, then, do we still have agents of the federal government keeping black teachers from teaching black children? This is entirely anathema to Du Bois's vision of a black America delivered by the best black leadership. Increasingly, blacks resent so condescending a paternalism. Wouldn't any of us in the same position?

LET SCHOOLS BE SCHOOLS

Schools should not continue to be used as arenas for the redesign of American society. Societies are made up of complex networks of individuals, informal groups, and organizations all seeking interests of their own. Societies—especially affluent ones like the United States—do not lend themselves to the designs of social engineers. Schools occupy a particularly important place in this complicated interweaving, since they are the places where families seek to promote the long-term benefits of their own children. They are also the institutions that bring families together in the important networks that help form the basis of strong communities. With this in mind, we advocate returning to neighborhood schools, strengthening the local social institutions around those schools, and maximizing opportunities within public school systems for individual minority families.

The reality of the new paradigm is our nation's increasing recognition of the appropriate place that race should hold in a truly multiracial and multiethnic society where "individuals are judged on the content of their character and not the color of their skin." This ideal is commensurate with the reality of social science, the American character, the American plan of government, and a society that is truly civil.

Notes

CHAPTER 1

1. "Harvard Report Says Nation's Schools Are Resegregating," *Black Issues in Higher Education* 16 (July 8, 1999): 16–17.

2. Peter Blau and Otis D. Duncan, *The American Occupational Structure* (New York: John Wiley & Sons, 1967).

3. James S. Coleman et al., *Equality of Educational Opportunity* (Washington, D.C.: U.S. Department of Health, Education, and Welfare, 1966).

4. Numbers are rounded off.

5. National Center for Education Statistics, "Percentage of Students in Grades 1–12 Who Were Black or Hispanic, by Control of School and Place of Residence: 1970–96," February 20, 2004, nces.ed.gov/quicktables; U.S. Bureau of the Census, *School Enrollment—Social and Economic Characteristics of Students: October 2000* (PPL–148), Table 5; U.S. Bureau of the Census, "Level of Enrollment below College for People 3 to 24 Years Old, by Control of School, Sex, Metropolitan Status, Race, and Hispanic Origin: October 2000" in *School Enrollment* (Washington, D.C.: U.S. Government Printing Office, 2000).

6. Gary Orfield, "Our Resegregated Schools," *Principal* 79, no. 5 (May 2000): 6–11.

7. Douglas S. Massey and Nancy A. Denton, *American Apartheid: Segregation and the Making of the Underclass* (Cambridge: Harvard University Press, 1993).

8. Carl L. Bankston III, "Demographics," in *African American Encyclopedia, Supplement*, ed. Kibibi Voloria Mack (New York: Marshall Cavendish, 1996), 1936–1941.

9. U.S. Bureau of the Census, *School Enrollment—Social and Economic Characteristics of Students: October 2000* (PPL–148), Table 5.

10. Gary Orfield, Susan E. Eaton, and the Harvard Project on School Desegregation, *Dismantling Desegregation: The Quiet Reversal of Brown v. Board of Education* (New York: The New Press, 1996).

11. Robert J. Sampson, Jeffrey D. Morenoff, and Felton Earls, "Beyond Social Capital: Spatial Dynamics of Collective Efficacy for Children," *American Sociological Review* 64 (1999): 633–660.

12. James S. Coleman, "Social Capital in the Creation of Human Capital," *American Journal of Sociology* 94 (1988): S95–S120; James S. Coleman, "Families and Schools," in *Equality and Achievement in Education*, ed. James S. Coleman (Boulder, CO: Westview Press, 1990), 325–340.

13. For a more complete explanation of this point of view, see James A. Banks, *Educating Citizens in a Multicultural Society* (New York: Teachers College Press, 1997).

14. U.S. Department of Justice, Bureau of Justice Statistics, "Homicide Trends in the U.S.," http://www.ojp.usdoj.gov/bjs/homicide/race.htm (retrieved January 7, 2004).

15. Associated Press, "Reports: Black Teens, Young Adults Face High Death Rates," *Duluth News Tribune.Com*, January 6, 2004, http://www.duluthsuperior.com/ (retrieved January 27, 2004).

16. Daniel Patrick Moynihan, *The Negro Family: The Case for National Action* (Washington, D.C.: Office of Policy Planning and Research, U.S. Department of Labor, 1965).

17. Coleman, "Social Capital in the Creation of Human Capital," S111.

18. Anne T. Henderson and Nancy Berla, *A New Generation of Evidence: The Family Is Critical to Student Achievement* (Washington, D.C.: National Committee for Citizens in Education, 1994); Anne T. Henderson, *The Evidence Continues to Grow: Parent Involvement Improves Student Achievement* (Columbia, MD: National Committee for Citizens in Education, 1987); Kathleen V. Hoover-Dempsey, Otto C. Bassler, and Jane S. Brissie, "Parent Involvement: Contributions of Teacher Efficacy, School Socioeconomic Status, and Other School Characteristics," *American Educational Research Journal* 24 (1987): 417–435.

19. Lee Coulon III, "Disagree with Busing Son from Milton to Vermillion," *The Advertiser*, January 27, 2004, A4.

20. Stephen J. Caldas and Carl L. Bankston III, "An Evaluation of the Consequences of School Desegregation in Lafayette, Louisiana," *Research in the Schools* 10, no. 1 (2003): 41–52.

21. Richard Burgess, "Parents Who Oppose Desegregation Plan Lose Battle," *The Advertiser*, March 17, 2004, B3.

22. *Brown v. Board of Education of Topeka*, 349 U.S. 294 (1955).

23. Alexis de Tocqueville, *Democracy in America*, trans. and ed. Harvey C. Mansfield and Delba Winthrop (Chicago: University of Chicago Press, 2000).

24. Pierre Bourdieu, "The Forms of Capital," in *Handbook of Theory and Research for the Sociology of Education*, ed. J. Richardson (Westport, CT: Greenwood Press, 1986), 241–258; Robert D. Putnam, "Bowling Alone: America's Declining Social Capital," *Journal of Democracy* 6, no. 1 (1995): 65–78; Robert D. Putnam, *Bowling Alone: The Collapse and Revival of American Community* (New York: Simon & Schuster, 2001); Robert D. Putnam, ed., *Democracies in Flux: The Evolution of Social Cap-*

ital in Contemporary Society (New York: Oxford University Press, 2002); James S. Coleman, "Social Capital," S95–S120.

25. R. McClain, "Ex-PAR Chief Doesn't Believe Education Can Reform Itself," *Sunday Advocate*, April 25, 1999, A1, A16, A17.

26. Let the reader note that the Baghdad of thirteen centuries ago has very little in common with the twenty-first-century city located on the same piece of real estate.

27. H. St. L. B. Moss, *The Birth of the Middle Ages* (London: Oxford University Press, 1974), 165.

28. This point of view is commonly associated with the Marxist tradition, but it can also be found among thinkers on the right. The classic example is John C. Calhoun, as described by Richard Hofstadter, "John C. Calhoun: The Marx of the Master Class," in *The American Political Tradition and the Men Who Made It* (1948; repr., New York: Vintage Books, 1989), 87–118.

29. For an overview of the failures of societies that have sought to abolish the market, see Joshua Muravchik, *Heaven on Earth: The Rise and Fall of Socialism* (San Francisco: Encounter Books, 2002).

30. As Raymond S. Franklin points out in his second chapter of *Shadows of Race and Class* (Minneapolis: University of Minnesota Press, 1991), one of the theoretical points debated by historians is whether Europeans and European Americans imposed slavery on people from Africa because they viewed Africans as inferior or whether racism came into existence as a justification for slavery. Some historians have suggested that as Europeans expanded their control over much of the world, they came into contact with many who were unlike themselves in appearance and in culture. Ethnocentrism may have led Europeans to see the people of Asia and Africa as inferior to themselves and encouraged enslavement. The historian George M. Frederickson argues in *White Supremacy: A Comparative Study in American and South African History* (New York: Oxford University Press, 1981) that racial oppression created ideas of racial inferiority, rather than the reverse. In either case, though, the cultivation of plantation crops resulted in an identifiable group of people becoming associated with forced labor. For a particularly good examination of how slavery was connected to the plantation economy, readers are referred to Sidney Mintz, *Sweetness and Power: The Place of Sugar in Modern History* (New York: Penguin Books, 1985).

31. Joseph J. Ellis, *American Sphinx: The Character of Thomas Jefferson* (New York: Knopf, 1997).

32. This point about the contradiction between an ideology of liberty and the practice of slavery giving rise to racism in American history has been made often. But an articulate if somewhat preachy exposition of the point can be found in Joe R. Feagin's *Racist America: Roots, Current Realities, and Future Reparations* (New York: Routledge, 2000). We agree with Feagin on this particular issue, although we reject his blanket condemnation of white America and his utterly unrealistic proposals for radically redesigning American political structures.

33. Henry Hughes, *Treatise on Sociology: Theoretical and Practical* (Philadelphia: Lippincott, Grambo, 1854); George Fitzhugh, *Cannibals All! Or, Slaves without Masters* (Richmond, VA: A. Morris, 1857).

34. For example, in Gerald Doppelt, "Illiberal Cultures and Group Rights: A Critique of Multiculturalisms in Kymlicka, Taylor, and Nussbaum," *Journal of Contemporary Legal Issues* 12 (2002): 661–692; and in Jude P. Dougherty, "Thesis: Antithesis," *Modern Age* 44 (Winter 2002): 18–20. Dougherty maintains that support for group rights over individual rights is a defining characteristic of liberalism, and he argues this gives liberalism an authoritarian nature. For a consideration of whether group rights can be thought of as a form of citizens' rights, see David Miller, "Group Rights, Human Rights, and Citizenship," *Review of Metaphysics* 55 (2002): 661–662. Miller argues that special treatment based on disadvantaged group membership in most cases cannot be considered as rights of citizenship.

35. See Forrest McDonald, *States Rights' and the Union: Imperium in Imperio* (Lawrence: University Press of Kansas, 2002), for a more elaborated argument of this perspective.

36. Eric Foner, *Reconstruction: America's Unfinished Revolution: 1863–1877* (New York: Harper & Row, 1989), 88.

37. Eric C. Lincoln and Lawrence H. Mamiya, *The Black Church in the African American Experience* (Durham, NC: Duke University Press, 1990), 8.

38. Eric Arnesen, *Brotherhoods of Color: Black Railroad Workers and the Struggle for Equality* (Cambridge: Harvard University Press, 2002).

39. Minnie Finch, *The NAACP: Its Fight for Justice* (Metuchen, NJ: Scarecrow Press, 1981).

40. *Brown v. Board of Education of Topeka,* 349 U.S. 294 (1955).

41. Office of the Assistant Attorney General, Civil Rights Division, *Civil Rights Division Activities and Programs* (Washington, D.C.: Civil Rights Division, 2002).

42. Stephen J. Caldas, Roslin Growe, and Carl L. Bankston III, "African American Reaction to Lafayette Parish School Desegregation Order: From Delight to Disenchantment," *Journal of Negro Education* 71, no. 2 (2002): 43–59.

CHAPTER 2

1. *Plessy v. Ferguson,* 163 U.S. 537, 16 S. Ct. 1138 (1896).

2. *Cumming v. Board of Education of Richmond County,* 175 U.S. 528, 20 S. Ct. 197 (1899).

3. *Berea College v. Commonwealth of Kentucky,* 211 U.S. 45, 29 S. Ct. 33 (1908).

4. *Missouri ex rel. Gaines v. Canada,* 305 U.S. 337, 59 S. Ct. 232 (1938).

5. *Sweatt v. Painter,* 339 U.S. 629, 70 S. Ct. 848 (1950).

6. Carl L. Bankston III and Stephen J. Caldas, *A Troubled Dream: The Promise and Failure of School Desegregation in Louisiana* (Nashville, TN: Vanderbilt University Press, 2002).

7. Florent Hardy, *A Brief History of the University of Southwestern Louisiana: 1900 to 1960* (Baton Rouge, LA: Claitor's Publishing, 1973).

8. "First African American Graduate Dies at 87," in *La Louisiane* (Lafayette: University of Louisiana, 2003).

9. *Brown v. Board of Education of Topeka*, 349 U.S. 294 (1955), 469.

10. *Brown v. Board of Education II*, 349 U.S. 294 (1955).

11. *Griffin v. County School Board of Prince Edward County*, 377 U.S. 218, 84 S. Ct. 1226 (1964).

12. Christine H. Rossell, "The Evolution of School Desegregation Plans since 1954," in *The End of Desegregation?* ed. Stephen J. Caldas and Carl L. Bankston III (New York: Nova Science Publishers, 2003), 51–72.

13. *Green v. County School Board of New Kent County, Virginia*, 391 U.S. 430, 88 S. Ct. 1689 (1968).

14. Charles A. Reich, *The Greening of America* (New York: Random House, 1970).

15. *Swann v. Charlotte-Mecklenburg Board of Education*, 402 U.S. 1 (1971).

16. Reich, *The Greening of America*, 14.

17. *Keyes v. School District No. 1, Denver*, 413 U.S. 189 (1973).

18. Ibid.

19. Rossell, "The Evolution of School Desegregation Plans."

20. Ibid.

21. *Boston's Children First v. Boston School Committee*, 183 F. Supp. 2d 382 (1999).

22. David Armor, "The Evidence on Busing," *The Public Interest* 28 (1972): 90–126.

23. David Armor, "Reflections of an Expert Witness," in *The End of Desegregation*, ed. Stephen J. Caldas and Carl L. Bankston III (New York: Nova Science Publishers, 2003), 3–23.

24. *Swann v. Charlotte-Mecklenburg Board of Education*.

25. *Milliken v. Bradley I*, 418 U.S. 717 (1974).

26. *Pasadena City Board of Education v. Spangler*, 427 U.S. 424, 96 S. Ct. 2697 (1976).

27. Ibid.

28. *Board of Education of Oklahoma City Public Schools, Independent School District No. 89 v. Dowell*, 498 U.S. 237, 111 S. Ct. 630 (1991).

29. Ibid., 250

30. *Sheff v. O'Neill*, Connecticut Supreme Ct. 678 A. 2d 1267 (1996).

31. Connecticut Office of Legislative Research, "Questions about Sheff v. O'Neill Settlement," February 13, 2003, http://www.cga.state.ct.us/2003/olrdata/ed/rpt/2003-R-0214.htm (retrieved October 14, 2003).

32. Adam Cohen, "The Supreme Struggle," *New York Times, Education Life Supplement*, January 18, 2004.

33. Richard D. Kahlenberg, *All Together Now: Creating Middle-Class Schools through Public School Choice* (Washington, D.C.: Brookings Institute Press, 2001).

34. Richard D. Kahlenberg, "Economic School Integration," in *The End of Desegregation?*, eds. Stephen J. Caldas and Carl L. Bankston III (New York: Nova Science Publishers, 2003), 149–175.

35. Bankston and Caldas, *A Troubled Dream*.

36. *Grutter v. Bollinger*, 123 S. Ct. 2325, 156 L.Ed.2d 304 (2003).

37. *Gratz v. Bollinger*, 123 S. Ct. 2411, 156 L.Ed.2d 257 (2003).

38. Caroline Hendrie, "City Boards Weigh Rule on Diversity," *Education Week on the Web*, November 5, 2003, http://www.edweek.org/ew/ewstory.cfm?slug=10Deseg.h23.

39. Myrle Croasdale, "Texas Schools Ponder Race Role in Admissions," *Amednews.com*, February 9, 2004, http://www.ama-assn.org/amednews/2004/02/09/prsd0209.htm (retrieved June 1, 2004).

40. David Schimmel, "Affirming Affirmative Action: Supreme Court Holds Diversity to Be a Compelling Interest in University Admissions," *Education Law Reporter* 415 (November 6, 2003): 401–415.

41. Charles V. Willie, remarks made during "Third General Session," Education Law Association annual meeting, Hilton El Conquistador, Tucson, AZ, November 20, 2004.

CHAPTER 3

1. For a more in-depth discussion of this issue, see the following: Caldas and Bankston, *A Troubled Dream*; Carl L. Bankston III and C. Eddie Palmer, "The Children of Hobbes: Education, Family Structure, and the Problem of Social Order," *Sociological Focus* 31 (1998): 265–280; Stephen J. Caldas, Carl L. Bankston III, and Judy S. Cain, eds. "Social Capital, Academic Capital, and the 'Harm and Benefit' Thesis: Evidence from a Desegregating School District," in *The End of Desegregation?* (New York: Nova Science Publishers, 2003), 121–148.

2. U.S. Bureau of the Census, "Census Bureau Releases Population Estimates by Age, Sex, Race, and Hispanic Origin. 2003," http://www.census.gov/Press-Release/www/2003/cb03-16.html (press release retrieved January 24, 2003).

3. Min Zhou and John R. Logan, "Increasing Diversity and Persistent Segregation: The Challenges of Educating Minority and Immigrant Children in Urban America," in *The End of Desegregation?*, ed. Stephen J. Caldas and Carl L. Bankston III (New York: Nova Science Publishers, 2003), 177–194.

4. In its 2003 rulings on the University of Michigan cases *Grutter v. Bollinger* (law school admissions) and *Gratz v. Bollinger* (undergraduate admissions), the U.S. Supreme Court implicitly endorsed the position that Hispanics, as well as blacks and Native Americans, were historically disadvantaged minorities worthy of special consideration.

5. H. G. Reza, "Historic School Bias Suit Nearly Forgotten," *Los Angeles Times*, September 10, 1996, A3.

6. For a detailed look at how an immigrant minority manages to succeed academically in the face of many disadvantages, see Min Zhou and Carl L. Bankston III, *Growing up American: How Vietnamese Children Adapt to Life in the United States* (New York: Russell Sage Foundation, 1998).

7. Roslyn R. Mickelson, "Subverting Swann: First and Second Generation Segregation in the Charlotte-Mecklenburg Schools," *American Educational Research Journal* 38 (2001): 215–252.

8. For more on how whites do academically in majority black schools, see Carl

L. Bankston III and Stephen J. Caldas, "Majority African American Schools and the Perpetuation of Social Injustice: the Influence of Defacto Segregation on Academic Achievement," *Social Forces* 72 (1996): 534–555; Carl L. Bankston III and Stephen J. Caldas, *A Troubled Dream: The Promise and Failure of School Desegregation in Louisiana* (Nashville, TN: Vanderbilt University Press, 2002).

9. Zhou and Logan, "Increasing Diversity and Persistent Ségregátion."

10. Ibid., 184.

11. Teresa C. Martin and Larry L. Bumpass, "Recent Trends in Marital Disruption," *Demography* 26 (1989): 37–51.

12. See, for example, how the issue is dealt with in Stanley Elkins, *Slavery: A Problem in American Institutional and Intellectual Life* (Chicago: University of Chicago Press, 1959); and E. Franklin Frazier, *The Negro Family in the United States*, rev. ed. (New York: Macmillan, 1957).

13. Herbert W. Gutman, *The Black Family in Slavery and Freedom, 1750–1925* (New York: Pantheon, 1976).

14. John W. Blassingame, *The Slave Community: Plantation Life in the Antebellum South* (New York: Oxford University Press, 1982); Eugene D. Genovese, *Roll, Jordan, Roll: The World the Slaves Made* (New York: Vintage, 1974).

15. George Akerlof, Jane Yellen, and Michael L. Katz, "An Analysis of Out-of-Wedlock Childbearing in the United States," *Quarterly Journal of Economics* 111 (1996): 277–317.

16. Gary S. Becker, *A Treatise on the Family* (Cambridge, MA: Harvard University Press, 1981); Gary S. Becker and Elisabeth M. Landes, "An Economic Analysis of Marital Instability," *Journal of Political Economy* 85 (1977): 1141–1187.

17. As argued by Robert Moffitt, "The Effect of the U.S. Welfare System on Marital Status," *Journal of Public Economics* 41 (1990): 101–124; Charles Murray, "Welfare and the Family: The U.S. Experience," *Journal of Labor Economics* 11 (1993): S224–S262; Robert D. Plotnick, "Welfare and Out-of-Wedlock Childbearing: Evidence from the 1980s," *Journal of Marriage and the Family* 52 (1990): 735–746; Lionel Tiger, *The Decline of Males* (New York: Golden Books, 1999).

18. James S. Coleman, "Families and Schools," *Equality and Achievement in Education*, ed. James S. Coleman (Boulder, CO: Westview Press, 1990), 325–340; James L. Collier, *The Rise of Selfishness in America* (New York: Oxford University Press, 1991); Gertrude Himmelfarb, *The De-moralization of Society: From Victorian Virtues to Modern Values* (New York: Knopf, 1995).

19. Allen C. Acock and K. Jill Kiecolt, "Is It Family Structure or Socioeconomic Status? Family Structure during Adolescence and Social Adjustment," *Social Forces* 68 (1989): 553–571.

20. Sarah McLanahan and Karen Booth, "Mother-Only Families: Problems, Prospects, and Politics," *Journal of Marriage and the Family* 51 (1989): 557–579; Nancy Vaden-Kiernan, Nicholas S. Ialongo, Jane Pearson, and Sheppard Kellam, "Household Family Structure and Children's Aggressive Behavior: A Longitudinal Study of Urban Elementary School Children," *Journal of Abnormal Child Psychology* 23 (1995): 553–568; Darin R. Featherstone, Bert P. Cundick, and Larry C.

Jensen, "Differences in School Behavior and Achievement between Children from Intact, Reconstituted, and Single-Parent Families," *Adolescence* 27 (1992): 1–12.

21. David Popenoe, "The Institution of Marriage Is Weakening Society," *Society* 36 (September/October 1999): 26.

22. U.S. Bureau of the Census, *Survey of Income and Program Participation*, Table 1, "Detailed Living Arrangements of Children by Race and Hispanic Origin" (Washington, D.C.: U.S. Government Printing Office, 1996).

23. Carl L. Bankston III and Stephen J. Caldas, "Family Structure, Schoolmates, and the Racial Inequalities in School Achievement," *Journal of Marriage and the Family* 60 (1998): 715–723.

24. Mike Hasten, "State Officials Pleased with Accountability Ranking," *The Advertiser*, January 7, 2004, B3.

25. U.S. Bureau of the Census, *Census of Population and Housing* (Washington, D.C.: U.S. Government Printing Office, 1990, 2000).

26. John R. Logan, *The New Latinos: Who They Are, Where They Are* (Albany: Lewis Mumford Center for Comparative Urban and Regional Research, State University of New York at Albany, 2001); Carl L. Bankston III, "Immigrants in the New South: An Introduction," *Sociological Spectrum* 23, no. 2 (2003): 123–128.

27. Zhou and Logan, "Increasing Diversity and Persistent Segregation," 179.

28. Jesse McKinnon, *The Black Population, 2000: Census 2000 Brief* (Washington, D.C.: U.S. Government Printing Office, August 2001), 5.

29. Ibid.

30. Betsy Guzman, *The Hispanic Population, 2000: Census 2000 Brief* (Washington, D.C.: U.S. Government Printing Office, May 2001).

31. Jesse McKinnon, *The Black Population, 2000, Census 2000 Brief* (Washington, D.C.: U.S. Government Printing Office, 2001).

32. Jessica S. Barnes and Claudette E. Bennett, *The Asian Population, 2000: Census 2000 Brief* (Washington, D.C.: U.S. Government Printing Office, February 2002).

33. U.S. Bureau of the Census, *October Current Population Surveys, 1972–2000* (Washington, D.C.: U.S. Department of Commerce).

34. Elaine Woo, "Court Action Ends 26-Year L.A. School Desegregation Case," *Los Angeles Times*, March 28, 1989, M4.

35. Ibid.

36. "Latino Segregation in Schools Increases," *Los Angeles Times*, July 27, 1987, I9.

37. Ibid.

38. See, in particular, the collection in Gary Orfield, Susan E. Eaton and the Harvard Project on School Desegregation, *Dismantling Desegregation: The Quiet Reversal of Brown v. Board of Education* (New York: The New Press, 1996).

39. The details of this "bilingual experiment" were published in the following articles: Stephen J. Caldas and Suzanne Caron-Caldas, "A Sociolinguistic Analysis of the Language Preferences of Adolescent Bilinguals: Shifting Allegiances and Developing Identities," *Applied Linguistics* 23 (2002): 490–514; and "The Influence of Fam-

ily, School and Community on 'Bilingual Preference': Results from a Louisiana/Quebec Case Study," *Journal of Applied Psycholinguistics* 21 (2000): 365–381.

40. Donna Christian, *Two-Way Bilingual Education: Students Learning through Two Languages* (Santa Cruz, CA: National Center for Research on Cultural Diversity and Second Language Learning, 1994).

41. U.S. Bureau of the Census, *Current Population Survey: October 2000*, "Dropout Rates in the United States, 2000" (Washington, D.C.: U.S. Department of Commerce, National Center for Education Statistics), http://nces.ed.gov/pubs 2002/droppub_2001/ (retrieved September 1, 2004).

42. Patricia Ward Biederman, "Blacks and Latinos Lag in Readiness for College," *Los Angeles Times*, October 23, 1988, sec. 2, 1, 4.

43. Readers may wonder why the UC system seems to regard Filipinos as non-Asians. If so, we share the perplexity.

44. University of California Application, "Application, Admissions, and Enrollment of California Resident Freshmen for Fall 1995 through 2002," www.ucop.edu/news/factsheets/flowfrc9502.pdf (retrieved December 20, 2003).

45. Pamela Ferdinand, "Suit Calls Diversity Policy Unfair," *Washington Post*, January 29, 1998, A10; Boston Public Schools Enrollment, boston.k12.ma.us/bps/enrollment.asp; Pamela Ferdinand, "Critics Fear Schools Have Turned back the Clock in Boston," *Washington Post*, July 18, 1999, A3.

46. Pamela Ferdinand, "Suit Calls Diversity Policy Unfair," A10.

47. Pamela Ferdinand, "Critics Fear Schools," A3.

48. For a summary of the competing explanations, see Carl L. Bankston III, "The Academic Achievement of Vietnamese American Adolescents: A Community Perspective," *Sociological Spectrum* 16 (1996): 109–127.

49. Carl L. Bankston III, "Being Well vs. Doing Well: Self-esteem and School Performance among Immigrant and Non-immigrant Racial and Ethnic Groups," *International Migration Review* 36 (2002): 389–415.

50. Carl L. Bankston III, "Youth Gangs and the New Second Generation: A Review Essay," *Aggression and Violent Behavior: A Review Journal* 3 (1998): 35–45.

51. Massachusetts Comprehensive Assessment System (MCAS), "Annual Comparisons for Specific Schools," www.profiles.doe.mass.edu.

52. Ibid.

53. Erol Ricketts and Ronald Mincy, *The Growth of the Underclass: 1970–1980* (Washington, D.C.: Urban Institute Press, 1988).

54. See, for example, Ken Auletta, *The Underclass* (New York: Random House, 1982); Nichlas Lemann, "The Origins of the Underclass," *Atlantic*, June 1986, 31–61.

55. Herbert J. Gans, "Deconstructing the Underclass: The Term's Danger as a Planning Concept," *Journal of the American Planning Association* 56 (1990): 271–277; Herbert J. Gans, *The War against the Poor: The Underclass and Antipoverty Policy* (New York: Basic Books, 1995).

56. Gene L. Maeroff, "City Schools Hint Suburbs Are Needed in Integration," *New York Times*, February 27, 1974, 1.

57. William Julius Wilson, *When Work Disappears: The World of the New Urban Poor* (New York: Knopf, 1996).

58. See ibid., 51–86.

59. Chris Adams, "Can Schools Save Black Boys?" *New Orleans Times-Picayune*, February 2, 1992, A1ff. Quotation from A5.

60. Heather Knight, "S.F. Parents Rekindle Desegregation Debate: Issue of Diversity vs. Neighborhood Schools," *San Francisco Chronicle*, October 7, 2003, A1.

CHAPTER 4

1. Robert J. Sampson, Jeffrey D. Morenoff, and Felton Earls, "Beyond Social Capital: Spatial Dynamics of Collective Efficacy for Children," *American Sociological Review* 64 (1999): 633–666.

2. Rodney Finke and Roger Finke, *Acts of Faith: Explaining the Human Side of Religion* (Berkeley: University of California Press, 2000), 118.

3. James S. Coleman, *Foundations of Social Theory* (Cambridge: Belknap Press of Harvard University Press, 1990), 318.

4. James S. Coleman, "Social Capital in the Creation of Human Capital," *American Journal of Sociology* 94 (1988): S95–S120; James S. Coleman, "Families and Schools," in *Equality and Achievement in Education*, ed. James S. Coleman (Boulder, CO: Westview Press, 1990), 325–340.

5. Alexis de Tocqueville, *Democracy in America*, trans. and ed. Harvey C. Mansfield and Delba Winthrop (Chicago: University of Chicago Press, 2000). For a brief discussion of the Tocquevillean roots of Putnam's thought, see Carl L. Bankston III, "No Bowling at All: Television, the Vita Inactiva, and Social Capital," *Sociological Focus* 36 (2003): 99–110.

6. Robert D. Putnam, "Bowling Alone: America's Declining Social Capital," *Journal of Democracy* 6 (1995): 65–78. Robert D. Putnam, *Bowling Alone: The Collapse and Revival of American Community* (New York: Simon & Schuster, 2001).

7. For an argument against Putnam's declining social capital view, see Everett C. Ladd, "The Data Just Don't Show Erosion of America's 'Social Capital,'" *Public Perspective* 7 (1996): 1–30.

8. Putnam, *Bowling Alone*.

9. Douglas B. Downeu, "Parental and Family Involvement in Education," in *School Reform Proposals: The Research Evidence*, ed. A. Molnar (Tempe, AZ: Information Age, 2002).

10. Meredith Phillips et al., "Family Background, Parenting Practices, and the Black-White Test Score Gap," in *The Black-White Test Score Gap*, ed. C. Jencks and M. Phillips (Washington, D.C.: Brookings Institution, 1998), 127.

11. B. Hart and T. R. Risley, "American Parenting of Language-learning Children: Persisting Differences in Family-Child Interactions Observed in Natural Home Environments," *Developmental Psychology* 28, no. 6 (1992): 1104.

12. Meredith Phillips et al., "Family Background."

13. C. Crain-Thoreson and P. S. Dale, "Do Early Talkers Become Early Readers?

Linguistic Precocity, Preschool Language, and Emergent Literacy," *Developmental Psychology* 28 (1992): 421–429.

14. Eileen W. Ball and Benita A. Blachman, "Does Phoneme Awareness Training in Kindergarten Make a Difference in Early Word Recognition and Developmental Spelling?" *Reading Research Quarterly* 26, no. 1 (1991): 49–66.

15. Phillips et al., "Family Background."

16. Vincent J. Roscigno and J. W. Ainsworth-Darnell, "Race, Cultural Capital, and Educational Resources: Persistent Inequalities and Achievement Returns," *Sociology of Education* 72 (1999): 158–178.

17. For the best-known statement of this latter position, see the "cultural capital" argument made by the late French sociologist Pierre Bourdieu, in *Distinction: A Social Critique of the Judgment of Taste*, trans. Richard Nice (Cambridge: Harvard University Press, 1984).

18. Laurence D. Steinberg, *Beyond the Classroom: Why School Reform Has Failed and What Parents Can Do* (New York: Simon and Schuster, 1997).

19. James S. Coleman, "Social Capital"; James S. Coleman, *Foundations of Social Theory*.

20. Coleman, *Foundations of Social Theory*, 595.

21. Judith Baer, "The Effects of Family Structure and SES on Family Processes in Early Adolescence," *Journal of Adolescence* 22 (1999): 341–354.

22. Min Zhou and Carl L. Bankston III, *Growing up American: How Vietnamese Children Adapt to Life in the United States* (New York: Russell Sage Foundation, 1998).

23. Quotation from Min Zhou, "Social Capital in Chinatown: the Role of Community-based Organizations and Families in the Adaptation of the Younger Generation," in *Beyond Black and White: New Voices, New Faces in the United States Schools*, ed. Lois Weis and Maxine S. Seller (Albany: State University of New York Press, 1997), 181–206. For a revealing look into the social structure of New York City's Chinatown, the reader should also check out Min Zhou's *Chinatown: The Socioeconomic Potential of an Urban Enclave* (Philadelphia: Temple University Press, 1995).

24. Soh Ji-young, "Measures Unveiled for Cutting Soaring Private Education Costs," *Korea Times*, February 17, 2004, http://times.hankooki.com/lpage/200402/kt2004021716532810230.htm (retrieved July 15, 2004).

25. Personal communication, Seong Man Park, July 14, 2004.

26. Carol Stack, *All Our Kin: Strategies for Survival in a Black Community* (New York: Harper & Row, 1974).

27. M. Patricia Fernandez-Kelly, "Social and Cultural Capital in the Urban Ghetto: Implications for Economic Sociology and Immigration," in *Economic Sociology of Immigration: Essays on Networks, Ethnicity, and Entrepreneurship*, ed. Alejandro Portes (New York: Russell Sage Foundation, 1995).

28. Child Trends Data Bank, http://www.childtrendsdatabank.org/family/thefamily/39parentalinvolvementinschools.htm, cites A. T. Henderson and N. Beria, *A New Generation of Evidence: The Family Is Critical to Student Achievement* (Washington, D.C.: National Committee for Citizens in Education, 1994).

29. Carl L. Bankston III and Stephen J. Caldas, *A Troubled Dream: The Promise and Failure of School Desegregation in Louisiana* (Nashville, TN: Vanderbilt University Press, 2002).

30. Ibid.

31. Debbie Burrow, Letter to the Editor, *Lafayette Daily Advertiser*, May 25, 2000.

32. Stephen J. Caldas, Carl L. Bankston III, and Judith S. Cain, "Social Capital, Academic Capital, and the 'Harm and Benefit' Thesis: Evidence from a Desegregating School District," in *The End of Desegregation?* eds. Stephen J. Caldas and Carl L. Bankston III (New York: Nova Science Publishers, 2003), 121–148.

33. For an excellent investigation of parental involvement and of some of the barriers to parental involvement on the part of families that are not middle class, see Annette Lareau, "Social Class and Family-School Relationships: The Importance of Cultural Capital," *Sociology of Education* 56 (April 1987): 73–85.

34. Caldas, Bankston, and Cain, "Social Capital."

35. John U. Ogbu and Astrid David, *Black American Students in an Affluent Suburb: A Study of Academic Disengagement* (New York: Lawrence Erlbaum Associates, 2003).

36. Roger D. Goddard, "Relational Networks, Social Trust, and Norms: A Social Capital Perspective on Students' Chances of Academic Success," *Educational Evaluation and Policy Analysis* 25 (Spring 2003): 59–74.

37. James S. Coleman, *The Adolescent Society* (New York: Free Press of Glencoe, 1961).

38. Ralph W. Emerson, "Culture," in *The Conduct of Life* (Boston: Ticknor and Fields, 1860, rev. 1876).

39. Steinberg, *Beyond the Classroom*, 159.

40. Summarized in Bankston and Caldas (2002), our rigorous statistical studies found average school peer socioeconomic status to be a more powerful predictor of individual student achievement than even a student's own background. Likewise, in *Beyond the Classroom*, Laurence Steinberg (1997) provides compelling justification for the relative greater influence of peer groups on adolescent behavior than the adolescent's own family.

41. Robert Putnam and Kristin A. Goss, "Introduction," in *Democracies in Flux: the Evolution of Social Capital in Contemporary Society*, ed. Robert Putnam (New York: Oxford University Press, 2002), 5.

42. Goddard, "Relational Networks," 61.

43. Signithia Fordham, *Blacked Out: Dilemmas of Race, Identity, and Success at Capital High* (Chicago: University of Chicago Press, 1995).

44. John McWhorter, "How Hip-Hop Holds Blacks Back," *City Journal* (Summer 2003): 28, http://www.city-journal.org/html/13_3_how_hip_hop.html (retrieved May 11, 2004).

45. Clarence Page, "Ignoring Black Political Correctness," *Daily Advertiser*, May 29, 2004: A9.

46. Ibid.

47. Lee Tee Jong, "Prolonged Economic Slump Forces Parents to Stop Extra Coaching for Their Children Which May Boost Chances of Entering Top Varsi-

ties," *The StraitsTimes Interactive*, June 30, 2004, http://www.straitstimes.com/eyeoneastasia/story/0,4395,259071,00.html (retrieved July 16, 2004).

48. L. Hudson and William M. Gray, "Formal Operation, the Imaginary Audience, and the Personal Fable," *Adolescence* 21 (1986): 751–765.

49. Stephen J. Caldas and Suzanne Caron-Caldas, "A Sociolinguistic Analysis of the Language Preferences of Adolescent Bilinguals: Shifting Allegiances and Developing Identities," *Applied Linguistics* 23 (2002): 490–514.

50. Steinberg, *Beyond the Classroom*, 158.

51. Personal communication, Stephanie Caldas, June 4, 2004.

52. See Laurence Steinberg's *Beyond the Classroom*.

53. David J. Armor, Christine H. Rossell, and Herbert J. Walberg, "The Outlook for School Desegregation," in *School Desegregation in the Twenty-first Century*, ed. Christine H. Rossell, Herbert J. Walberg, and David J. Armor (Westport, CT: Praeger, 2002), 323–333. The authors make this statement in summarizing a chapter in this same volume, by Charles M. Achilles, "Racial Disparities in School Discipline," 235–265.

54. Bankston and Caldas, *A Troubled Dream*.

55. Reported in Caldas, Bankston, and Cain, "Social Capital," 120–148.

56. Stephen J. Caldas, Carl L. Bankston III, and Judith Cain, "A Case Study of Teachers' Perceptions of School Desegregation and the Redistribution of Social and Academic Capital," in review for publication.

57. David G. Savage, "Many Minority Students Back in Their Old Schools," *Los Angeles Times*, April 11, 1982, 6.

58. "Both Races Distressed 5 Years after Coast Integration Order," *New York Times*, June 18, 1975, 22.

59. Putnam, "Bowling Alone," 69.

60. Ibid., 72.

61. Reported in Bankston and Caldas, *A Troubled Dream*, 93.

62. Tip O'Neill and Gary Hymel, *All Politics Is Local and Other Rules of the Game* (New York: Crown Publishers, 1994).

63. Steinberg, *Beyond the Classroom*, 153.

64. Christine H. Rossell, *Improving the Voluntary Desegregation Plan in the Baton Rouge School System*, a report to the court in the case of *Davis et al. v. East Baton Rouge School Board et al.*, October 27, 1999. The quotation is from a footnote on p. 6 of the report.

65. Marlene Cimons, "Dual School Systems in South Thrive," *Los Angeles Times*, March 1, 1982, 6.

66. See Bankston and Caldas, *A Troubled Dream*, 163.

67. Stephen Casmier, "Sorrow and Joy: Mingle in Death of Woodland School," *New Orleans Times-Picayune*, June 1, 1990, B1, B2. Retired principal Emily Watkins quoted on p. 2.

68. Stephen J. Caldas, Roslin Growe, and Carl L. Bankston III, "African American Reaction to Lafayette Parish School Desegregation Order: From Delight to Disenchantment," *Journal of Negro Education* 71, no. 2 (2002): 43–59.

69. Information provided by school board member David Thibodaux, February 4, 2004.

70. Sebreana Domingue, "Board: Keep Vermilion Open," *Daily Advertiser*, February 5, 2004, A1.

71. Frederick A. Rogers, *The Black High School and Its Community* (Lexington, MA: D. C. Heath & Co, 1975).

72. Ibid., 73.

73. Vivian Gunn Morris and Curtis L. Morris, *The Price They Paid: Desegregation in an African American Community* (New York: Teachers College Press, 2002).

74. Ibid., 79.

75. Asa G. Hilliard III, Foreword to Vivian Gunn Morris and Curtis L. Morris, *The Price They Paid*, x.

76. David E. Thigpen, "An Elusive Dream in the Promised Land," *Time*, May 10, 2004, 32.

77. Richard Burgess, "Schools Remain Tough Issue in Civil Rights: Local Efforts on Desegregation Reviewed by Those Who Remember Struggle," *Sunday Advertiser*, January 18, 2004, A4.

78. Ibid.

79. See, in particular, Carl L. Bankston III and Stephen J. Caldas, "Majority African American Schools and the Perpetuation of Social Injustice: The Influence of Defacto Segregation on Academic Achievement," *Social Forces* 72 (1996): 534–555.

CHAPTER 5

1. For the view that none of the arguments in favor of the public provision of education are persuasive, readers may want to look at John R. Lott, Jr., "Why Is Education Publicly Provided? A Critical Survey," *Cato Journal* 7, no. 2 (Fall 1987): 475–501.

2. See the classic article by Milton Friedman, "The Role of Government in Education," in *Economics and the Public Interest*, ed. Robert Solow (New Brunswick, NJ: Rutgers University Press, 1955), 123–155.

3. Anthony Downs, *An Economic Theory of Democracy* (New York: Harper, 1957).

4. Among the best-known criticisms of this sort are Samuel Bowles, "Schooling and Inequality from Generation to Generation," *Journal of Political Economy* 80 (June 1972): S219–S251; and Samuel Bowles and Herbert Gintis, *Schooling in Capitalist America: Educational Reform and the Contradictions of Economic Life* (New York: Basic Books, 1976).

5. Joel H. Spring, *The Sorting Machine Revisited: National Educational Policy since 1945* (New York: Longman, 1989).

6. Charles M. Tiebout, "A Pure Theory of Local Expenditure," *Journal of Political Economy* 64 (October 1956): 416–424.

7. For a summary and critique of the intellectual development argument for

education in a democratic society and of the inculcation of values arguments, see Lott, "Why Is Education Publicly Provided?"

8. Jonathan Kozol, *Savage Inequalities: Children in American Schools* (New York: Harper Perennial, 1992).

9. Thorstein Veblen, *The Theory of the Leisure Class: An Economic Study of Institutions* (New York: Macmillan, 1902).

10. Dave Barry, "Preschool Panicking," *Miami Herald*, http://www.miami.com/mld/miamiherald/living/columnists/dave_barry/ (retrieved November 25, 2004).

11. Eric A. Hanushek, "The Economics of Schooling: Production and Efficiency in Public Schools," *Journal of Economic Literature* 24 (1986): 1141–1177.

12. Gary Burtless, "Introduction and Summary," in *Does Money Matter? The Effect of School Resources on Student Achievement and Adult Success*, ed. Gary Burtless (Washington, D.C.: Brookings Institution Press, 1996), 1–42, 43.

13. Anonymous communication, April 1, 2004.

14. Cited in Kristen King, "Expert: BR Losing Its White Students," *The Advocate*, July 13, 1999, A1.

15. *Missouri v. Jenkins*, 115 S. Ct. 2038 (1977/1978/1984/1987/1990/1995/1997).

16. Paul Ciotti, "Money and School Performance: Lessons from the Kansas City Desegregation Experiment," *Cato Policy Analysis No. 298* (Washington, D.C.: Cato Institute, 1998).

17. Ibid., 1.

18. Ibid.

19. *Missouri v. Jenkins II*, 515 U.S. 70, 115 S. Ct. 2038 (1995).

20. Tracy Allen, "Judge Grants School District Unitary Status," *The Call*, August 15, 2003, http://www.kccall.com/news/2003/0815/Front_Page/027.html (retrieved October 9, 2003).

21. See, for example, Stephen J. Caldas and Carl L. Bankston III, "The Effect of School Population Socioeconomic Status on Student Academic Achievement," *Journal of Educational Research* 90 (1997): 269–277.

22. Geraint Johnes, *The Economics of Education* (New York: St. Martin's Press, 1993), 5.

23. Adam Smith, *The Wealth of Nations* (1776. repr., New York: Random House, 1977). Smith argued that the whole country benefited when everyone was free to pursue his or her own best economic self-interests without government interference.

24. Among the many works that have found this are James S. Coleman and Thomas Hoffer, *Public and Private High Schools: The Impact of Communities* (New York: Basic Books, 1987); James S. Coleman, Thomas Hoffer, and Sally Kilgore, *High School Achievement: Public, Catholic, and Private Schools Compared* (New York: Basic Books, 1982); Valerie Lee, Todd K. Chow-Hoy, and David T. Burkam, "Sector Differences in High School Course-taking: A Private School or Catholic School Effect?" *Sociology of Education* 71 (1998): 314–335; William Sander and Anthony C. Krautmann, "Catholic Schools, Dropout Rates, and Educational Achievement," *Economic Inquiry* 33 (1995): 217–233.

25. Robert J. Franciosi, *The Rise and Fall of American Public Schools: The Political Economy of Public Education in the Twentieth Century* (New York: Praeger, 2004), 90.

26. Julian R. Betts and Robert W. Fairlie, "Explaining Racial and Immigrant Differences in Private School Attendance," *Journal of Urban Economics* 50 (2001): 26–51; Richard J. Buddin, Joseph J. Cordes, and Sheila Nataraj Kirby, "School Choice in California: Who Chooses Private Schools?" *Journal of Urban Economics* 44 (1998): 110–134; Bruce W. Hamilton and Molly K. MacCauley, "Determinants and Consequences of the Private-Public School Choice," *Journal of Urban Economics* 29 (1991): 282–294.

27. Our calculations from Steven Ruggles and Matthew Sobek, *Integrated Public Use Microdata Series, Version 3.0* (1% Census Sample) (Minneapolis: Historical Census Projects, University of Minnesota, 2003).

28. Our calculations for Ruggles and Sobek, *Integrated Public Use Microdata Series*.

29. Quoted in Franciosi, *Rise and Fall of American Public Schools*, 141.

30. David Brasington, "Which Measures of School Quality Does the Housing Market Value?" *Journal of Real Estate Research* 18 (1999): 395–413; Donald R. Haurin and David Brasington, "School Quality and Real Estate Prices: Inter- and Intrametropolitan Effects," *Journal of Housing Economics* 5 (1986): 351–368.

31. Quoted in Carl L. Bankston III and Stephen J. Caldas, *A Troubled Dream: The Promise and Failure of School Desegregation in Louisiana* (Nashville, TN: Vanderbilt University Press), 70.

32. Wendy Mansfield and Elizabeth Farris, *Office of Civil Rights Survey Redesign: A Feasibility Survey* (NCES 92–130) (Washington, D.C.: National Center for Education Statistics, U.S. Department of Education, September 1992).

33. National Center for Education Statistics, *Digest of Education Statistics, Tables, and Figures*, Table 54 (Washington, D.C.: NCES, U.S. Department of Education, 1997).

34. Spyros Konstantopoulos, Manisha Modi, and Larry V. Hedges, "Who Are America's Gifted?" *American Journal of Education* 109 (2001): 344–382.

35. Franciosi, *Rise and Fall of American Public Schools*, 142.

36. Ibid.

37. Myron Lieberman and Charlene K. Haar, *Public Education as a Business: Real Costs and Accountability* (Lanham, MD: Scarecrow Press, 2003), 83.

38. Ibid., 86.

39. Ibid.

40. See Carl L. Bankston III and Stephen J. Caldas, "White Enrollment in Nonpublic Schools, Public School Racial Composition, and Student Performance," *The Sociological Quarterly* 41 (2000): 539–550.

CHAPTER 6

1. Rone Tempest, "Troubled Arkansas School Becomes Best in State," *Los Angeles Times*, February 28, 1982, 1.

2. Peter Baker, "40 Years Later, 9 Are Welcomed," *Washington Post*, September 26, 1997, A1+. Quotation taken from p. A9.

3. Vanessa Everett, "Campuses Journey through Desegregation," *Beaumont Enterprise*, August 24, 2003, 1.

4. Ibid., 4.

5. Ibid.

6. Associated Press, "Judge Ends Desegregation Order in Dallas Schools," *CNN.com*, June 6, 2003, http://www.cnn.com/2003/EDUCATION/06/06/dallas.schools.ap/ (retrieved December 12, 2004).

7. "Busing of 17,328 Ordered in Dallas," *New York Times*, April 11, 1976, 33.

8. Dallas Independent School District Adopted Budget, 2000–2001.

9. Dallas Independent School District Salary Report, January 11, 2001.

10. We are indebted to Josh Benton of the *Dallas News* for passing along to us up-to-date information on the desegregation experience in the Dallas Independent School District.

11. These figures add to more than 100 percent because Latinos can also be classified as whites.

12. Texas Education Agency, *Academic Excellence Indicator System, 2002–03 District Performance* (Austin, TX: Texas Education Agency, 2004).

13. Associated Press, "Judge Ends Desegregation."

14. Ibid.

15. Events in the Baton Rouge case are drawn primarily from one of our earlier books and articles. See Carl L. Bankston and Stephen J. Caldas, *A Troubled Dream: The Promise and Failure of School Desegregation in Louisiana* (Nashville, TN: Vanderbilt University Press, 2002); Stephen J. Caldas and Carl L. Bankston III, "Baton Rouge, Desegregation, and White Flight," *Research in the School* 8, no. 2 (2001): 21–32.

16. Quoted in Carl L. Bankston III and Stephen J. Caldas, *A Troubled Dream: The Promise and Failure of School Desegregation in Louisiana* (Nashville: Vanderbilt University Press, 2002), 86.

17. In Louisiana, the parish (county) is in most cases identical with the school district.

18. Quoted in Bankston and Caldas, *A Troubled Dream*, 96.

19. See ibid., 92.

20. Quoted in ibid.

21. Louisiana Department of Education, *Annual Financial and Statistical Report, 2002–2003* (Baton Rouge: Louisiana Department of Education, 2004).

22. On the "lavish praise" heaped on the Charlotte school system after desegregation, see Stephen Samuel Smith, *Boom for Whom? Education, Desegregation, and Development in Charlotte* (Albany: State University of New York Press, 2004).

23. Quoted in ibid., 60.

24. Ibid., 62.

25. Ibid., 63.

26. Roslyn Arlin Mickelson, "White Privilege in a Desegregating School Sys-

tem: The Charlotte-Mecklenburg Schools Thirty Years after Swann," in *The End of Desegregation?* ed. Stephen J. Caldas and Carl L. Bankston III (New York: Nova Science Publications, 2003), 97–119.

27. Smith, *Boom for Whom?*, 83.

28. Quoted in Alison Moranta, "Desegregation at Risk," in *Dismantling Desegregation: The Quiet Reversal of Brown v. Board of Education*, ed. Gary Orfield, Susan E. Eaton, and the Harvard Project on School Desegregation (New York: The New Press, 1996), 195.

29. Sue Anne Presley, "Charlotte Schools Are Scrambling," *Washington Post*, November 8, 1999, A3.

30. Smith, *Boom for Whom?*, 6.

31. Test results are taken from the Charlotte-Mecklenburg Schools website, http://www.cms.k12.nc.us/departments/instrAccountability/schoolPerforman ce.asp (retrieved February 15, 2004).

32. "Louisville Busing Found to Alter Housing Pattern," *New York Times*, May 27, 1977, A9.

33. *Steven V. Roberts*, "Mixed Results of Integration Typified in Louisville School," *New York Times*, March 16, 1978, A23.

34. Ibid.

35. Iver Peterson, "Louisville, Once Violent, Then Calm, Is Now Edgy," *New York Times*, November 18, 1979, D1.

36. U.S. District Court, Western District of Kentucky at Louisville, Civil Action No. 3:98-CV-262-H.

37. Kentucky Department of Education, *Spring 2003 Kentucky Performance Report* (Frankfort, KY, 2003).

38. Bankston and Caldas, *A Troubled Dream*.

39. Lisa Frazier, "P.G. Braces for Major Changes," *Washington Post*, June 24, 1996, B1.

40. Lisa Frazier, "P.G. Schools Struggle with Racial Plan," *Washington Post*, April 2, 1996, C1. Quotation of Ms. Teasdale taken from p. C1.

41. Ibid., C6.

42. Lisa Frazier, "Judge Blocks Move by P.G. School Board to Ease Magnet Racial Quotas," *Washington Post*, July 9, 1996, B1.

43. Peter Pae, "In P.G., A New School of Thought," *Washington Post*, July 28, 1996, B1+.

44. Lisa Frazier, "Prince George's School Plan Hurt by Tax Revolt," *Washington Post*, December 1, 1996, B1.

45. Charles Babington and Lisa Frazier, "Proposal Would End Busing, Settle Suit in Prince George's," *Washington Post*, October 21, 1997, A1+.

46. Lisa Frazier, "Judge Ends Busing in Prince George's," *Washington Post*, September 2, 1998, A1+.

47. 2004 Maryland Report Card. Data available online at www.mdreportcard. org/Enroll_ByGenderRace.

48. 2004 Maryland Report Card. Data available online at www.mdreportcard. org/msa.

49. Mark Nichols and Kim L. Cooper, "Segregation Creeps Back In," *Indianapolis Star*, May 16, 2004. Available online at www.indystar.com.

50. Jon Jeter, "Integrated Magnet School Leaves Students Poles Apart," *Washington Post*, February 13, 1998, A1.

51. Nichols and Cooper, "Segregation Creeps Back In."

52. Data on the racial composition of Indiana schools are taken from the school data information on the website of the Indiana Department of Education, www.ideanet.doe.state.in.us.

53. Indiana Department of Education, www.ideanet.doe.state.in.us.

54. Where not otherwise noted, much of our discussion of the St. Louis case is drawn from Amy Stuart Wells and Robert L. Crain, *Stepping over the Color Line: African American Students in White Suburban Schools* (New Haven, CT: Yale University Press, 1997). Wells and Crain provide an excellent case study of St. Louis, although their perspective and conclusions differ from ours. We admire their work, yet we take issue with their ad hominem characterizations of the white suburbanites who disagreed with interdistrict busing as simply historically uninformed "resistors," contrasted with the "visionaries" who supported the program.

55. Hon. William Clay in the House of Representatives, July 16, 1999.

56. Joy Kiviat, "Could School Choice Save St. Louis?" *School Reform News*, December 1, 2000. Available online at http://www.heartland.org/Article.cfm? artId=10832.

57. Missouri Assessment Program (MAP), 1997–2004. St. Louis City Disaggregate Data by Race/Ethnicity. Available online at http://dese.mo.gov/schooldata/ four/115115/mapdnone.html.

58. Wells and Crain, *Stepping over the Color Line*. See the map on p. 254.

59. Paul Delaney, "Chicago to Attempt to Integrate Schools after Success in Other Cities," *New York Times*, September 4, 1977, A6.

60. Lesley Oeslner, "Court Backs Zoning That in Effect Bars Low Income Blacks," *New York Times*, January 12, 1977, A1.

61. "3 Chicago Youths Injured at an Anti-busing Rally," *New York Times*, September 12, 1977, A18.

62. "500 Chicago Students Walk out over Busing," *New York Times*, September 14, 1977, A16.

63. Nathaniel Sheppard, Jr., "Effort to Integrate Chicago Schools Has Had Little Effect, Study Finds," *New York Times*, March 6, 1979, A14.

64. "Chicago Board Rejects School Desegregation under U.S. Conditions," *New York Times*, October 18, 1979, B24.

65. Casey Banas, "City Must Involve Most Schools in Integration Plan," *Chicago Tribune*, September 28, 1980, sec. 1, p. 2.

66. Casey Banas, "School Board Oks New Bias Plan," *Chicago Tribune*, April 30, 1981, sec. 1, p. 1.

67. John McCarron and Stanely Ziemba, "Still Highly Segregated, Data Show," *Chicago Tribune*, April 7, 1981, sec. 1, p. 1.

68. "School Bill $87,732 for Bias Pact," *Chicago Tribune*, February 11, 1981, sec. 5, p. 1.

69. Jean Latz Griffin, "Schools Sue US for Integration Aid," *Chicago Tribune*, June 2, 1983, sec. 1, p. 1.

70. John Schmeltzer and John McCarron, "City School Aid Vetoed," *Chicago Tribune*, August 14, 1983, sec. 1, p. 1.

71. Casey Banas, "379 Schools Vie for U.S. Funds," *Chicago Tribune*, December 29, 1983, sec. 2, p. 1.

72. Mary Ann Zehr, "Close to Home," *Education Week* 23, no. 6 (2004): 30–34.

73. "Excerpts from Supreme Court Decision Barring Detroit-Suburban School Merger," *New York Times*, July 26, 1974, 17.

74. Warren Weaver, Jr., "Dual Schools Still a Problem but Now It Is in the North," *New York Times*, April 21, 1974, B5.

75. "U.S. Submits Brief in Integration Case," *New York Times*, February 24, 1974, 35.

76. "Excerpts from Supreme Court Decision Barring Detroit-Suburban School Merger," *New York Times*, July 26, 1974, 17.

77. Agis Salpukas, "Joy Is Expressed in the Suburbs, Reactions in Detroit Divided," *New York Times*, July 26, 1974, 17.

78. Ibid.

79. Much of the account of the Wisconsin case is drawn from Jack Dougherty, *More than One Struggle: The Evolution of Black School Reform in Milwaukee* (Chapel Hill: University of North Carolina Press, 2004).

80. Ibid., 36–39.

81. Ibid., 149.

82. Paul Delaney, "Wisconsin Ponders a Plan for State to Legislate Desegregation of Four Schools in Milwaukee and Suburbs," *New York Times*, April 13, 1975, 22.

83. Dougherty, *More than One Struggle*, 153.

84. Ibid.

85. Jim Mann, "18 Years En Route, LA Busing Arrives at the Highest Court," *Los Angeles Times*, March 31, 1982, 1–2.

86. Robert Lindsey, "Anger in California," *New York Times*, March 5, 1978, E4.

87. David G. Savage, "School Integration, Crowding: Solutions in Conflict?" *Los Angeles Times*, October 27, 1985, sec. 2, p. 1.

88. "14,000 Apply for 'Magnet' Schools," *Los Angeles Times*, March 28, 1982, 25.

89. Ibid.

90. William Trombley, "Major Problems Face Magnet Schools," *Los Angeles Times*, April 12, 1982, 2.

91. Lee Harris and Tendayi Kumbula, "Many Parents Giving up on Black Public Schools," *Los Angeles Times*, September 1, 1982, 1+.

92. Pamela Moreland, "Armor Doesn't Miss a Beat in Battle against Busing," *Los Angeles Times*, June 6, 1985, 3.

93. Pamela Moreland, "Board Raises Ratio of Minority Enrollments for 48 L.A. Schools," *Los Angeles Times*, May 19, 1987, 1.

94. Pamela Moreland, "Valley Is 'Getting Shafted,' Weintraub Says of Magnet Proposal," *Los Angeles Times*, November 14, 1987, 3.

95. Pamela Moreland, "L.A. Schools' White Limits at 11 Schools Is Reinforced," *Los Angeles Times*, June 7, 1988, 1.

96. Elaine Woo, "Judge Tells NAACP to Settle Lawsuit," *Los Angeles Times*, June 21, 1988, 1.

97. Sandy Banks, "Minority Gains Limited in L.A. Busing Program," *Los Angeles Times*, June 17, 1990, 1.

98. Tom Wicker, " 'Stifling' Pasadena's Integration," *New York Times*, April 29, 1973, 17.

99. Tom Wicker, "Integration in Pasadena," *New York Times*, April 27, 1973, 37.

100. Ibid.

101. William Trombley, "Public Schools in Pasadena Achieve Gains as Strife Ends," *Los Angeles Times*, June 8, 1986, sec. 1, p. 3.

102. Ibid.

103. Anica Butler, "Pasadena Superintendent Wants to Phase out Busing," *Los Angeles Times*, January 20, 2002, B10.

104. Anica Butler, "Pasadenans Debate Plan to End Busing," *Los Angeles Times*, February 9, 2002, B1.

105. John Herders, "Challenge to the North on School Segregation," *New York Times*, February 15, 1970, sec. 4, p. 2.

106. "Antibusing Law for State Voided by Federal Court," *New York Times*, October 2, 1970, 1.

107. Lesley Oelsner, "Queens School Plan Stirs Racial Controversy," *New York Times*, April 12, 1971, 48.

108. Martin Arnold, "Racial Outbreak at South Shore High School in Brooklyn Is Traced to Earlier Tensions," *New York Times*, April 30, 1971, 40.

109. Mia Vickers and Mitchell Vickers, *New York Times*, October 17, 1970, Letter to Editor.

110. "Integration Plan Hailed at School," *New York Times*, May 18, 1974, 35.

111. Gene I. Maeroff, "City Schools Hint Suburbs Are Needed in Integration," *New York Times*, February 27, 1974, 1.

112. Marcia Chambers, "School Integration Goals Elusive in Changing City," *New York Times*, April 23, 1979, B1.

113. "Abandoning Andrew Jackson High," *New York Times*, April 27, 1979, A30.

114. Marcia Chambers, "U.S. Tells Queens to Desegregate a School," *New York Times*, August 30, 1979, B3.

115. Ibid.

116. Ari L. Goldman, "Macchiarola Orders Whites Shifted to Nearly All-Black Queens School," *New York Times*, June 19, 1980, B5.

117. Gene Maeroff, "Imbalance in the Schools and the Dilemmas of Integration," *New York Times*, December 27, 1980, 25.

118. Ibid.

119. Ari L. Goldman, "Queens Parents Defy Macchiarola on Pupil Transfer," *New York Times*, February 2, 1981, B3.

120. Serge Schmemann, "Rosedale School Dispute: The Parents Feel Abused," *New York Times*, February 6, 1981, B1.

121. Edward A. Gargan, "Police Evict Protestors Occupying Queens School in Integration Case," *New York Times*, February 8, 1981, 1.

122. Ibid., 30.

123. Howard Sertan, letter, *New York Times*, February 18, 1981, 30.

124. Serge Schmemann, "White View of Schools Clash," *New York Times*, February 17, 1981, B1+, quotation on B1.

125. Gene L. Maeroff, "U.S. May Aid Queens Racial Plan," *New York Times*, September 11, 1981, B2.

126. Enrollment data available online at www.nycenet.edu/daa/SchoolReports.

CHAPTER 7

1. Arthur R. Jensen, "How Much Can We Boost IQ and Scholastic Achievement?" *Harvard Educational Review* 39 (1969): 1–123.

2. Arthur R. Jensen and Frank Miele, *Intelligence, Race, and Genetics: Conversations with Arthur R. Jensen* (Boulder, CO: Westview Press, 2002); Arthur R. Jensen, *The G Factor: The Science of Mental Ability* (Westport, CT: Praeger, 1998).

3. Richard Herrnstein and Charles Murray, *The Bell Curve* (New York: The Free Press, 1994).

4. One of the authors' graduate students, Kevin McGowen, wrote an outstanding research paper about *The Bell Curve*, wherein he coined the expression "the Bell Curve Curse" to describe the book's somewhat macabre beginnings.

5. Christopher Jencks and Meredith Phillips, *The Black-White Test Score Gap* (Washington, D.C.: Brookings Institution, 1998); Paul E. Barton, *Parsing the Achievement Gap: Baselines for Tracking Progress* (Princeton, NJ: Educational Testing Service, 2003).

6. National Center for Education Statistics, U.S. Department of Education. All information on the NAEP was retrieved from the website of the National Center for Educational Statistics, http://nces.ed.gov/nationsreportcard/about/trend.asp.

7. National Center for Education Statistics, "The Nation's Report Card," http://nces.ed.gov/nationsreportcard/reading/results2003/raceethnicity.asp (retrieved July 10, 2004).

8. Laurence D. Steinberg, *Beyond the Classroom: Why School Reform has Failed and What Parents Need to Do* (New York: Simon and Schuster, 1997).

9. From the College Board website, http://www.collegeboard.com/prod_downloads/about/news_info/cbsenior/yr2004/2004_CBSNR_total_group.pdf (retrieved November 28, 2004).

10. ACT news release, http://www.act.org/news/releases/2003/8-20-03.html (retrieved July 16, 2004).

11. Percentages rounded off to nearest whole number.

12. High school graduation rates obtained from U.S. Department of Commerce, Bureau of the Census, *March Current Population Surveys, 1971–2001* in *The Condition of Education, 2002* (Washington, D.C.: National Center for Education Statistics, U.S. Department of Education, 2003).

13. From the College Board website, http://www.collegeboard.com/prod_downloads/about/news_info/cbsenior/yr2004/graph_11_most_gaps.pdf (retrieved November 28, 2004).

14. College attendance figures obtained from U.S. Department of Commerce, Bureau of the Census, *March Current Population Surveys, 1971–2001* in *The Condition of Education, 2002* (Washington, D.C.: National Center for Education Statistics, U.S. Department of Education, 2003).

15. U.S. Department of Education, National Center for Education Statistics, *Postsecondary Institutions in the United States: Fall 2002 and Degrees and Other Awards Conferred: 2001–02* (Washington, D.C.: NCES, 2004), 154.

16. Jerome E. Morris, "Can Anything Good Come from Nazareth? Race, Class, and African American Schooling and Community in the Urban South and Midwest," *American Educational Research Journal* 41, no. 1 (2004): 69–112.

17. Barton, *Parsing the Achievement Gap.*

18. U.S. Department of Health and Human Services, Indicators of Welfare Dependency, *Annual Report to Congress, 2002,* 111–119. Data come from the *CPS Current Population Survey of Food Security,* with calculations made by the Economic Research Service of the Department of Agriculture.

19. Ulric Neisser et al., "Intelligence: Knowns and Unknowns," *American Psychologist* 51 (1996): 77–101; R. Karp et al., "Growth and Academic Achievement in Inner-City Kindergarten Schools," *Clinical Pediatrics* (Philadelphia) 31 (1992): 336–340; A. F. Meyers et al., "School Breakfast and School Performance," *American Journal of Diseases of Children* 143 (1989): 1237.

20. J. A. Martin, B. E. Hamilton, P. D. Sutton, S. J. Ventura, F. Menacker, and M. L. Munson, "Births: Final Data for 2002," *National Vital Statistics Reports* 52, no. 10 (Hyattsville, MD: National Center for Health Statistics, 2003).

21. Research studies available at Child Trends Data Bank, http://www.childtrendsdatabank.org/indicators/57LowBirthweight.cfm.

22. Nielsen Media Research, "African American Television Usage: Late Night," http://www.nielsenmedia.com/ethnicmeasure/african-american/AAlatenight.html (retrieved August 24, 2004).

23. Stephen J. Caldas and Carl L. Bankston III, "Black and White TV: Race, Television Viewing, and Academic Achievement," *Sociological Spectrum* 19, no. 1 (1998): 39–61.

24. ACT news release, http://www.act.org/news/releases/2003/8-20-03.html (retrieved July 16, 2004).

25. SAT website, http://www.collegeboard.com/prod_downloads/about/news_info/cbsenior/yr2003/pdf/graph8.pdf (retrieved July 16, 2004).

26. J. D. Anderson. *The Education of Blacks in the South, 1860–1935* (Chapel Hill: University of North Carolina Press, 1988).

27. James A. Johnson, Victor L. Dupuis, Dianne Musial, Gene E. Hall, and Donna M. Gollnick, *Introduction to the Foundations of American Education*, 12th ed. (Boston: Allyn & Bacon, 2001).

28. Ibid.

29. See Chapter 1 in Carl L. Bankston III and Stephen J. Caldas, *A Troubled Dream: The Promise and Failure of School Desegregation in Louisiana* (Nashville, TN: Vanderbilt University Press, 2002), for a detailed discussion of the quality of black education in Louisiana prior to the *Brown* decision of 1954.

30. Kenneth Clark and Mamie M. Clark, "The Development of Consciousness of Self and the Emergence of Racial Identity in Negro Children," *Journal of Social Psychology* 10 (1939a): 591–599; and Kenneth Clark and Mamie M. Clark, "Segregation as a Factor in the Racial Identification of Negro Pre-school Children," *Journal of Experimental Education* 8 (1939b): 161–163.

31. Morris Rosenberg and Roberta G. Simmons, *Black and White Self-esteem: The Urban School Child* (Washington, D.C.: American Sociological Association, 1971); and Judith R. Porter and Robert E. Washington, "Black Identity and Self-esteem," *Annual Review of Sociology* 5 (1979): 53–74.

32. Nancy St. John, *School Desegregation* (New York: Wiley, 1979); and Walter G. Stephan, "The Effects of School Desegregation: An Evaluation 30 Years after Brown," in *Advances in Applied Social Psychology*, ed. M. Saxe and L. Saxe (Hillsdale, NJ: Erlbaum, 1986), 181–206.

33. James S. Coleman, S. D. Kelley, and J. A. Moore, *Trends in School Integration* (Washington, D.C.: Urban Institute, 1975).

34. Bankston and Caldas, *A Troubled Dream*.

35. Stephen J. Caldas, Carl L. Bankston III, and Judith S. Cain, "Social Capital, Academic Capital, and the 'Harm and Benefit' Thesis: Evidence from a Desegregating School District," in *The End of Desegregation?* ed. Stephen J. Caldas and Carl L. Bankston III (New York: Nova Science Publishers, 2003), 121–146.

36. Unfortunately, we did not define for the teachers what we meant by "benefited," so in the teachers' minds this could have meant either "academically" or "socially" or "psychologically" benefited.

37. Thomas Cook et al., *School Desegregation and Black Achievement* (Washington, D.C.: National Institute of Education, U.S. Department of Education, 1984).

38. David J. Armor, "Black Achievement 50 Years after Brown," paper presented at the Harvard University Kennedy School of Government conference "50 Years after Brown, What Has Been Accomplished and What Remains to Be Done?" (April 23–24, 2004); David J. Armor, "Desegregation and Academic Achievement," in *Desegregation in the Twenty-first Century*, ed. Christine H. Rossell, Herbert J. Walberg, and David J. Armor (Westport, CT: Praeger, 2002), 147–188.

39. Roslyn Arlan Mickelson, "White Privilege in a Desegregating School System: The Charlotte-Mecklenburg Schools Thirty Years after *Swann*," in *The End of*

Desegregation?, ed. Stephen J. Caldas and Carl L. Bankston III (New York: Nova Science Publishers, 2003), 105–129; Jeannie Oakes, *Keeping Track: How Schools Structure Inequality* (New Haven, CT: Yale University Press, 1986).

40. Jerome E. Morris, 2004; T. Beauboeuf–La Fontant, "A Movement against and Beyond Boundaries: 'Politically Relevant Teaching' among African American Teachers," *Teachers College Record* 100, no. 4 (1999): 702–723; E. V. Siddle Walker, *Their Highest Potential: An African American School Community in the Segregated South* (Chapel Hill: University of North Carolina, 1996).

41. Elizabeth G. Cohen and Rachel A. Lotan, *Working for Equity in Heterogeneous Classrooms: Sociological Theory in Practice* (New York: Teachers College Press, 1997).

42. Stephen J. Caldas and Nicole Boudreaux, "Poverty, Race, and Foreign Language Immersion: Predictors of Academic Achievement," *Learning Languages* 5, no. 1 (1999): 4–15.

43. The following clause is from the NCLB Act, Sec. 1111 (b),(3),(c),(ix),III: "the inclusion of limited English proficient students, who shall be assessed in a valid and reliable manner and provided reasonable accommodations on assessments administered to such students under this paragraph, including, to the extent practicable, assessments in the language and form most likely to yield accurate data on what such students know and can do in academic content areas, until such students have achieved English language proficiency." From the U.S. Department of Education website, http://www.ed.gov/policy/elsec/leg/esea02/pg2.html#sec1116 (retrieved September 2, 2004).

44. Ibid.

45. Richard Kahlenberg, "Economic School Integration," in *The End of Desegregation?*, ed. Stephen J. Caldas and Carl L. Bankston III (New York: Nova Science Publishers, 2003), 149–175.

46. Carl L. Bankston III and Stephen J. Caldas, "Majority Black Schools and the Perpetuation of Social Injustice: The Influence of De Facto Segregation on Academic Achievement," *Social Forces* 75, no. 2: 535–555 (1996).

47. Morris, "Can Anything Good Come from Nazareth?"

48. Cited in Rebecca Winters, "No Long Separate, but Not Yet Equal," *Time*, May 10, 2004, 21.

49. J. D. Anderson, *The Education of Blacks in the South, 1860–1935* (Chapel Hill: University of North Carolina Press, 1988); V. Dempsey and G. Noblit, "The Demise of Caring in an African American Community: One Consequence of School Desegregation," *Urban Review* 25, no. 1 (1993): 47–61; R. Irving and J. J. Irving, "The Impact of the Desegregation Process on the Education of Black Students: Key Variables," *Journal of Negro Education* 52, no. 4 (1983): 410–422; E. V. Siddle Walker, *Their Highest Potential: An African American School Community in the Segregated South* (Chapel Hill: University of North Carolina Press, 1996).

50. Personal communication, Essie Thibodeaux-Lyles, February 23, 2002.

51. Personal communication, anonymous, September 6, 2004.

52. For more on the need for black teachers, see Carolyn Talbert-Johnson,

"Structural Inequities and the Achievement Gap in Urban Schools," *Education and Urban Society* 37, no. 1 (2004): 22–36.

CHAPTER 8

1. We do indeed mean "paradigm" in much the same sense as Thomas S. Kuhn's *The Structure of Scientific Revolutions,* 3rd ed. (Chicago: University of Chicago Press, 1996).

2. Gary Orfield and N. Gordon, *Schools More Separate: Consequences of a Decade of Re-segregation* (Cambridge: Harvard University, Civil Rights Project, 2001); Gary Orfield and Susan E. Eaton and the Harvard Project on School Desegregation, *Dismantling Desegregation: The Quiet Reversal of Brown v. Board of Education* (New York: The New Press, 1996).

3. Kuhn, *The Structure of Scientific Revolutions,* 5.

4. Christine Rossell's study of hundreds of districts shows quite clearly that the more coercive the desegregation plan, the less racially integrated a school or district was likely to become. Christine H. Rossell, "The Evolution of School Desegregation Plans since 1954," in *The End of Desegregation?,* ed. Stephen J. Caldas and Carl L. Bankston III (New York: Nova Science Publishers, 2003), 51–72.

5. Roslyn R. Mickelson, "Subverting Swann: First and Second Generation Segregation in the Charlotte-Mecklenburg Schools," *American Educational Research Journal* 38 (2001): 215–252.

6. Charles Lussier, "Amount of Attorneys' Pay May Be up to Federal Court," *The Advocate,* April 11, 2004, A1.

7. Richard D. Kahlenberg *Althoughter Now: The Case for Economic Integration of the Public Schools* (Washington, D.C.: The Brookings Institution Press 2001).

8. In almost all the authors' research studies, race and socioeconomic status of students correlate at r > .700—a strong correlation.

9. Robert Putnam, "Bowling alone: America's Declining Social Capital," *The Journal of Democracy* 6 no. 1 (1995): 65–78.

10. Laurence D. Steinberg, *Beyond the Classroom: Why School Reform has Failed and What Parents Can Do* (New York: Simon and Schuster, 1997).

11. Ricardo D. Stanton-Salazar, "A Social Capital Framework for Understanding the Socialization of Minority Children and Youths," *Harvard Educational Review* 67 (1997): 1–40; Ricardo D. Stanton-Salazar and Sanford M. Dornbusch, "Social Capital and the Reproduction of Inequality: Information Networks among Mexican-Origin High School Students," *Sociology of Education* 68 (1995): 116–135; Roger D. Goddard, "Relational Networks, Social Trust, and Norms: A Social Capital Perspective on Students' Chances of Academic Success," *Educational Evaluation and Policy Analysis* 25 (Spring 2003): 59–74.

12. Recently published research by Barbara Nye, Spyros Konstantopoulos, and Larry V. Hedges in a highly regarded education journal continues to strengthen the empirical evidence that effective teaching truly does lead to measurable student improvement, especially among low-SES students. See their "How Large Are

Teacher Effects?" *Educational Evaluation and Policy Analysis* 26, no. 3 (2004): 237–257.

13. W.E.B. Du Bois, "The Talented Tenth," from *The Negro Problem: A Series of Articles by Representative Negroes of To-day* (New York: James Pott and Company, 1903).

Index

tion, 102–4, 206; disenchantment with desegregation, 102; educational expectations of, 83, 85, 86, 88, 90; enrollment in private schools, 122; flight from desegregating districts, 96; high school graduation rates, 192; higher educational achievement levels, 193–95; historical roots of black-white gap, 197–98; literacy rates, 198; parent to child reading rates, 77; parental school involvement, 81–82; population concentrations, 55; poverty rates of, 65, 214; preparation for college, 197; school suspensions and expulsions, 88, 90–91; self-esteem of, 198–99; television watching patterns, 196; unemployment, 68–69

Boston, 34–35, 37, 38, 72

Brown v. Board of Education of Topeka (*Brown* decision), 3, 10, 19, 23, 30, 43, 65, 87, 104, 136, 146, 166–67, 206, 209; details of case, 27–28; endorsement of neighborhood schools, 28; historical context, 23, 218

Brown II, 28. *See also* "All deliberate speed"

Buffalo, 31

Busing, 41, 161–63, 170–72; anti-busing laws, 170–71, 174; endorsement by Supreme Court, 33. *See also* Forced busing

California, 54–57, 111; Proposition 1, 170–71

Catholic schools. *See* Private schools (and nonpublic)

Charlotte-Mecklenburg, NC, 11, 33, 39, 146–49, 180, 212. See also *Swann v. Charlotte-Mecklenburg Board of Education*

Chicago, 55, 161–65, 167, 179–80

Chinese Americans: discrimination against, 17

Civil Rights: Act of 1866, 16; Act of 1871, 17; Act of 1875, 17; Act of 1957, 20; Act of 1960, 20; Act of 1964, 20, 29, 155; Act of 1968, 20; changing paradigm of, 210; definition, 12; as dominant paradigm, 211; as espoused by John Locke, 12; of groups, 16; history, 12; and immigration, 53

Civil Rights Movement, 21, 31, 33, 161, 186, 198, 209, 210; heyday, 211; moral momentum of, 212

Civil Society, 106, 209, 219. *See also* Social capital

Civil War, 16

Clay, William, 159

Clustering ("pairing"): as a desegregation strategy, 144, 147

Coercive desegregation, 180, 214. *See also* Forced busing

Coleman, James, 1, 2, 6, 8, 74, 78, 84, 106, 117, 198–99. See also *The Coleman Report*

The Coleman Report, 1, 2, 5, 97, 198–99

Colorblind attitudes, 25, 28, 32

Combat pay, 206, 218

Command and Control Economy, 4, 34, 133, 135, 215

Community schools. *See* Neighborhood schools ("community schools")

Compensatory education programs, 162, 167

Connecticut, 39

Consent decree, 145, 158

Controlled choice, 145, 215

Cosby, Bill, 87

Cross-district busing, 36–37, 40, 67, 149, 156, 159, 166

Daley, Richard J., 161

Dallas, 37, 57, 141–43, 180, 213

Davidson, Thomas W., 141

Socioeconomic status, and association with parenting styles, 76; connection with academic achievement, 201

South Carolina, 17

South Korea, 79, 87

Steinberg, Laurence, 78, 85, 89, 100, 190

Suspensions and expulsions, 90–92

Swann v. Charlotte-Mecklenburg Board of Education, 33, 35, 36, 37, 116, 146–48. *See also* Charlotte-Mecklenburg, NC

Sweatt case, 27

"Talented Tenth," 218–219. *See also* Du Bois, W.E.B.

Target ratios. *See* Racial target ratios

Tennessee, 17

Test bias, 202

Test gap. *See* Achievement gap

Test scores, 143, 145–47, 149, 152, 155. *See also* Achievement gap

Texas, 17, 54–55, 111

Thurmond, Strom, 211

Tiebout, Charles, 110

Tipping point. *See* Racial tipping point

Tocqueville, Alexis de, 10, 75, 97, 106

Topkea, Kansas, 104

Tracking. *See* In-school segregation (also within classroom)

Unintended consequences, 179, 214, 216

Unitary status, 32, 34, 36, 38, 39, 164; of Baton Rouge, LA, 146, 213; of Charlotte-Mecklenburg, NC, 149, 212; of Dallas, TX, 141; of Kansas City, MO, 117; of Los Angeles, CA, 172; of Louisville, KT, 151; of Prince George's County, MD, 155; of St. Louis, MO, 159

U.S. Department of Justice, 139, 155, 158–59, 162

University of Louisiana, 27

University of Michigan, 42. *See also Grutter v. Bollinger*

University of Texas, law school, 27; medical school, 42. *See also Sweatt* case

Veblen, Thorstein, 113

Vietnam War, 30–31

Vietnamese students, 79

Violence in schools, 92–94

Virginia, 17

Voting Rights Act of 1965, 20

Vouchers, 178

Wallace, George, 211

Washington, Booker T., 198, 218

Washington, D.C., 31

Weinstein, Jack B., 175

West Virginia, 17

White flight, 34, 46, 115–17, 128, 136, 144–45, 147–48, 151, 154–58, 163, 166, 168, 170–73, 176–79, 181, 183, 199, 212

Whites: academic performance, 61, 146, 149, 152, 155, 157, 160, 187–95; achievement in majority black schools, 201; enrollment in private schools, 121–24; parent to child reading rates, 77; parental school involvement, 81; poverty rates of, 65; suspensions and expulsions, 90–91; television watching patterns, 196

Wilson, William Julius, 50, 67–68

Within-school segregation. *See* In-school segregation (also within classroom)

About the Authors

STEPHEN J. CALDAS is Professor of Educational Foundations and Leadership at the University of Louisiana, Lafayette. He has authored or co-authored more than 45 publications, including the book titled *A Troubled Dream: The Promise and Failure of School Desegregation in Louisiana*, which was awarded the Louisiana Library Association Literary Award for 2002.

CARL L. BANKSTON III is Professor of Sociology at Tulane University. He has been author or co-author of several previous books, including *Growing Up American: How Vietnamese Children Adapt to Life in the United States* (winner of the 1999 Thomas and Znaniecki Award, and the Mid South Sociological Association's 2000 Distinguished Book Award), *A Troubled Dream: The Promise and Failure of School Desegregation in Louisiana*, and *Blue Collar Bayou: Louisiana Cajuns in the New Economy of Ethnicity*. He has also edited 6 books and authored over 85 journal articles and book chapters.